The Struggle in the Air 1914-1918

A SQUADRON FLING OVER THE ALPINE PEAKS

The Struggle in the Air
1914-1918

The Air War Over Europe During the First World War

Charles C. Turner

LEONAUR

The Struggle in the Air 1914-1918
The Air War Over Europe During
the First World War

by Charles C. Turner

First published under the title
The Struggle in the Air 1914-1918

Leonaur is an imprint
of Oakpast Ltd

ISBN: 978-0-85706-333-5 (hardcover)
ISBN: 978-0-85706-334-2 (softcover)

http://www.leonaur.com

Publisher's Notes

The opinions of the authors represent a view of events in which he
was a participant related from his own perspective,
as such the text is relevant as an historical document.

The views expressed in this book are not necessarily
those of the publisher.

Contents

Preface

This is an attempt to describe the great achievements during the war of our air services, and to present them in due relation to the rapid developments in the mechanics of flight and in the art of flying. It should, therefore, be more than a mere story of aerial adventure: it is an endeavour to present, but without technicalities, the development step by step of aircraft, of the art of flying, and of the various functions of aircraft in war. An ambitious programme; and, conscious though I am of inability to do full justice to it, I can at any rate claim the possession of one or two advantages. I knew personally most of the pre-war aeroplane designers and flyers; watched the birth and the growth of the Flying Services; and served in the latter throughout the great struggle.

One of the earlier aviators (No. 70 in the British list), and previously a balloonist, and associated with the aeronautical movement in England from 1907, I offered my services to the authorities two days before England declared war against Germany. I was granted a commission as sub-lieutenant, Royal Naval Volunteer Reserve, in October, 1914, and was attached to the Royal Naval Air Service.

My Service life, which ended soon after the termination of hostilities, was varied. During the first few months my official obsession was Zeppelins; but although technically "in action" against the "Leviathan of the Sky" on two occasions, London's anti-aircraft defence fought no battles during my association with it. I was then transferred to observation balloons to instruct officers under training, with a certain amount of practical as well as theoretical and experimental work thrown in. This included a good deal of "free" ballooning.

My next appointment took place at one of the re-organizations of the Royal Naval Air Service, when I was asked to give instruction to flying officers in theory of flight, the compass, aerial navigation, map-reading, and meteorology; rather "a large order," but proving a most valuable experience, which brought me into contact with a large number of men who had before, or did afterwards distinguish themselves in the war, or who played a big part in the developments of aeronautics.

I paid only one brief visit to France; but it was an eventful visit to me, for I examined by day from an aeroplane the British and German lines from the sea to far south of Ypres, and I took part in a night raid by Handley-Page bombers.

This is not an attempt to write a complete history of the aerial war, or to record all the wonderful and brave deeds of our airmen. A book that would include all these would be valuable as a work of reference, but it would be essentially different in aim from this small effort. A certain number of the incidents here related have been told elsewhere, and in some cases there has been no need to go beyond the official reports. Some are here published for the first time, and to some I have been able to add hitherto unpublished details.

I am indebted to the Controller of His Majesty's Stationery Office *(London Gazette)*, and to the Editors of the *Times, Daily Telegraph, Morning Post, Daily Chronicle, Daily Mail, Daily Express, Observer*, and the *Aeroplane* for permission to quote from these newspapers; and also to the publishers (Messrs. W. Blackwood and Sons) of *An Airman's Outings*, by "Contact";—(Messrs. Longmans) *of Flying; Some Practical Experiences*, by Hamel and Turner; and *Tales of the Great War*, by Sir H. Newbolt; and—(Messrs. Cassell and Co.) of *Plane Tales from the Skies*, by "Wing Adjutant,"(also published by Leonaur.)

CHAPTER 1

Capabilities of Aircraft

Before the war aviation interested a very small minority. The heavy expenses of private flying, dangers real and imagined, the dread of vertigo and other physical ills, were sufficient to convince most people that flying—glorious triumph admitted—was for a few specially gifted men and women. Even enthusiasts who peeped into the future, and realized that with all its limitations aerial travelling was destined to play a big part in the affairs of men and nations, said that flying might someday be safe and enjoyable, but at that period its discomforts alone were sufficient to outweigh its attractions. The author remembers Lord Northcliffe remarking that, so far as he was concerned, what with the cramped position, the noise of the motor, the cold, and the rush of air, the passenger or the pilot of an aeroplane had a most unpleasant time.

With this in mind, then, it is particularly worthy of record that the only thing that kept alive in England the first feeble flame of aviation enthusiasm was not the care of far-seeing Governments, but the energy of a little band of inventors and flyers, professional and amateur, who loved it for its own sake. The sacrifices of time, money, and comfort were outweighed by the promise and, in their case, the delights of flying. True, they looked forward to the removal of most of the dangers and discomforts: meanwhile, they were glad to be able to play their part in the work and to carry on with the primitive craft then available.

The aeroplane of pre-war days—and these remarks apply generally to those of war-time too—were of numerous types, but were all craft with very limited accommodation for pilot or passenger. They had to be started by an assistant outside the machine, they were driven by unsilenced motors (self-starters and silencers had been used, but their time had not yet come), they required a skilful man at the wheel, they were prone to unwarned stoppage at the caprice of the engine, in which case a landing-place of considerable size and fair smoothness had to be found quickly, failing which a broken undercarriage was the almost inevitable penalty. Further, the question of sufficient structural strength of various parts of the machine was still unsolved, so that the breakage of aeroplanes in the air was not uncommon; albeit this danger was being overcome. It cannot be said that all machines in use even now are free from all these limitations.

One sat inside, either as pilot or passenger, much time and anxiety having been spent in getting the engine ready for work, and in looking carefully over every part of the machine for any sign of dangerous wear and tear. The engine started with an appalling roar, and the signal to "let go" having been given, the chariot of the air sped forward along the ground and after running from 50 to 250 yards, during which the vibration decreased, attained "flying speed." The din created by the motor, at first distracting, one could become indifferent to; but conversation was out of the question. Once clear of the ground, with increasing altitude a greater and greater expanse of country unfolded itself below, although the ordinary sensation of altitude, as in looking down from a "sky-scraper," was absent.

The wide view, the knowledge of the triumph of a machine produced by the science and obstinate struggles of aspiring men, the rush of air, the realization of speed, all this was exhilarating to certain temperaments; although occasionally one heard of pilots and passengers who became bored by these things. Sensation of altitude leading to giddiness there was none; nor can there be in aircraft. The imagination may, however, be busy; and if it be allowed morbidly to dwell upon possible dangers it may affect the nerves and make flying a misery. This, however, is exceptional. The normally healthy man, even if possessing a keen imagination, has nerves sufficiently in hand to avert over-anxiety.

Let us recall what aircraft of all kinds were able to do when the war began, as regards speed, duration of flight, load-carrying, climbing, and manoeuvring; remembering, however, that Service machines carrying a "war load" were not "stripped" for record-breaking.

The greatest speed that had been attained on an aeroplane, not aided by the wind, was 126½ miles per hour; but this was on a machine that had very little range of speed, and that could not land safely except on a smooth ground about 600 or 800 yards long. It was not a war machine, and comparatively few pilots could fly it. Aeroplanes were, however, being made with a maximum speed of 100 miles per hour, and even slightly more, that would keep in flight at 45 miles per hour; and these were, therefore, by no means mere racers. There were several types having a big range of speed, with the maximum over 90 miles per hour. To this class belonged the Sopwith and Bristol "scouts."

The altitude record stood at 25,756 feet, but such a height could not be attained without special preparations, and was merely serviceable as showing that there was no actual impossibility, either to man or machine, in flying at very great altitudes. Far more important was the fact that heights of 10,000 and 12,000 feet were commonly attained, and that a climbing speed of 1,000 feet in a minute for the first 1,000 feet, carrying a fair load, had been realized.

Flights of over 20 hours' duration had been made on a few occasions; of course, with every ounce of spare carrying capacity given to fuel and oil. Against these extreme cases may be set the fact that many aeroplanes, besides pilot and passenger and something to spare for ammunition, could carry enough fuel for a six hours' flight.

In passing, it is worthy of note that types of aeroplanes seen at aviation meetings in pre-war days were, with very few exceptions, not the types that survived the tests and demands of campaigning after the first six months of war. Aeroplane design was, in fact, more advanced than it would have seemed to be to the casual onlooker. It was passing through some very interesting changes.

The monoplane, all unsuspected by the general public, was declining in favour, a fact due to the potential superiority, on every side of practical capability, of the biplane. Curiously, up to the outbreak of war the mono-plane was the favourite division at aviation meetings, where it won most of the "events," just as, up to that time, it held most of the flight records. In the summer of 1914 it was rumoured in the inner circles of flying that a biplane had exceeded the 126J miles per hour record. At that time preparations were being made for the Gordon-Bennett aviation contest, the conditions of which required that in addition to the highest speed necessary to win the race, each machine should have been proved capable of maintaining flight at a speed of only 44 miles per hour.

This condition had spurred designers to produce high-speed machines that could also fly and land at a moderate speed, not the kind of craft that flew the race in 1913. These latter were monoplanes. In the biplane, however, superior lifting capacity, resolvable into a lower minimum speed, could be combined with great speed secured by the cutting down of head-resistance by refinement of shape and the elimination of most of the external bracing wires. What was known as the "scout" biplane was the result. Gustav Hamel, whose name was associated in the public mind with brilliant monoplane flying, was fully alive by theory and practice to the coming of the biplane, a little fact which helps to illustrate the situation. It was confidently believed that the Gordon-Bennett of 1914 would fall to England, whose far-seeing designers had produced the Sopwith, Bristol, and other types of high-speed and good speed-range biplanes.

Now it was the type of aeroplane that was being designed for the Gordon-Bennett that proved the forerunner of machines most successful in war as regards some of the most important of the services rendered by aircraft. But the issue was confused somewhat by two curious circumstances. First, the surprising lack of organization of the French Flying Services, and the undue preference that had been given to the monoplane by our skilful, daring flying brothers across the Channel. Just before the war, indeed, one or two of the biggest monoplane makers were struck off the French War Office list, one of several indications that the French Government were beginning to feel uneasy with regard to the developments of national aviation.

It may be recalled that in 1912 the distressing frequency of monoplane disasters induced the French Government to suspend monoplane flying, a course of action which the British War Office soon after followed. Technical inquiries were held. The simple fact is that monoplane wings, even when many external bracing wires are used, are weaker than biplane wings weight for weight, because they lack the mutual support afforded by the wings of the biplane. Moreover, in a short-span biplane some of the external wire supports can be eliminated, the reduction of head-resistance making for increasing speed, with the danger of collapse in the air reduced.

The French Flying Service was, nevertheless, to some extent tied to the monoplane, and a considerable number of monoplanes were in use, more especially in the first eighteen months of war. Some of them were of the "parasol" type, designed to avoid one of the disabilities of the monoplane by giving the pilot a better view than that obtained from ordinary monoplanes, the wings of which shut out so much of the landscape. But the "parasol" monoplane is somewhat unstable and unmanoeuvrable. It requires "managing" on a turn, and in a vol plane or glide, *i.e.* descent with engine stopped. Nor has it any outstanding advantage. An interesting sequel was the transformation of some of this series into biplanes by the building of a very small wing under the main wing. This increased the lift, as well as improving controllability. The converted "parasol" rather resembled some of the "scout" biplanes designed about the same period.

There was a further lesson in the fate of a few mono-planes of the "parasol" type exposed to high-explosive shell fire. The wings are partly supported by a system of bracing wires upwards and outwards from the body of the machine. In the concussion of shells bursting below the machine, but not near enough to incapacitate the pilot, these wires have broken, the pressure of air on the outspread wings being too much for them. The result was total collapse in some cases in which biplanes might have escaped.

All these remarks, of course, refer to the early months of the war. Design and construction developed rapidly, and for certain special purposes monoplanes were in 1917 and 1918 used with success. The Bristol and Fokker are examples.

The second of the two confusing issues brought about the extensive use of a biplane designed by the Royal Aircraft Factory. This was the famous B.E.2C, a self-balancing machine which lacked the high speed that war conditions soon demanded of aircraft and, besides, lacked other requisites of the fighting machine. It was distinctly useful for night work, since the piloting entailed very little labour. But here, again, it proved too slow both on the level and in climbing to tackle Zeppelins. Another drawback—one belonging to all self-righting machines—was its inability to dive steeply and fast, a useful quality in a fight. The self-balancing machine, too, is, if anything, a less controllable machine in landings than many ordinary types; and since there are numerous small breakages due to rough landings, entailing repairs and delays, this is not an unimportant item.

Many misunderstandings prevailed then, and some of these still survive. One was due to the enthusiastic advocacy of the self-balancing machine, advocacy which too often assumed that the general public possessed expert knowledge. Thus a War Minister hailed the self-balancing machine in terms which suggested that a child could fly it; and he was taken quite seriously by many people!

Particular types of aircraft used will be referred to in the accounts of aerial adventures which occupy the bulk of this book, but a few words on the general arrangement of pilots' and passengers' seats and the controls may be acceptable.

Besides his controls—a lever, or a wheel, for elevating and for lateral balance, and a footbar for steering by means of the rudder—a number of flying and engine instruments are arranged on the instrument-board, and a compass either low down and in front of the pilot or, if of the vertical type, on a level with his head, in front. By the aid of the compass the pilot can keep the head of the machine on some desired bearing, which may be at quite a large angle to the actual course in relation to fixed landmarks; in other words, aircraft commonly have to go on their way crabwise on account of wind more or less across their path.

As winds are often of great velocity, besides being variable, it is difficult enough in clear weather and over familiar country to fly a straight course; and in misty weather, or when flying above the clouds or over the sea, it is a common experience to make a great deal of leeway in some unexpected direction. Even in ordinary cross-country flying, when the pilot's attention is not diverted to enemies or to anti-aircraft gunfire, losing the way, or at least making an unintentional zigzag or curved course, was, at the time the war began, the rule rather than the exception. When a journey in the air included fighting a duel or two, involving all sorts of twists and turns, the difficulties may be imagined.

A "drift" indicator that could be used in these conditions was until towards the end of the war regarded as almost inconceivable; such an instrument that would, even with close attention from the pilot, be of the slightest practical use in misty weather, or for oversea work, was scarcely less inconceivable. Attempts had been made to produce instruments of the kind, but the least impracticable depended upon keeping observation on some fixed point. Imagine how limited this was likely to be when the most tangible object in view was a wave on the ocean. Approximate estimates of "drift" may now be obtained by observation of smoke bombs fired from the machine; and there are one or two excellent instruments for observing fixed landmarks.

The other instruments employed are the air-speed indicator, sufficiently described by its name, but one of the uses of which is to guard the airman, when immersed in fog or cloud, against unconsciously climbing or descending. A side-slip indicator warns him, in similar circumstances, against unconsciously getting the machine too steeply banked, or insufficiently banked, on a turn. An altimeter gives him his approximate height either above sea-level, or above any zero at which he chooses to set the dial at the start. An inclinometer (now seldom used) showed the general attitude of the machine in flying in relation to the horizontal.

All these instruments are imperfect and liable to disorder, and each is limited as to its usefulness. Thus, the compass gives the bearing of the machine, not the actual path it is travelling; the altimeter takes no note of the hills and valleys below, and is of no value for informing .a pilot in fog or at night the moment he should level out to land.

A pilot does not fly with his eyes glued on the instrument-board. No pilot could ever attain skill in that way. Indeed, the author has had experience of pupils who acquired this bad habit in the early days of their tuition and never overcame it, with the result that they had to give up flying. The good pilot knows his instruments thoroughly, but uses them, except for practice purposes, only when he cannot trust his physical sensations, knowledge of speed, and balance. The compass should, how-ever, be attended to on a cross-country flight even over familiar country in clear weather.

The field of vision, although extensive, is hindered by the mists of distance; and the field of effective vision, except when flying at small altitudes, has a much smaller radius than that of the horizon. At the greater heights of possible reconnaissance even objects almost directly below the machine appear too small for more than general observation. Training and experience are required to make the best of this; and in favourable atmospheric conditions photography under expert treatment reveals details illegible to the eye.

With such vehicles the airmen of the Allies and of their enemies "took the skies" in August, 1914, prepared to fly "under fire" from batteries below, and facing the possibility of attack by hostile craft in the air. But the war saw numerous improvements, and as time went on machines were more and more highly specialized. This was particularly noticeable in the development of the high-speed single-seater fighting scout, and the early elimination of many types, including the slower of the "pusher" biplanes.

On general principles seaplanes are like land aeroplanes, but in those days were less satisfactory on account of unavoidable features in their design. The under-carriage of floats was a serious complication from the aeronautical point of view. These craft were not generally so fast, and not so sensitive on the controls as overland types, the big vertical distribution of load and of side-surface accounting for this. The record speed of a seaplane was about 90 miles per hour, when that of the ordinary machine was about 130. Again, the seaplane with floats was not capable of remaining in the water for more than 24 hours, or so, without serious damage, even in calm water. A very different case could be made out for the flying boat of today, (*at time of original publication.*)

Airships, instead of depending for their lift upon the resistance of the air on "wings" as do aeroplanes, are upheld by static buoyancy. Carrying a large quantity of light gas—hydrogen they are lighter than the air they displace on the ground. They are squeezed upwards by the pressure, and continue to rise until the air becomes so thin that it is equal in weight, volume for volume, to that of the airship. They are shaped with a view to reducing head-resistance. Most modern airships have elevating planes which, inclined at an upward angle to the path of flight, enable these craft under the influence of forward speed to ascend above their static level. These elevating planes are used to some extent to regulate altitude, but altitude control is chiefly secured by valving out some of the gas, or by dropping ballast.

At the outbreak of war the Zeppelin was the best air-ship type, and the Germans, who had experimented on it for many years, had brought it to a high degree of efficiency. They were rapidly building up a considerable fleet of Zeppelins and of their other rigid airship, the Schütte Lanz, a somewhat smaller and less capable type.

The best type of Zeppelins then in use could attain a maximum air-speed (net speed, *i.e.* without help from wind) of about 54 miles per hour, the economical speed being in the neighbourhood of 40 miles per hour. They could climb to a height of 10,000 feet by discharging a large quantity of ballast; but their usual navigating height was about 4,000 to 6,000 feet. Their rigidity was secured by enclosing gas-containers in a sheath of aluminium built up like a lattice girder. They were served by a crew of from 18 to 28. They carried machine-guns; and experiments had been made with a machine-gun on top of the envelope, access to which was attained by a kind of chimney running right through the "hull." These experiments had not been successful, although at a later date they were. Zeppelins could, at best, remain aloft for a period of about 80 hours, but their usual voyages were of 6 to 12 hours. The Zeppelin airship had been tried extensively, and a good attempt at regular passenger services had been made in Germany.

Great Britain had done very little in airship work, the reason being primarily the indifference of the public and the reluctance of any

Government to spend money on any form of experiment on armament not definitely approved by the public. The Government, however, by 1912 had admitted that airships ought to be built, and small grants of money were voted annually for the purpose. In the spring of 1914 the Government professed itself satisfied with what was being done, and the public were assured that ere midsummer a fleet of British air-ships would manoeuvre together over the Houses of Parliament. The promise could not be fulfilled.

Our very small fleet of non-rigid airships, until the submarine war developed, were of no value at all for any offensive operations, their sole use being in reconnaissance. The ordeal of war resulted in the designing of a small non-rigid British airship that proved to possess unexpected good qualities of speed and control. This type consisted of an aeroplane fuselage and engine attached to a streamline-shaped gas-container. Although very small—at first only about 60,000 cubic feet capacity—it rivalled the Zeppelins in speed.

Airships of all kinds require a large ground staff. They are subject to the same navigation limitations as aeroplanes, but have the advantage of not being compelled to descend by engine failure. This, and their greater duration capacity, made them more suitable for night work than aeroplanes.

CHAPTER 2

Theory in 1914

A month before the war there were naval and military experts who believed that aircraft were merely trick machines, for serious work not to be considered: in the field they would give more trouble than service, and would use up labour and transport far beyond their value. Each aeroplane, it was objected, required shed-room and half a dozen attendants. They were so fragile and delicate that they continually needed tinkering, adjustment, and repair. The engines were never ready at the moment required. In flight the pilot was ever haunted by the fear of engine failure and other troubles; and even if all these faults could be overcome there was no machine that, besides carrying fuel for more than six hours' flying, could lift enough ammunition to do serious damage.

It was agreed that aerial reconnaissance, if it could be carried out with accuracy, would be valuable; but it was considered very doubtful in the light of manoeuvres experiences whether reconnaissance by aircraft would be trustworthy; and untrustworthy reconnaissance is worse than no reconnaissance at all. Troops on the ground would screen and disguise their movements. Also, it was objected, aircraft would be easily shot down. The idea that airships could be usefully employed in war was ridiculed; indeed, it was firmly believed that Great Britain possessed defensive weapons so accurate and powerful that enemy aircraft would never dare to approach our skies. A War Minister had solemnly assured Parliament to that effect!

Unfortunately many of the enthusiasts who opposed these views were enthusiastic without knowledge. They ignored the difficulties, and glossed over the disabilities under which aircraft laboured. A very small handful of officers and aeronautical students, besides being mindful of the shortcomings of aircraft, perceived that they must nevertheless play a big part in war, and foresaw the means by which many of the defects would be overcome. One looks back with satisfaction to having been one of that small band of prophets.

As long ago as November 27, 1912, General Sir James Grierson said,[1] "Warfare will be impossible unless we have the mastery of the air."

But what a task was faced by the Air Services when war broke out! Fairly to understand that, indeed, one must know something about the machines available and the conditions under which they entered the conflict. Unquestionably they were fragile, delicate craft, needing the constant care of trained "nurses." Yet we have seen their swift triumph. After six months of war those who had scoffed acknowledged that aircraft were indispensable.

After the manoeuvres of 1913 instructions were issued for use in army training, in which it was laid down that aircraft were to fly, as a rule, at not less than 3,000 feet when exposed to rifle fire; and when artillery was present this altitude was to be increased by another 1,000 feet. Under misty conditions it was left to the pilot to fly lower if objects could not be distinctly seen. In these manoeuvres both the 3rd and 4th Divisions succeeded in escaping observation, and some of the cavalry were also able to remain undetected.

Further revealing the anticipations of British military authorities may be quoted the War Office tests for the guidance of manufacturers, issued in February, 1914. The tests, set out here, included an examination of workmanship and materials, rolling test, and one hour's flight.

For purposes of calculation, weights of pilot and passenger were to be 160 lbs. each.

This is of extraordinary interest now, as illustrating the general possibilities of aircraft at the time, and particularly in view of the fact that two classes of fighting aeroplanes were specified. At that time many experts supposed that aeroplanes of the types then extant would never fight in the air; that they would, on the contrary, always avoid conflict. It is a fact that the British Third Arm entered the field with many machines better adapted to fighting than those of the other Powers, and the tests quoted above are proof that the British authorities had, in one detail at any rate, a clearer conception of the coming aerial war. Duels in the air occurred immediately after the outbreak of war.

A few weeks before the war, Army manoeuvres in England, France, and Germany were the occasion for trials of aircraft on a larger scale

---

1. Aeronautical Society Meeting.

PERFORMANCES REQUIRED FROM VARIOUS MILITARY TYPES.

	Light Scout.	Reconnaissance Aeroplane (a).	Reconnaissance Aeroplane (b).	Fighting Aeroplane (a).	Fighting Aeroplane (b).
Tankage to give an endurance of	300 miles.	300 miles.	200 miles.	200 miles.	300 miles.
To carry	Pilot only.	Pilot and observer plus 80 lb. for wireless equipment.	Pilot and observer plus 80 lb. for wireless equipment.	Pilot and gunner plus 300 lb. for gun and ammunition.	Pilot and gunner plus 100 lb.
Range of speed ..	50 to 85 miles per hour	45 to 75 miles per hour.	35 to 60 miles per hour.	45 to 65 miles per hour.	45 to 75 miles per hour.
To climb 3,500 ft. in	5 minutes.	7 minutes.	10 minutes.	10 minutes.	8 minutes.
Miscellaneous qualities	Capable of being started by the pilot single-handed.	—	To land over a 30 ft. vertical obstacle and pull up within a distance of 100 yards from that obstacle, the wind not being more than 15 miles per hour. A very good view essential.	A clear field of fire in every direction up to 30 degrees from the line of flight.	A clear field of fire in every direction up to 30 degrees from the line of flight.

Instructional aeroplanes with an endurance of 150 miles will also be tested under special conditions; safety and ease of landing will be of first importance in this type.

than before.

A test of the organization of the German Flying Corps was made in May. Three aeroplanes were ordered to be sent to Doeberitz from each of the centres at Cologne, Posen, Königsberg, Halberstadt, Metz, Strasburg, Darmstadt, and Graudenz, each about 300 miles distant. With the exception of the three from Darmstadt, which were stopped by a storm, all the machines reached their destination in good order. In France squadron flights were at all times in progress. In England a concentration of aeroplanes was made on Salisbury Plain. Five squadrons, each of 12 machines, were assembled, with transport. Three of the squadrons had their complete road transport, namely, 38 vehicles each. There were other, but incomplete, units; and altogether about 70 aeroplanes and 200 motor vehicles were assembled. The exercises included speed tests, reconnoitring for named objects, climbing tests, wireless, photographing, and night flying.

The Royal Naval Air Service at about the same time had an assembly of machines at Spithead, about 20 seaplanes taking part. Striking displays over the fleet were made, and a "flight past" the King during his inspection was duly performed.

The Royal Naval Air Service had control of all lighter-than-air craft and all seaplanes, and possessed in addition a number of "land" aeroplanes; and the Royal Flying Corps was confined to "land" aeroplanes.

Meanwhile tentative steps had been taken to protect warships against aerial attack. The new *Temeraire* was fitted with light horizontal armour plates over her magazine. The magazine is obviously a vulnerable point, and once made safe the armoured ship had little to fear from such aerial attacks as were then considered possible. Later ships were similarly protected, and a few high-angle guns were distributed among the Fleet.

As to pilots, French airmen were undoubtedly more brilliant than German, but German organization was superior. Britain had pilots that rivalled the best of France, and had applied an organization no whit inferior to Germany's, but her Air Service was ridiculously small. There never had been sufficient pressure of public opinion to overcome the inertia of officials and politicians. Beside the lukewarmness of public opinion, the administrative evils resulting in too little encouragement being given to private manufacturers was a comparatively small matter. Democracy was paying the price of a low average public interest and intelligence; for a democracy to be secure it must be well-informed and intelligent.

There was, nevertheless, and as already pointed out, a very creditable side of the British Flying Services. In details of training our men had the advantage. They became hardier flyers, helped by the more difficult climatic conditions in which they trained. They were not discouraged from the attainment of supreme flying skill. Even looping the loop was permitted to pilots who sought complete mastery of their craft; and in the flying schools, after war broke out, notices were exhibited to that effect.

German training was different, and aimed rather at solidity. The German Services, although large, lacked fast machines, and the German Staff apparently never anticipated the necessity for providing aeroplanes with guns. It would be more correct to say that aeroplane design was as yet a matter of exigence rather than of choice. It seemed most likely that airmen would avoid conflict, being so ill-furnished for it. That view, as we have seen, was held by the British War Office, but with certain important reservations.

Aircraft for employment in naval warfare had received less attention. Perhaps the most authoritative pronouncement on the subject was that of a distinguished naval officer.[2]

> The coming of the seaplane has in no way revolutionized naval warfare, but has assisted at a revolution which had been already started before its advent. The beginning of this revolution was the power of controlling the narrow seas which commenced with the advent of the torpedo-boat, making cruising in such waters for large vessels an unhealthy occupation during the night-time. The submarine increased a hundredfold the anxieties of the large vessel when within 1,000 miles of an enemy's base.
>
> Now comes the seaplane to give eyes and ears to the short-sighted and deaf submersible. Both by night for the destroyer and by day for the submarine, the difficulty is not to sink its adversary when located, but to locate him and get into his proximity. At night the difficulty is very little lessened by the help of aircraft, but by day the assistance is enormous; waterplanes, when intelligently worked, can give instant notice by wireless to the mother-ship of the submarines, and enable her to send out her comparatively slow-moving children to arrive, unseen, across the track of their large and speedy enemy.

2. *Flying: Some Practical Experiences.* Hamel and Turner.

The next role which the waterplane will be called upon to play in war-time is the hunting of the submarine. From the difference of size and background, it is certain that the aeroplane will always see the submarine before she is herself discovered for the submarine, like the whale, cannot always remain under water. It will, therefore, be one of the duties assigned to aircraft to find the submarines, and either knock away their periscopes by automatic gunfire, or to assist the destroyer to hunt them in order to make them run their batteries down; for, when a submarine's batteries are exhausted, she becomes a surface craft, and is at the mercy of the smallest destroyer that floats on the ocean.

In this latter way, the seaplane becomes an offensive craft, but undoubtedly its principal duty will be to act as a scout. Although its great speed enables it to cover a large area of water in a very short space of time, yet lifting power being limited, it cannot carry sufficient fuel to be a very long-distance scout.

It is therefore very important to have ships specially built to enable the planes to be carried out to sea to a point of vantage from which they can start on their duties. The problem of landing on one of these vessels has not yet been satisfactorily solved, but it is most important that it should be, for the hoisting in of the seaplane can only be safely accomplished in fairly smooth water, and, as the supply of pilots and seaplanes must necessarily be limited, it is of great importance that they should be preserved as much as possible.

For Great Britain it is essential that aeroplane ships should be built; although the cost undoubtedly will be great, it must be remembered that, for over half the days of the year, at the lowest estimate, aeroplanes will do the work of ten cruisers.

CHAPTER 3

The Flight to France and the Baptism of Fire

Everybody knew that the First Army Corps had been brought to a degree of efficiency not excelled, probably not quite equalled, by any in the world. Even so the swift, silent "march" of our Expeditionary Force in the early days of August, 1914, justly afforded the nation reason for pride. It was so much more soldier-like than popular, but often erroneous, ideas of War Office managing expected. The South African War had taught lessons, which subsequent reforms in administration had carried into effect. But few people imagined that the very new and inexperienced Royal Flying Corps would prove equal to a real test. War Office Administration of the Royal Flying Corps had been the subject of bitter Press and Parliamentary criticism, and the criticism was so far justified by the fact that no more than three squadrons and an incomplete fourth, were ready for the field—a ridiculously inadequate number. On the score of equipment and skill, however, those three squadrons might have served as a pattern both for our Allies and for the enemy.

The first proof was afforded by the flight across the Channel on August 14th, at a moment when almost frantic efforts were being made to prepare further squadrons for the field. It is now acknowledged that the supply of aeroplanes was so limited that Lieutenant-Colonel (later Major-General) Brancker requisitioned the best of the school aeroplanes from the Central Flying School at Upavon to supply the squadrons going to the Front. On that memorable 14th of August 37 machines crossed the Straits of Dover in a period of two hours. Others, singly, had been flying across before that time, and others continued the stream afterwards. Indeed the stream never ceased, except at night and during tempest, throughout the war; and towards the end of the war night did not interrupt it. The Straits became an aerial highway; the pilots whose work it was frequently to make the journey, became known as "ferrymen."

The historic flight of August 14th was one of the most remarkable events in military history, and a great aeronautical achievement and turning-point, the nearest approach in peace time having been during the "European Circuit," a race held in July, 1911, when eleven aviators flew from France to England. Hurried preparations had been made near Amiens to establish a headquarters for the Flying Corps. Already a staff of officers and mechanics had been dispatched thither. Supplies were being sent across the Channel and were accumulating at the French ports and on the railways. Farnborough and Upavon were in a state of unprecedented bustle, and apparent confusion. The flyers themselves were testing machines, and the squadron and wing commanders directing arrangements.

No one knew for certain the hour, or the day, that the journey to France would be made. Indeed, there were rumours that the machines would be packed up and sent by rail and steamer, the aviators accompanying them. Private correspondence containing news of movements and intentions was, of course, forbidden; and the anxious families and friends of officers of the Corps were in complete ignorance until the flight was an accomplished fact and they received letters, sometimes not until a month later, from France. To a few no word came between a letter posted in England and an item in the casualty list showing that the loved one had been killed in France.

No word of this leaked out, but the crowd of machines was observed by thousands of people at Folkestone and, Dover, and created an indelible impression on their minds merely as a spectacle; comparatively few of the fortunate onlookers understood the tremendous significance of the event. Seasoned pilots some, young and ardent others, it is literally true that not one held any hope of seeing England again. Whatever illusions were entertained at that time by a few optimists as to the course of the war, the flying men knew that to the ordinary risks of their calling were to be added the fire of artillery, and inevitable stresses of real campaigning that would add heavily to the peace casualties rate.

The newspapers had for the past three days been full of accounts (as we know now, many of them purely imaginary) of German and French airmen shot down by artillery. As we shall see, the casualties, although heavy, were not so heavy as some people expected.

And the flight was made without mishap, although few of the pilots had flown the Channel before. All the machines landed safely at, or close to Amiens, that city being the first base of operations. The machines flown were chiefly B.E.'s and B.E.2C 's; although other types, including a few monoplanes, were included.

At that time the Royal Flying Corps was commanded as follows:— Brig.-General Sir David Henderson, K.C.B., D.S.O., hitherto Director-General of Military Aeronautics at the War Office, was gazetted Colonel-Commander, and commanded the Corps until November, Lieutenant-Colonel Brancker, R.A., taking his place at the War Office. Lieu-tenant-Colonel Trenchard, C.B., D.S.O., previously Assist-ant-Commander, Central Flying School, took command of headquarters at Farnborough, Lieutenant-Colonel Sykes being appointed a General Staff Officer with Headquarters in the Field.

One of the most terrible ordeals for a new and untried arm, most of whose members had never been under fire, was endured in the retreat from Mons, when our flyers flew over the advancing hordes of Germans and brought back reports of their movements. Grotesquely inaccurate stories of this retreat were published at the time. Thus, one correspondent asserted that the British Army was a "broken" army, and that it was pursued by aeroplanes and Zeppelins! He said that aeroplanes, Zeppelins, armoured motors, and cavalry were loosed like an arrow from the bow, and served to harass the retiring columns and to keep the German Staff fully informed of the movements of the Allied Forces. The work of the British airmen was ignored in these accounts, which ought never to have seen the light. It is a fact that no Zeppelin took part in the German advance. Dealing with these panic-distorted narratives the official report dated September 18, 1914, stated:—

In view of the many statements being made in the Press as to the use of Zeppelins against us, it is interesting to note that the Royal Flying Corps, who have been out on reconnaissances on every day since their arrival in France, have never seen a Zeppelin, though airships of a non-rigid type have been seen on two occasions. Near the Marne, late one evening, two such were observed over the German forces. Aeroplanes were despatched against them, but in the darkness our pilots were uncertain of the airships' nationality and did not attack. It was afterwards made clear that they could not have been French. A week later an officer reconnoitring to the flank saw an airship over the German forces and opposite the French. It had no distinguishing mark, and was assumed to belong to the latter, though it is now known that it also must have been a German craft. The orders of the Royal Flying Corps are to attack Zeppelins at once, and there is some disappointment at the absence of those targets.

Again, at the end of the storm and stress of the great retreat—the first experience of war for our airmen, who came through it with fewer losses than seemed possible—but before rest and reorganization were possible, they were able by devoted labour to observe Von Kluck's unaccountable swerve to the South-east right across the British Front. The enemy's airmen should have observed, and perhaps did report that our army was in no such sad plight that its existence could be so ignored.

For a few weeks, owing to the retreat, dire confusion reigned; There was no proper base, or storage and repair depot. All the preparations to establish organization for the repair of aeroplanes and their engines had broken down. Carpenters, fabric workers, electricians, photographers, dark-room operators, stores, and cleaning staffs were not available. Machines were flying all day and every day, and very often to avoid capture by the enemy were sent up in perilously bad condition.

In spite of this appalling and disheartening state of affairs our airmen "carried on." It was due to their observation—at first distrusted—that General Sir Horace Smith-Dorrien knew that at least three German Army Corps were attacking at Le Cateau instead of one, priceless information which prevented a complete disaster. During the retreat it was often "touch and go," our aeroplanes getting off the ground at times under fire from German guns.

CHAPTER 4

Early Surprises

Supremacy in the air is of little use if you are not on something like level terms with the enemy on the ground. When the thunderbolt of war burst, and the "islanders" for a moment reeled under the shock, no man, not even the greatest military or aeronautical experts, knew how the aerial arm would fare, or what effect it would have on the mighty conflict, or whether the Allies or their enemy would achieve any sort of settled ascendancy. Despite a soon-acknowledged personal superiority over enemy airmen, our aviators had to join in the retreat from Mons. Yet even in that retreat the work they did was an earnest of the triumph they won when the Allied armies recovered from the first blow and pressed the Huns back again.

At times during the war that ascendancy was gravely threatened, so that it could only just be held at the cost of disproportionate casualties, but it was never actually lost. In the first three weeks of their work in France the Royal Flying Corps, by their initiative and daring, had caused the Germans to fear them. The retreat of the enemy from the Marne was as hurried as had been his advance after Mons, and it was not effected without the sacrifice of much material including, at one haul, a score of aeroplanes, and on other occasions smaller captures of the kind.

Undoubtedly the German airmen did not render such valuable service to their side during the retreat from the Marne as ours had in somewhat similar circumstances. Certainly in point of speed we had a number of machines superior to average enemy craft, but the difference was not so-marked as to account for the ascendancy we achieved over a numerically stronger enemy. Sir Horace Smith-Dorrien, (*Smith-Dorrien* by Horace Smith-Dorrien also published by Leonaur.) referring to the squadron of the Royal Flying Corps attached to his Staff, wrote on September 9th:

> Our aeroplane officers are real heroes. Not only do they appear to have put the fear of God into the German airmen, for they hunt them wherever they see them, with the result that there have been none in the air for two days, but in spite of being shot at every time they go up, they continue their reconnaissances and bring back quite invaluable—and what always proves to be true—information.

The officers concerned included, by the way, Major Salmond and Captains Jackson, Charlton, Conran, and Cruikshank.

Aerial tactics and aircraft methods generally were but little understood by the great body of the troops at that period of the war, and the accounts which appeared in the newspapers were often grotesquely inaccurate. Weighing the evidence, however, it appears that the enemy had been able to prepare certain effective methods that were subsequently copied or improved upon by the French and British.

The Royal Flying Corps at first worked day and night, by day in the air, by day and night in the sheds: no leave, and very little leisure. Repairs and casualties in large numbers had to be dealt with immediately, and amid the confusion of unexpected war followed by the dire menace to the safety of Paris itself, the Royal Flying Corps base first established at Amiens had to be moved. That, at any rate, had been foreseen for a few days previously, rumours of the condition of the retreating Allies reaching the Aircraft Depot in alarming form. Preparations were already under way, but ordinary transport facilities were unequal to the task, and at the last the order was given to burn a huge quantity of petrol and some minor stores.

All this time the ideas of aerial warfare formed during peace were being tested, and in many cases found wrong; and the men at the head were readjusting their plans and methods, and preparing for the long strenuous campaign that lay ahead. Above all, they had to build up schemes for co-operation with the other arms of the Service, and to an extraordinary extent teach the other arms, which in many cases were sceptical, as to the ways by which the flying arm could help them.

An English aviator relating some of his experiences in September, 1914, said that in one flight he was shelled about 100 times, but there were only a dozen holes in the planes. He was fired at both by friend and enemy.

The following extract from a letter from an officer, published in the *Aeroplane*, refers to the same period:—

You have heard by now of the battle of Mons. I was over that. We were reconnoitring roads behind, and when we went out the guns were getting to work. I saw two German batteries with our shells bursting over them like little bits of cotton-wool, while our guns didn't seem to have been found. Later the German aeroplanes flew over and found them out. When we came back houses were burning at Jemappes and Mons, and stacks were burning all over the place from shell fire. I saw one of our trenches, and a German attack coming off. They were coming up in a long, dense column, with the head all spread out in front like a large human tadpole.

Just after this they got on to us with anti-aircraft guns, and burst shells round us. We got off with nothing worse than a small splinter through the elevator. These guns are rather terrifying, but do very little damage. Fellows have had shells burst all round them for quite a long time without being hurt at all. So far the machine I've been in has not been touched by bullets. We fly high now, 5,000 feet or so, and are quite safe, but at first two or three machines came in pretty well riddled.

During the great German advance in 1914, and later in similar big movements, our airmen saw a remarkable spectacle. The long line of the advance could be clearly seen by the chain of burning villages, woods and farms, the big belt of flame and smoke moving a few miles each day.

In the early days of the war many of our artillery commanders would not believe in the efficiency of aerial observation of artillery fire, and their location of new batteries, and they often disregarded reports obtained at great risk by our flyers. There were cases of active prejudice on the part of artillery commanders against aircraft! Another instance of our backwardness was afforded by the slowness with which our authorities applied the lesson that shrapnel was of no use against troops in trenches. The Germans knew all this long before, and we had to follow their example, namely, to shell with high explosive shells and then follow up with shrapnel on the troops driven out of cover.

In anti-aircraft artillery, the Germans were far in advance. They had been building up this arm for many years. Even in 1909 half a dozen different types of anti-aircraft guns were publicly exhibited at the Frankfurt aeronautical exhibition. In England at the time nothing was being done, and the official attitude towards aircraft was one of lukewarmness, if not positive antagonism. The enemy had an excellent range-finding method for anti-aircraft work, and a system of "bracketing" aircraft in the air—covering a wide and deep region with shell fire—which sometimes secured direct hits at a great height.

Contrary to the belief that fighting in the air would be the exception rather than the rule, there were several duels in the air during the first two months of the war, carbines, automatic pistols, and revolvers being the principal weapons employed. The first credible report of aerial fighting relates to an inconclusive fight between a French and a German machine on August 14th, the Frenchman being armed with a Browning pistol. Another relates to an Anglo-German duel, date not given, described in a letter in the *Morning Post*, August 28th, as follows:—

An English pilot, emerging from a cloud, found immediately beneath him a German aeroplane. Swooping down to within revolver shot, he emptied all his chambers, with an effect he could not observe, because the cloud once more enveloped him. Later on, when he emerged from the cloud again, he saw underneath a small crowd gathered round a smashed aeroplane, and he came to the conclusion that his revolver shots had not been without effect.

One of the earliest encounters in the air was that in which Captain G. W. Mapplebeck was wounded. He was unarmed, but carried a load of bombs. The German was armed with a rifle. Captain Mapplebeck received an extraordinary wound in which a severed muscle acted as a tourniquet on an artery and prevented fatal loss of blood. He lost consciousness, however, immediately on landing.

The career of this pilot, who was killed in a flying accident in England on August 14, 1915, calls for a note, his adventures in the field being so typical of the fortunes of the Flying Arm in France in 1914-1915. One of the 37 pilots who made the memorable flight to the Front at the outbreak of war, he had already won distinction by destroying a train of German ammunition lorries with a bomb dropped from his machine. He was on the wing above the advancing enemy, all through the retreat from Mons. Three months after the wound received in the fight mentioned above he returned to duty, and was one of three pilots whose machines were shot down during a bombing expedition. One died of his wounds. One was made prisoner. Captain Mapplebeck managed to elude capture, and with the aid of a Frenchman he made up a disguise which got him into Lille, where he managed to procure a little money. He then made his way on foot to Holland, and, passing for an English electrician, escaped being interned and eventually got across to England.

These were among the first incidents in the aerial war which, in the course of a few months, was to develop into battles in which sometimes more than 100 machines were engaged, exerting a profound influence on the designing of aeroplanes and on the methods of training pilots in aerial formations and tactics.

Among Sir John French's earliest references to the work of the Royal Flying Corps was the following, in the despatch published September 10, 1914.

> I wish particularly to bring to your Lordship's notice the admirable work done by the Royal Flying Corps under Sir David Henderson. Their skill, energy, and perseverance have been beyond all praise. They have furnished me with the most complete and accurate information, which has been of incalculable value in the conduct of the operations. Fired at constantly both by friend and foe, and not hesitating to fly in every kind of weather, they have remained undaunted throughout.

The reference to the danger from our own artillery was only too well justified. In the first months of the war some of our battery commanders were liable to make mistakes as to the identity of airmen, and in one or two painful instances exercised so little discrimination that courts of inquiry had to be held. In a great many cases, however, it is impossible to prevent entirely the firing at friendly airmen: that is one of the risks that the flyer on war service must take. As the fighting proceeded, moreover, the German types of aeroplane included fewer "taube" and "arrow" forms which early made a broad distinction between theirs and ours, and at 10,000 feet and higher it was exceedingly difficult, even with powerful glasses, to see identification marks.

An unexpected phase of the war was afforded by the bombing by German aeroplanes on August 3, 1914, of Lunéville, an "open" town. This was a foretaste of the indiscriminate bombing of undefended places by the nations into a demand for an early peace, another amazing example of the curious ignorance of psychology which, in the German leaders, went hand in hand with a really wonderful capacity for material organization and forethought.

A glimpse is given of the conditions under which air-men fought, and the experiences they went through under enemy fire, by a letter from a Royal Flying Corps officer early in March, 1915, published in the *Daily Chronicle*:—

Last month I certainly did have some very exciting experiences. One day when troops were being moved up we were sent out to patrol the lines and prevent German aeroplanes coming over. We met one coming over, and as soon as he saw us he turned and made for home in an almost straight line. The only reason he did not go in an absolutely straight line was that he wanted to lead us over the two anti-aircraft guns in this area. They shot at us, but they were afraid to aim in front, and their shells burst miles behind us. We chased him all the way back to his aerodrome, but, although we were a bit faster, we couldn't catch him, as he went down gradually while we had to keep up. We saw another machine, but he went straight down too. We were so annoyed with these that we dropped two bombs, and then I fired about 50 rounds with the machine-gun at them on the ground.

Another day, when there was a strong west wind blowing, I had a near shave of not being able to get home. We knew the wind was about as strong as we could manage, and we hovered about a long time before we settled to go over. We went over a little way once, and got back fairly easily. Then we went about ten miles over, and turned round to get home. For nearly a quarter of an hour we made no headway at all. The pilot put the nose of the machine down, and we came down to 3,000 feet, and were able to make headway. But it would have been madness to go over the trenches at that height, making hardly any headway at all, so we climbed up again before we got to the trenches. Meanwhile there was a big storm cloud coming up from the west, and it was an exciting race. If we got into the cloud we. should have to come down or else lose our way hopelessly, and probably be blown back 10 miles in half as many minutes.

When we were almost over the trenches a bullet came through the bottom of the machine, through my *puttee* and leather coat, and out through the top plane. Next moment the clouds swept down on us. The pilot went straight down, and we roared through the cloud. I hadn't the slightest idea whether we were going straight or turning round (you never can tell in a thick cloud), but when we emerged at about 800 feet we saw we were comfortably this side of the trenches, and we got home safely. We had only 10 minutes' petrol left, so we were lucky.

Next day we had to go over an area where we well knew there was a very good gun. We were particularly told to have a good look at this bit, so we had to go right over it. They soon began to shell us, and the concussion of the very first shot shook us, and gave me quite a headache. They then got five or six very unpleasantly-close shots at us, and then one a few feet below us, which fairly spluttered us all over with bullets and splinters. One bit of shell passed between the pilot's legs, through the petrol tank, and just grazed past my shoulder.

The petrol was spilt all over the place, and half-suffocated the pilot. The engine stopped, and we swung round to the right and down. We soon got out of range, and then the engine picked up. Luckily there was an auxiliary petrol tank, and we pointed for home as hard as we could go. Before we landed the pilot shouted to me to have a look over and see if the wheels were still there.

Apart from questions relating to the need for specialized machines for specific purposes; whether small swift scouts were or were not to be supplemented by big heavily-armed "battle-planes"; whether "formation" flying was or was not desirable; as well as large numbers of technical and constructional questions; there was the much-debated problem of the possible checkmating of aircraft by the employment of screens, concealments, and ruses.

On this point, if aircraft compelled an enemy to take elaborate measures of concealment, and to restrict all except the most trivial movements to the hours of darkness, their employment would be fully justified. How vividly was this illustrated in the great climax of battle in 1918! On that basis alone, the side possessing aircraft would have an enormous advantage over an enemy without the "bird's-eye view." It will be admitted, looking back to the opinions expressed by experts immediately before and after the outbreak of war, that always the view that has sought to belittle the influence of aircraft has been proved to be the wrong view, just as wrong as the wilder anticipations of ill-informed aeronautical enthusiasts.

One of our generals is reported to have declared, "The aeroplane has done a lot for us, but we are going to outlive it. The aeroplane finds its business harder every day."

Lord Sydenham, on the subject of screens against aircraft observation, in the course of a long interview in the *Observer* on December 20, 1914, said:—

When you come to handle enormous masses of men—immense armies—the command becomes extraordinarily difficult. To command 100,000 men in the field effectively was a task that comparatively few generals were able to accomplish. But when an army exceeds a million it is possible that we may have got beyond the capacity of the directing brain to exercise an effective control, not only over such enormous masses of men, but also over such an immense and varied extent of country as they must occupy.

This fact, together with the extreme effectiveness of modern weapons, led to troops 'digging themselves in'—that is, digging light shelter trenches—for the purpose even of a small action, and a force attacking might lightly entrench a position won preparatory to further advance. If such a force found itself unable to advance, or if a local advance would not serve the object of the whole army, then it became desirable to dig in more and more, until we ultimately arrived at the very elaborate field fortifications such as are now opposed to each other on the plains of France and Flanders.

An additional difficulty to advancing under such conditions in the present day is that any large body of troops intended to strike or break through the enemy's lines in force is almost certain to be discovered by aviators, an entirely new factor in warfare. This explains the difficult position in which the Allies find themselves, even though they must now be numerically stronger than the enemy, over whom they have certainly obtained moral ascendancy. It also explains why their advance seems at present to be possible only by local progress in detail.

CHAPTER 5

Fighting in the Air in 1914-1915

It has been explained how unprepared were airmen and how un-suitable were their craft for fighting in the air, the reasons being that flying was in its infancy, and the military authorities, almost without exception, believed that airmen could do their work best by avoiding fighting.

For some months after the outbreak of war machine-guns were not carried in aeroplanes. The first encounters were between airmen armed only with pistols or carbines, and most of them were inconclusive. The majority of the machines in active service were tractors.

The history of fighting in the air is fascinating because of its swift development, stage by stage, to the highly specialized business it became towards the end of 1916. Of the various aspects of the aerial war this is the most difficult to deal with properly. But if, whilst relating a number of the more remarkable encounters, the author is able to present the matter with some regard to their technical sequence and their bearing upon the successive stages of the war of which they were an accompaniment, he will have achieved his object.

For material there are reports, letters and mess yarns dealing with thousands of air fights ranging from duels between man and man to fights between large formations, and the labour of sorting these out and classifying them is almost as great as that of faithfully describing them. Fighting is necessarily often referred to in other parts of the book, where it was incidental to artillery observation, reconnaissance, bombing, or other air work. Here the subject is considered by itself, although some of the battles described were by airmen on machines not employed exclusively for fighting.

Much entertainment will be found in a perusal of the newspapers at the outbreak of the war. Until a rigid censorship was established the imaginative newsman did as he pleased. He made battles in the air; he killed famous airmen; he invented wonderful new types of aircraft. Even when the censorship had been established, for a time there was little check on rumour provided it exerted no influence on military operations. On occasion the military authorities for their own ends may have started canards in the press.

The first fight in the air was reported from Nancy on August 2, 1914. Garros, the famous French aviator, it was declared, rammed a Zeppelin airship with his machine, sacrificing his own life in the act of destroying the enemy. This story was probably a mere repetition of the excited talk of the cafes. It was entirely untrue.

Very early in the war aeroplanes and airships were brought down by artillery. But the first authentic report of a duel in the air came from Renter's correspondent on August 15th. It ran:—

In another place a French aeroplane yesterday encountered a German aeroplane. The French pilot chased the German, firing with a Browning. The German aviator did not reply, but fled.

In a previous chapter the first aerial fight of a British airman is recorded as having occurred on August 27th. The Englishman used a revolver. And belonging to the same phase of aerial fighting was the duel reported on October 16th. A Royal Flying Corps airman on a fast scouting monoplane, and carrying two rifles, gave chase to a hostile machine, but lost sight of the enemy in clouds. Then a German Otto biplane came on the scene, a slow "bus," but one having the engine behind, and, therefore, if well armed, a formidable opponent.

The Englishman offered battle. He knew that, owing to the position of the propeller on the hostile craft, he could not be fired at when astern. When within sixty yards he fired one rifle without result. His superior speed taking him ahead, he turned, and again getting astern emptied his magazine at the German, and the latter began to descend. Then the Englishman stopped his engine, and began a downward glide whilst reloading. Unfortunately the magazine jammed, but he managed to insert four cartridges and to fire them at his opponent, who disappeared into a bank of clouds. The Englishman followed but never saw him again; and by the way, one has never yet heard of a pilot who has been able to track another machine's path in the clouds.

Sir Henry Newbolt, in *Tales of the Great War*, gives the following account of a fight in December, 1914:—

An Albatross having a strong north wind behind him ventured

to rush our lines. His challenge was accepted by an English pilot, whom I am obliged to call X. Having a good Avro machine, our man climbed more quickly than his enemy expected, and the shots that were meant to get him before he was up all passed below him. The German, seeing that he had missed, then turned to go home, but found the wind heavily against him. It was against X too, but his Avro gained on the enemy, who dodged like a rook trying to escape from a peregrine. He succeeded in avoiding X's fire, but the chase was too much for him; when he found he could not shake off his pursuer, his heart failed and he came down and surrendered.

The names of the more famous airmen naturally became the subjects of sensational stories. It was difficult sometimes to separate the true from the false. Here, from the *Morning Post*, is a story of Garros who, as we have already seen, on August 2, 1914, had previously been reported killed.

One day recently a German aeroplane was seen approaching the French lines, and was duly received with a hail of bullets. To every one's surprise it proceeded to land quite calmly in the middle of the French troops, and the surprise was intensified when the famous aviator Garros sprang down to the ground.

'"This is madness,' said an officer. 'What on earth are you doing, Garros, on board a German aeroplane?'

'A mere accident,' said Garros. 'I was chasing a German Taube, and had almost got it when my motor broke down. So I had to land as quickly as I could. There were lots of Germans below, so I came down looping the loop in the wildest breakneck fashion. The German aviators evidently thought I had broken my neck, as they swept round and came down to see what papers they could find on me. I shammed dead until they were almost upon me, when I dropped them dead with a couple of shots from my revolver. Then I put my disabled aeroplane into a neighbouring shed and came back on board the Taube.'

Of the French bullets two had gone home; one had grazed the propeller and the other had made a hole in a wing.

As regards the adaptability of aeroplanes to fighting, the Germans were in no better case than the Allies. Indeed they had been less inclined than the French or the British to consider fighting as a very important matter. They had given a good deal of attention to the question of bomb-dropping from aircraft, but little or none to the aerial duel.

In the stress of the Great War with its pressing demands on all aeroplane makers to produce aircraft in ten times the quantity they could possibly turn out, there could be no thought of an immediate drastic change of type. The machines, such as they were, had to be made. There were the drawings, there was the plant. Beyond all that, inventors and designers could set to work with an eye to the future. But it is no simple matter to design a new type of aeroplane. It takes months to put it on a satisfactory manufacturing basis. So, ingenious minds were led to contrive adaptations and makeshifts.

At this early period it was supposed that a fighting aeroplane should be one from which a gun could be aimed. Therefore, the "pusher" type of aeroplane was indicated, whether single-seater or two-seater. Later on it became evident that for the fighting scout type a light single-seater is best, of a speed and manoeuvrability that are easiest attained in the tractor division; and in a few cases a machine-gun was carried on the top plane of such machines.

A better solution seems obvious now. At the time, however, it was wonderful enough. Secretly prepared and brought into use soon after the first battle of the Marne, the world at large knew nothing about it for two or three months. The solution, which appears to have been the work of several minds, made it possible to carry on a tractor aeroplane a machine-gun that could be fired directly ahead. The gun was mounted on top of the body of the machine, the muzzle pointing through the propeller, the end of the muzzle being a few inches from the blades of the screw. Of the stream of bullets proceeding from the gun a small percentage would, of course, hit one or the other of the blades.

There were two general ways of overcoming this difficulty; one which is attributed to Garros, the French adopting it, although the Germans afterwards copied it, consisted of armouring a portion of the propeller blades. The other appears first to have been used on Service by the Germans, although early French experiments were made in the same direction; it consisted of an interrupter gear timing the stream of bullets between the two whirling blades.

The action of this firing mechanism was really to pull the trigger of the machine-gun at the moments when neither of the propeller blades was in front of the muzzle, but so finely timed that the almost infinitesimal period of time occupied by the bullet's passage from the breach to the muzzle was allowed for. The number of revolutions of the propeller were normally 1,200 to 1,400 per minute; so that in one minute there would be 2,400 or 2,800 blade-cuttings of the line of fire. The machine-guns used in the period now under review fired 500 or 600 rounds per minute, or 8 to 10 per second. For short "bursts" of firing the interruption was scarcely worth considering. In rare cases a propeller has stopped dead with one blade covering the muzzle, thus preventing firing. It will be readily understood, however, that such an occurrence during a duel was so uncommon that it was not a serious drawback.

The deflector propeller had steel plates on each blade at the point opposite the muzzle of the gun, the faces of these plates being at an obtuse angle to the line of fire. The stream of bullets was not interrupted, but five or six in every hundred struck one or the other of the steel plates and was simply deflected out of the way; the others went to the mark. Nothing seemed more simple; but this device fell out of favour because the impact of the bullets so seriously interfered with the smooth, even rotation of the screw as to reduce the flying efficiency of the machine; also, several cases of propeller smashing occurred. And in any case, with the general introduction of "tracer" or explosive bullets for use in aeroplane machine-guns the deflector propeller was doomed.

At a later date two machine-guns with interrupter gear were often carried, either side by side on top of the fuselage, or one on either side of the fuselage.

It is of interest to note that until the end of 1915 whenever a German machine with a gun firing through the propeller was encountered the fact was noted in the official report of the fight, showing that even at that date it was not the universal practice.

Yet another alternative afterwards became possible with the employment of a certain type of engine having a large hollow crank-shaft on which was fixed the boss of the propeller. In this case a machine-gun was fixed in the crank-shaft, the muzzle thus pointing out directly forward from the centre of the screw.

With any of these fixed machine-gun devices in use, the airman had to aim his machine, and open fire when the sights told him he was "on."

As an item of historic interest the following Admiralty announcement of January 23, 1915, concerning one of the earliest squadron engagements of the war, may be quoted:—

On Friday, the 22nd, 12 or 13 German aeroplanes appeared over Dunkirk at 11.30 a.m. and dropped bombs. No particular damage was done, except that a shed in the docks was set on fire. One of the bombs fell just outside the United States Consulate, breaking all the windows and smashing the furniture. Belgian, French, and British naval and military airmen engaged the German aeroplanes, one of which was brought down by a British military machine, just over the Belgian frontier. The German aeroplane and its two occupants were captured. During the day visits were paid to Zeebrugge by Squadron Commander Richard P. Davies and Flight Lieutenant Richard Peirse, who dropped bombs (see Chapter 19). In making a reconnoitring flight before this attack Squadron-Commander Davies was on one occasion surrounded by seven German aeroplanes, but managed to elude them. He was slightly wounded in the thigh on his way to Zeebrugge, but continued his flight, and accomplished his mission.

"Eyewitness," the official chronicler, at a date, June, 1915, when few authentic descriptions of aerial duels had been seen, gave an example of a fight which at that time had striking characteristics.

While reconnoitring over Poelcapelle at a height of about 4,000 feet, two officers of the Royal Flying Corps engaged a large German biplane having a double fuselage, two engines, and a pair of propellers. The German machine at first circled round ours, shooting at it with a machine-gun, but not inflicting any damage. Then our observer fired about 50 rounds at less than 200 yards' range. This had some effect, for the hostile biplane was seen to waver. After some more shots its engines stopped, and it nose-dived to a level of 2,000 feet, where it flattened out, flying slowly and erratically.

Under a heavy fire from anti-aircraft guns down below our pilot turned towards our lines to complete his recon-naissance, when his machine was hit, and he decided to make for home. But the petrol tank had been pierced, and as the aeroplane glided downwards on the slant the petrol was set alight by the exhaust and ran blazing down to the front of the body of the aeroplane, which travelled on to the accompaniment of the rattle of musketry as the unexpended rounds of machine-gun ammunition exploded in the heat and those in the pilot's loaded revolver went off.

The pilot, however, did not lose control, and the aeroplane proceeded steadily on its downward course. Before it reached the ground a large part of the framework had been destroyed, and even the blades of the propeller were burnt as the propeller ceased to revolve.

When the machine finally landed behind our lines both the officers were severely burnt and the pilot, climbing hurriedly out of the blazing wreck, tripped over a wire stay, fell, and sprained his knee. The few still serviceable portions of the aeroplane were then salved and collected under the shrapnel fire of the German guns. As an example of terseness, the last words of the pilot's official report of this adventure are worthy of quotation:

... the whole of the nacelle (body) seemed to be in flames. We landed at W. 35 n. P. 16 (Z Serios 93 E. W.). 1/35,500.

"Beware of the Hun in the Sun," was an injunction dinned into the ears of newcomers. But in spite of the most insistent cautioning the first three months of a pilot's career at the Front was, throughout the war, the most critical. So many were shot down within a few weeks of leaving England. If a man survived this critical period, he had by that time learned enough to avoid being so easy a victim to the Hun.

There were other rules of the game which, the reader will understand, steadily developed with improving craft and appliances. Very soon these rules began to be formulated. Here, for example, is one of the earliest. In approaching end-on British pilots were advised to swerve under the enemy, then turning sharply and taking up position below and behind, and pursuing in the same direction. The enemy could thus be raked before he could locate you. It required highly trained judgment to make the turn, for if not done accurately, either the enemy could perceive the intention, or else at the end of it you were too far astern.

But a dozen situations called for quick-turning and diving, and the fighting scout became specialized as a light and very strong single-seater. The French had the Morane and Nieuport monoplanes, and the Germans adopted the former type and, slightly modifying it and giving it a bigger engine, they effected what was called the "Fokker surprise" in 1915. There was really nothing original about this machine, which was not exceptionally manoeuvrable, but there was a clear perception of the needs of the situation. For the rest, the enemy were indebted to the policy which enabled them to employ more powerful driving units on their aircraft, and that was a policy that dated back to pre-war days.

The Fokker achieved a brief and limited success. It was often

A CHASE IN CLOUD-LAND

downed by Nieuports, de Havilland pusher scouts, and by slower but well-handled craft, and it soon met a tartar in the Sopwith "1½ strutter." In the first days of the Fokker phase our two-seaters adopted the tactics of turning out of the enemy's line of fire and then raking him with the observer's rear gun. The Fokkers replied by attacking in a long dive. If they did not succeed they continued the dive until put of range, and broke off the action. Indeed, throughout the war, a single-seater attacking a two-seater had nothing to gain by continuing in action after the first rush. Before the end of 1915 Fokkers almost invariably worked in twos and threes. Soon there were improved Fokkers, Albatrosses, and other German scouts, as we shall see when reviewing the work of 1916. Here it may be recalled that the Sopwith "1½ strutter," a two-seater, for a few months did great execution; although many were shot down by the enemy.

Up high there is knowledge, but no sense, of speed. On a clear day with no objects close at hand, a machine might seem poised stationary in the blue: the country below rolls past almost imperceptibly. It is like being in an express train, and keeping the eye fixed on the distant hills, which appear to have scarcely any relative motion to the train. The foreground streaking past informs the mind of speed. Up aloft there is no foreground. The air-speed indicator records, say, 80 miles per hour. Sometimes a few isolated clouds are met. They appear as if suddenly created in the void. They approach the machine (it does not seem that the machine approaches them) with incredible swiftness, and rush silently past. Are they blown along by some mighty invisible wind? and is it this wind that is making your struts and wires hum and sing? Or are they still, and you moving? So far as your sensations go, it might as well be one as the other. But you know perfectly well that it is the machine that is in motion.

The passenger in an aeroplane runs precisely the same risks as the pilot. No invidious distinction, then, must be drawn between the two. In the Service, pilots wear the double wings, observers a single wing with a large O. The latter are not, as some people have imagined, men who have failed at piloting. To the contrary, they are men chosen very often for some special qualification. They are usually capable of piloting in an emergency. They must not suffer from nerves, because if anything is trying to the nerves it is sitting still and watching another man do the work.

Lieutenant Williams, and Lieutenant Hallam, his observer, who in this case was doing photography, in a B.E.2C near Lille were attacked by a Fokker at a height of about 8,000 feet. While bringing his gun into action Lieutenant Hallam was hit in the left hand so that he could not work the gun. The machines then manoeuvred round each other, when the pilot was hit in the arm and shoulder, and lost consciousness. Lieutenant Hallam's attention was called to this fact by the machine's spinning. He looked round and saw the condition the pilot was in, and had to make up his mind what to do.

Under circumstances like that a man very often does rather more than he would have thought possible. Lieutenant Hallam did not hesitate; he climbed out of his seat, gripping one of the short centre struts with his right hand, got one leg down by the pilot and, hanging on with his left arm, seized the pilot's lever and tried to get the machine into control. It would not answer to the control. It was engaged on a bad spin, with the engine "all out," and was in as bad a case as a machine can very well be. A thought flashed through Lieutenant Hallam's mind of the instrument-board, that sheet-anchor of the pilot, which informs him if the machine is going down head first, or tail first, or slipping sideways.

It was a half-humorous thought, and it chiefly had reference to the futility of things. The control-lever having failed, he tried to close the throttle, realizing that the engine must be stopped at all costs. But this had no effect, the wire having been broken. He then turned off the petrol tap, which of course had the effect of stopping the engine; and then he tried the control-lever again. In a few moments he got the machine nose-down, and thence into complete control; and soon after managed to land just behind the French trenches. It is not surprising, under the circumstances, and considering the roughness of the ground, that the machine turned over. The unconscious pilot was thrown out, and Lieutenant Hallam climbed out and assisted him until help arrived in the shape of the French Red Cross. The machine was still under fire, but Second-Lieutenant Gilbert, of another squadron, who saw the landing, ran out to it and rescued the Lewis gun and instrument-board.

The Distinguished Service Order was bestowed on Captain Amyas Eden Borton (who as Brigadier-General took part in the first flight to India in 1918), and Captain Anthony Marshall for the following:—

When on flying reconnaissance over the neighbourhood of Staden on June 7, 1915, Captain Borton was wounded in the head and neck by a bullet fired from a hostile aeroplane, and although suffering severely from loss of blood he contrived, with the assistance of the observer, to bandage his wounds and completed the reconnaissance on the prescribed course.

Captain Marshall continued his observations after rendering all possible aid to the pilot, who was gradually losing consciousness, notwithstanding that the German aeroplane was persistently attacking. The valuable report supplied by this officer is as detailed and complete for the last as it is for the first part of the reconnaissance.

A French airman brought down a German by aid of a simple stratagem. Flying at a height of 7,000 feet he saw an Aviatik approaching. The German pilot tried to escape, and the Frenchman went after him. After ten minutes' flying he caught him up, and flew above him. Then the fight began. His observer, when only about 18 yards from the enemy, opened fire. The enemy machine was only struck in a plane, and the German replied with his machine-gun. The Frenchman then let his machine fall in a steep dive; the German aviator, thinking that he was out of action, pursued. But the Frenchman suddenly rose again and came over the German, some five or six yards above him, and his observer fired his carbine, wounding the German pilot in the arm. The latter seemed to take no notice of his wound, and continued to direct his machine. A second bullet struck his petrol tank and the whole machine burst into flames, and crashed to earth.

Major L. W. Brabazon Rees was awarded the V.C. for gallantry described officially as follows:—

Whilst on flying duties, Major Rees sighted what he thought to be a bombing party of our own machines returning home. He went up to escort them, but on getting nearer discovered they were enemy machines, about 10 in all. Major Rees was immediately attacked by one of the machines, and after a short encounter it disappeared behind the enemy lines, damaged. Five others then attacked him at long range, but these he dispersed on coming to close quarters, after seriously damaging two of the machines. Seeing two others going westwards, he gave chase to them, but on coming nearer he was wounded in the thigh, causing him to lose temporary control of his machine. He soon righted it, and immediately closed with the enemy, firing at a close contact range of only a few yards, until all his ammunition was used up. He then returned home, landing his machine safely in our lines.

This was the same pilot who was awarded the Military Cross for the following:—

On September 21, 1915, when with one machine-gun, accompanied by Flight-Sergeant Hargreaves, he attacked a large German biplane with two machine-guns. The enemy, having the faster machine, manoeuvred to get him broadside on, and then opened heavy fire, but Captain Rees pressed his attack and succeeded in hitting the enemy's engine, for the machine made a quick turn, glided some distance, and finally fell just inside the German lines near Herbecourt.

On July 28th he drove down a hostile monoplane, in spite of the fact that the main spar of his machine had been shot through and the rear spar shattered.

On August 31st, with Flight-Sergeant Hargreaves, he fought a German machine more powerful than his own for three-quarters of an hour, then returned for more ammunition and went out to the attack again, finally bringing the enemy's machine down, apparently wrecked.

It was very soon found to be futile to expend ammunition of which but a very limited supply could be carried, at a range of more than a few yards, and skill in fighting depended largely upon reserving fire until it could be effective, and at the right moment on being on the "blind spot" of the enemy.

Captain L. G. Hawker, on a Bristol scout, encountered a German two-seater over Hooge, at a height of 10,000 feet. Approaching down sun, his opponent thus having the light in his eyes, he opened fire at a range of 100 yards, and the enemy craft took fire and was destroyed. The same pilot over Bixhoete, at a height of 9,000 feet, approached a German two-seater unperceived, and opened fire at 50 yards, bringing the enemy down. The observer fell out, and the machine and pilot crashed to earth in the British lines near Zillebeke. Captain Hawker had just before fought another enemy two-seater which, however, escaped.

Captain Hawker, who was awarded the V.C. had already won the D.S.O. for bombing (see Chapter 14).

Two R.F.C. officers on a B.E.2C were attacked north of Bapaume by an Aviatik, a much faster machine. The latter "made rings" round the British flyers, while both sides were firing continuously. The German then threw over two silver balls, which burst into smoke. The

British pilot guessed these were altitude indicators, and promptly flew to a higher level; and only just in time, for immediately the enemy anti-aircraft guns fired a number of shells which burst just below them. The German dived and landed apparently undamaged.

The official "Eyewitness" contributed the following narrative on May 14, 1915:—

On Monday, the 10th . . . one of our airmen had a thrilling experience. He was alone in a single-seater aeroplane, in pursuit of a German machine. While trying to reload his machine-gun he lost control of the steering gear, and the aeroplane turned upside down. The belt round his waist happened to be loose, and the jerk of his turn almost threw him out of the machine, but he saved himself by clutching hold of the rear centre strut—the belt slipping down round his legs.

While he hung thus, head downwards, making desperate efforts to disengage his legs, the aeroplane fell from a height of 8,000 feet to about 2,500, spinning round and round like a falling leaf. At last he managed to free his legs and reach the control lever with his feet. He then succeeded in righting the machine, which turned slowly over, looping the loop,[1] whereupon he slid back into his seat. This constitutes a record, even in a Service where hairbreadth escapes are of daily occurrence.

Still taking the period of the summer of 1915, here is an incident which gives a very clear picture of the nature of the work. This story of a fight in the air was published in the *Eton College Chronicle*. The British aeroplane contained Captain Loraine, of the Royal Flying Corps and the Hon. Eric Lubbock, and the extracts given are from letters from Mr. Lubbock:—

Yesterday Loraine and I had an exciting adventure. We sighted a German about four miles off and attacked. We both opened fire at about 50 yards. I fired again at about 25, firing 26 rounds, and then my gun jammed. I heard Loraine give a great shout, but felt neither fear nor triumph. Then our machine turned downwards. As I fired my last shot I had seen the German turn down. I knew that if he got below us my machine-gun was the only one that could fire at him. We were diving, I standing almost on the front of the body. Then we turned level. I finished my gun, but there was no German!

---

1. This appears to have been not the ordinary loop.

But our guns (Loraine's and mine) had jammed at the same moment. I spent another five minutes at Loraine's gun, and finally got both done. We saw another enemy coming in the distance. Loraine went all-out to climb and attack, while I put my stiff and aching hands in my mouth praying for sufficient life to come back to them; they were frozen. Then our engine stopped, and we were helpless, so we turned and glided homewards. Unable to reach the aerodrome we landed in a plough, a beautiful landing.

Loraine left me and went for help. Of course the crowd came from all sides. One Frenchman, remarking '*Vous avez l'air faim*,' fetched me some beefsteak and coffee, for which I was most grateful. A 'Tommy' gave me a cigarette. Well, the luckless *Boche* fell 20 yards behind our front-line trench. The pilot was shot through the stomach; the observer, a boy of seventeen, just grazed in the head. In spite of his fall he will be all right, but yesterday he was crying and absolutely nerve-broken. No wonder, poor thing! The pilot was dead before they got him away.

On the machine was found an old machine-gun. It had been taken from the Canadians months ago, and now has come back to them. It is absolutely unfit for aeroplane work. There was a camera with a Zeiss lens, which will be most valuable to us, although the camera was pierced by two bullets. There were some plates, which are being developed at this moment. The camera is heavy and clumsy, not a patch on ours. It is such that you cannot take a vertical photograph. There was a carbine—a very nice weapon. There was a pistol for firing coloured lights, which had been hit by us and spoiled. There was a priceless pair of binoculars, magnifying 18 times. I am to take all these things myself to the G.H.Q., which makes me very shy.

I went to a town last night to have my hair cut. I walked with some 'Tommies.' 'Lummy,' said one to the others, 'did yer see that fight in the air this morning? German fell 20 yards behind our trench.' Then followed a glowing account of the fight, with details I was unaware of. I went to a shop to buy a broom, and the shop woman asked me if I had seen the fight this morning. I said I had. But nevertheless she gave me a description, gesticulating and copying our every movement. So with everyone. The Frenchman who brought me breakfast after we landed had watched it all, seen the German fall, and followed us in. Altogether it is the excitement of the land.

I believe they are going to give me the German carbine. I was congratulated by the General Officer Commanding the Royal Flying Corps, who said he would get recognition for a 'very plucky effort.' Today I went to see and photograph the remains of the 'German 'bus.' It was rather destroyed, as they have taken out the engine. It was the latest type. The German observer says he was given to understand that we tortured all our prisoners, and wondered when it was going to be over. He was also much surprised to hear that he was going to be taken to England, as the German Navy has control of all the seas, and England is completely cut off! Now one can understand why they go on fighting.

If my gun had not been jammed after the fight, and if another Hun had not appeared in the distance, I'd have photographed him falling, but I was much too busy at the time, seeing that we were forced to land instead of fighting the second machine. I am sorry now, but one has to act so quickly; it is half-minutes which make the difference, and to get the gun going is the most important thing.

For this Captain Loraine was awarded the Military Cross and his observer received the same decoration. And in the same *Gazette* the award of the Legion of Honour to Captain James Valentine—like Loraine, one of the pioneers—was notified.

Our airmen were hard tried for a short period by the Fokkers which, as the following incident shows, were part of a general forward aerial fighting policy, including new methods and concerted attacks. Second-Lieutenant Horsburgh on a B.E.2C , with an observer, while on reconnaissance, was attacked by three Fokkers, one of which took up position over the British machine, one below, and the other by the side. As if this were not enough, another hostile, a pusher biplane, approached from behind and opened fire at short range. The observer, Lieutenant Haynes, replied; but the petrol tank of the British machine was pierced, and it had to make for our lines. It actually reached its aerodrome in spite of the superior force against it of faster machines.

In the autumn of 1915 a German two-engine three-seater type, promptly dubbed a "battle-plane" by the newspapers and made the subject of a typical "scare," appeared on the field. This type was first seen, the author believes, about the middle of September. One, at any rate, was tackled by a Vickers (pilot Lieutenant Powell) near Polygon

Wood. The engagement began with the enemy about 100 yards away and slightly above, coming straight on and firing two machine-guns. The British observer (Air Mechanic Shaw) reserved his fire till less than 20 yards, when the enemy at once dived with one of his engines stopped and the other apparently on fire.

The success of comparatively slow machines in fights with Fokkers at this period was due to the generally undeveloped condition of aerial fighting, and to the superior resource and daring of British airmen. At a later period the possession of slightly superior speed, or climb, made great difference to the result; although of course at all times the personal equation was important, as it always will be.

A B.E.2C was attacked by two Fokkers one day in September. The Germans dived down on the British machine from a superior height, and then kept behind firing their guns. The observer on the B.E.2C had to mount his gun for action rear; but the first burst he fired took effect, one of the enemy falling and eventually crashing into trees. The second Fokker went home.

From June 15th to October 15, 1915, the Royal Flying Corps had 240 fights in the air, most of which were behind the enemy lines. Four German machines were brought down behind our trenches, and at least a dozen in the German lines. Many others were damaged.

The Victoria Cross was awarded to Second-Lieutenant G. S. M. Insall for "most conspicuous bravery, skill, and determination on November 7, 1915, in France." He was patrolling in a Vickers fighter with Air Mechanic T. H. Donald as gunner, when a German machine was sighted, pursued, and attacked near Achiet. The German pilot led the Vickers machine over a rocket battery, but with great skill Lieutenant Insall dived and got to close range, when Donald fired a drum of cartridges into the German machine, stopping its engine. The German pilot then dived through a cloud, followed by ours. Fire was again opened, and the German machine was brought down heavily in a ploughed field four miles south-east of Arras.

On seeing the Germans scramble out of their machine and prepare to fire, Lieutenant Insall dived to 600 feet, thus enabling Donald to open heavy fire on them. The Germans then fled, one helping the other, who was apparently wounded. Other Germans then commenced heavy fire, but in spite of this, Lieutenant Insall turned again, and an incendiary bomb was dropped on the German machine, which was last seen wreathed in smoke. Lieutenant Insall then headed west in order to get back over the German trenches, but as he was at only

2,000 feet altitude he dived across them for greater speed, Donald firing into the trenches as he passed over.

The German fire, however, damaged the petrol tank, and, with great coolness, Lieutenant Insall landed under cover of a wood 500 yards inside our lines. The Germans fired some 150 shells at our machine on the ground, but without causing material damage. Much damage had, however, been caused by rifle fire, but during the night it was repaired behind screened lights, and at dawn Lieutenant Insall flew his machine home with his gunner.

A typical letter from the Front about this period is quoted here from the *Morning Post*:—

Yesterday I had my first really trying experience. We did a long reconnaissance, which took us nearly to Mons, taking us four hours and five minutes. When we left the ground it was freezing hard, and *en route* we encountered two snow-storms. The cold was absolutely excruciating, my eyes got frozen up; the water in my eyes turned to ice. I had to keep on brushing it out of my eyes. A great sheet of ice formed over the mouth outlet of my mask, so that I had to smash it to breathe. We finished off by fighting a German machine and chasing it from Arras to Douai, where he dived down under cover of his 'Archies' and 'Horaces.'

We arrived back, and the pilot, being nearly dead with cold, crashed the machine on landing. Fortunately neither of us was damaged. When we got in we found that they were just preparing to pack our kits, as they thought that we must have been brought down in Germany. I have added one of the propeller blades of the crashed reconnaissance machine to my collection.

On Sunday I was just getting up at a.m., having had a lazy morning, when a message came down from the office to say that two Huns were on their way to ——. I ordered out one of my machines, the one I always go with—and we left the ground to cut them off. When we were over B——, well in our own lines, at about 5,000 we spotted a Hun at about 11,000. We chased it, climbing all the time, till, when just near Lille, or about 10 miles into the German lines, we got level with it. By this time the Hun (an Albatross) had been joined by two other Huns.

We swept past the Albatross (a big white machine), and I got

40 rounds into it at close range; he banked, then rose, dived to earth, and crashed, apparently turning over. By now the other two machines had turned to engage us, and on turning we found two more coming from over Lille. Four to one—good odds. Fairly long odds; but still we thought we'd have a good smack at it. Rather to our annoyance, we saw what we took to be a sixth German—a tiny little single-seater.

On they came; they came in line, sweeping past us on the left, round our tail, and back on the right. To our surprise the little tiny machine fastened on to the tail of one of the Boches and chased it round and round, and proved to be a little Morane scout. They came on time and time again, pouring machine-gun fire on us, but for every one shot we got they got one back; but at one time we were getting the fire of four machines at once.

My hands began to lose all feeling, but I kept the gun going. *Bang! bang!* came their shots; we could feel the little jars as our machine was hit. But apparently they got more than they gave, as after 25 minutes' fighting two machines cleared off towards Lille, and the other two, not liking to be left to fight two British machines (although one was only a little single-seater), flew off southwards. The scout and we at once gave chase to one of them, but had to give up 20 miles further south, and gracefully retired to our own lines to the accompaniment of much 'Archy.'

Lieutenant-Observer J. F. P. Harvey, who was captured by the Germans, sent the following description, which appeared in the *Morning Post*, of a battle in mid-air and how he was treated after capture:—

I had had a fight with two German aeroplanes when a shell burst very close to us, and I heard a large piece whizz past my head. Then the aeroplane started to come down head first, spinning all the time. We must have dropped about 5,000 feet in about twenty seconds. I looked round at once and saw poor ——, with a terrible wound in his head, dead. I then realized that the only chance of saving my life was to step over into his seat and sit on his lap, where I could reach the controls. I managed to get the machine out of the terrible death-plunge, switched off the engine, and made a good landing on *terra firma*.

I shall never forget it as long as I live. The shock was so great that I could hardly remember a single thing of my former life for two days. Now I am getting better, and my mind is practically normal again. We were 10,000 feet up when poor —— was killed, and luckily it was this tremendous height that gave me time to think and act.

I met one of the pilots of the German machines that had attacked us. He could speak English well, and we shook hands. I had brought down his machine with my machine-gun, and he had had to land quite close to where I landed. He had a bullet through his radiator and petrol tank, but neither he nor his observer was touched. I met two German officers who knew several people I knew, and they were most awfully kind to me. They gave me a very good dinner of champagne and oysters, etc., and I was treated like an honoured guest.

CHAPTER 6

Fighting in the Air in 1916

The "Ace"—the airman who counts heads as so many enemy machines shot down to certain destruction—began to appear just before the Fokker monoplane. No doubt there were previously a few airmen on both sides who had brought down two or three enemies and were therefore distinguished; but until the single-seater scout became one of the most highly cultivated types there were not many of these individual scores. The early famous "Aces" included Major Hawker, Guynemer, Boelcke, and Immelmann. Von Richthofen became a pilot about Christmas, 1915. The size of the "bags" increased not because it became easier to bring down aeroplanes than formerly; quite the contrary. But there were more fights, the machine-gun had been speeded up, and the art of the air fighter more carefully cultivated.

At the end of 1915 we had a few two-seater fighting "pusher" aeroplanes, and a few tractor scouts with guns either firing over the top of the propeller or through a deflector propeller. We were so badly off for fighting scouts that our two-seater reconnaissance machines often had to work in pairs, or threes, for mutual protection. This was a point gained by the enemy by their "Fokker policy," that of attacking by groups of twos or threes. There had been a good deal of fighting between two-seaters, the British types including the Vickers, the B.E.2C and the B.E.2B. The year 1915 saw the beginning of the reign of the single-seater fighting scout designed for high speed, manoeuvrability, and steep diving.

Later on high altitude capacity became one of the most important qualities. Of single-seater machines the British used Morane "parasols" and biplanes. Sopwith "tabloids," Bristol "bullets," a Nieuport biplane, and a Martinsyde, none of which with the engines then employed on them could much exceed 95 miles per hour.

No sharp chronological division can be made in the methods of aerial fighting. There was never any long winter cessation of activity at the Western Front; but winter was usually a transition period from one to a bigger development, if only for the reason that each Spring saw an offensive launched by one side or the other, and for each offensive elaborate preparations had to be made.

Early in 1916 a distinct advance was observable. Our designers had set to work on the problem, and the Flying Service by the middle of the year possessed its first purely fighting squadrons mounted on two-seater tractors or on small fast single-seaters. Amongst the new British machines were the Sopwith 1½ strutter, the two-seater already mentioned, and the De Havilland pusher scout. The pusher two-seater known as the F.E., also put in an appearance; and it may be remarked here that the pusher, although never quite so fast as the fastest contemporaneous tractor, was a machine respected by the enemy on account of the freedom of movement for the forward gun.

In 1914 and 1915 machines were used at the front as they were available. Thus reconnaissance and artillery observation were performed on various types more or less unsuitable. In 1916, however, specialization in various directions began to show itself; although, except in the heavy bomber type and the fighting scouts, the lines drawn were never absolutely sharp. For example, one of our best two-seater fighters was used for artillery observation and also as a fast raider. The R.E.8, although the "R" stands for "reconnaissance," was used for bombing and a variety of other services.

This, by the way, was a machine with a very bad early record, which to some extent it lived down. It developed bad flying habits and structural weakness, and was further handicapped by the early R.A.F. engine which became notorious for its proneness to catch fire. Perhaps only an official-designed machine could have survived the home casualties alone caused by this type; which is the more regrettable because it kept back better designs that were, as a matter of fact, available. The R.E.8 was afterwards altered, and the engine improved.

This being one of the chapters on aerial fighting single-seaters will figure largely in it. With few exceptions, single-seater fighters at this period were driven by rotary engines, one reason being that this type of engine disposes the heaviest item in the machine in a small space longitudinally, thus giving quick manoeuvring. Later on, with the more exacting demands for speed and high altitude (in both qualities the rotary falls off rather rapidly), synchronizing with a difficulty in increasing the size of rotary engines, fixed engines were used with success both by the enemy and ourselves for the more powerful fighting scouts. But, notwithstanding, there was a demand for a high-power rotary, and the B.R. motor was much used in our scouts in 1917 and 1918. One advantage of the rotary is that it quickly gets off the ground.

In the year under review the Sopwith triplane, a quick and high climber that was very much liked by pilots, the redoubtable Sopwith "Camel," the Bristol two-seater fighter, and D.H. two-seaters became available. The S.E.5, a fixed-engine single-seater tractor scout of fine capabilities, one of the two undisputed successes of the Royal Aircraft Factory, also came into use.

One of the first things the air-fighter had to acquire was the ability to distinguish between friend and foe at a distance, and long before the tricolour rings of the Allies, or the black Maltese cross of the enemy became visible. Two French pilots on one occasion fought each other on a misty day, and both came back with their machines riddled with bullets. A comparison of notes discovered that each had mistaken the other for an enemy! And that was by no means the only instance of friend fighting friend in the sky.

Often it happened that a strange machine approached and the pilot found when quite close that it was marked with the concentric red, white, and blue rings of a friend. In that case each of them proceeded on his errand, whatever it might be. They could not exchange a word, or even much in the way of signalling, although if there should be anything special to communicate you could fly alongside for a few moments and, chiefly by gestures, intimate this or that. As a rule, a wave of the hand was the only greeting.

In 1916 formation flying was in its infancy. Signals between the leader and his followers were primitive. Thus a Very light was fired to signal stragglers up; there could be no attempt to keep perfect formation during complicated manoeuvres. To bold attack even by inferior force the protection afforded by flying in formation easily broke down; and the rule in the British Service was to attack vigorously and separate the leader from his followers. At this period the enemy rarely attacked a well-flown squadron with vigour.

Before a patrol or a squadron set out it was necessary to arrange a rendezvous for reformation in the event of a fight; but circumstances often made the keeping of this appointment impossible. And unfortunately it was a fairly common incident to lose pilots who strayed out of formation. When left to their own resources they either lost their way and were captured, or fell an easy prey to enemy formations.

Methods of fighting steadily developed. Many well-worn tricks and ruses were practised, but the air-fighter had ever to be alert for new tactics and new types of machines, and prompt to report them to his Squadron Commander for circulation throughout the Services. Thus our pilots soon discovered, at first to their cost, that if they saw a Fokker, almost invariably another machine was far overhead—a distant speck—watching for an opportunity to pounce. As soon as the Englishman was engaged with his more obvious opponent, down would come number two upon him.

As to fighting methods, a full dissertation upon them would be out of place anywhere than in a Service manual. Suffice to say, each type of aeroplane possessed its own particular qualities in terms of speeds at various heights, highest altitude attainable (or "ceiling"), rate of climb, armament, view, field of fire, "blind spot," and so on. The expert air-fighter—and woe betide the inexpert!—had to be familiar with all these details. The reader need be acquainted only with the more general considerations as, for example, that the aim is always helped by firing at a machine pursuing the same path, rather than trying to bag a machine flying in the opposite direction or across the bows. In the case of a single-seater scout attacking a pusher—even a two-seater—from behind, the latter is at a disadvantage, the observer's field of fire being cut off by the planes, the propeller, and the tail—a fact which often enabled an enemy to approach unseen. Considerable ingenuity was displayed in design.

Thus, the French produced a tractor single-seater, the pilot of which was seated behind the top plane, and able, by standing up, to see all around. The bottom plane was so small that a very slight turn enabled the pilot to see in all directions. The gun being mounted high, on the top plane, shot over the propeller; it was slightly inclined upwards, but not enough to make aiming difficult. The gun was fired from the control lever, and the pilot, at will, could point it upwards at a steeper angle than the normal.

Most of the two-seater fighters had the pilot in front working the fixed machine-gun, or guns; and the observer behind with a field of fire very little obstructed by parts of the machine. These two-seaters were often used on bombing raids, and being well armed did not need escorting provided they travelled in groups. In the two-seaters the only "blind spot" was behind and under the tail.

It was customary, even before the battle of the Somme, to allocate a portion of the line to a fighting squadron to patrol at a definite period in the day. This was done in order to secure freedom from molestation for our artillery observation, and also in order to beat off enemy photographic reconnaissance.

Before perusing descriptions of aerial battles the reader should be familiar with terms commonly employed. Thus, an Immelmann turn (there were various so-called "Immelmann" turns; and the name seems to have been given quite capriciously) consists in getting the machine up on one side without turning, and then letting it fall on its back; after a moment the nose drops, the machine dives vertically and recovers the correct flying position, but now travelling in the opposite direction; "returning on its own track like a whiplash." The terms "looping" and "spiral" are sufficiently well known. "Stalling" is loss of air-speed, deliberately provoked on occasion by heading the machine up so steeply that all way is lost, and it either slips back on its tail, ultimately swinging aft and then getting its head down, or immediately drops its head to the diving position, in which it is again in full control.

It was, and always will be, a cardinal maxim to get to lightward of your enemy; also to keep an eye on the amount of leeway due to wind lest, during the excitement of an action, you were carried far to the east; and, of course, whenever possible to get your attack home before you were perceived. Surprise in the air can, however, only be of very brief effectiveness, a matter of five or six seconds only; and then, unless you had fired to good purpose, your opponent would have a turn at you. It was a very sound rule that a single-seater should never attack a two-seater; or, if it attacked a two-seater tractor, it should never approach from either side astern, thus enabling the observer in the larger machine to take almost leisurely aim.

It was perfectly sound tactics, however, to chase up from directly astern. As a rule, the surprise attack on a two-seater having failed, it was the right course for a single-seater to dive out of the way, on the principle that "*he who fights and runs away lives to fight another day.*"

The danger of drifting over the enemy's lines was greater for the Allies than for the enemy, the prevailing winds in N.W. Europe being from the westerly half of the circle. This is a circumstance that considerably increased our Air Services casualties throughout the war.

The following account was published as a supplement to a Corps Summary at the beginning of 1916.

One of our machines, to which another was acting as escort, was engaged in reconnaissance work over Cambrai on the morning of December 29th. They were attacked by six Fokker monoplanes, firing through the propeller. As a result of the machine-gun fire of the six Fokkers, our escorting machine was immediately shot down, but its occupants seemed to reach the ground safely, so landing as to effect intentionally the destruction of their machine without injury to themselves. It was followed to the ground by two of the Fokkers. Our remaining machine succeeded in driving off and apparently seriously injuring by its fire the first Fokker which had attacked it. It was out of control when last seen, and was nose-diving with every prospect of injury or death to its occupants.

Our machine was then attacked by the three other Fokkers, which it fought for 15 minutes, and then, its machine-guns being temporarily out of action, its pilot decided that escape could only be sought by a very risky dive to within 20 feet of the ground—risky in that it necessitated a descent by very steep spirals at a speed of quite 100 miles an hour, with little room to recover. Only very delicate and confident handling could ensure the success of this manoeuvre, which only the absence of other means of escape could justify.

It was prompted by two other considerations. In the first place, a Fokker, being less handy, would not dare to pursue within 20 feet of the ground, the margin for recovery after the nose-diving being so very restricted; and, secondly, if our machine was once more to reach friendly territory in safety it was desirable that it should conceal from armed enemies to be surmounted in its front its nationality, and this it could only do by skimming over the ground at as low an elevation as possible.

Skimming along just above the ground, as skims a grouse under a hawk, our machine, hard pressed, turned westward for home, whereupon one of the German machines, all of which had maintained an elevation of 1,000 feet, swooped towards it, but was promptly driven off by rapid fire, one gun by that time having been repaired.

The fight continued half-way to the British lines, when two Fokkers gave it up. The British pilot and observer at once started climbing to attack the single remaining Fokker, but this brought back the two companions, and our machine resumed its original elevation. The three German machines ultimately turned back, giving up the chase when about a mile from the German lines, before crossing which the British pilot naturally sought to climb; but, our aeroplane being unable to rise higher than 800 feet owing to the engine having been hit in the fight, pilot and observer were subjected to very heavy rifle, machine-gun, and field artillery fire, which the machine fortunately survived, although its planes and spars were damaged, and some of its stays nearly severed.

The anxieties of the position had for long been greatly increased by the knowledge that only sufficient petrol remained in the tank to bring the machine just within the friendly lines if a direct course was pursued, so that to be driven in any degree out of that course would have been fatal. Early in the engagement the oil feed had been shot away, and, with an engine injured by rifle fire, the chances of ever reaching home had seemed remote, but an expiring effort landed the machine just within the French lines south-west of Arras.

On February 29th, near Merville, Lieutenant Leggatt with his observer, Lieutenant Howe, were on patrol at a height of 10,000 feet. Seeing an enemy aeroplane making for the German lines 6,000 feet up, Lieutenant Leggatt dived his machine down at a speed of well over 100 miles an hour, while Lieutenant Howe fired, and the enemy, apparently hit, dived and disappeared behind the German lines. A full account of the fight was given in the *Daily Chronicle*, from which the following particulars are taken.

Rising again to 9,000 feet, the British sighted an Albatross biplane, making towards the British aerodrome. Lieutenant Leggatt gradually overhauled the enemy until they were flying at the same level. When only 150 yards separated the two planes, Lieutenant Leggatt turned his machine slightly so that his observer could fire effectively. Hard firing continued for some time between the two machines, when suddenly the Albatross dived and turned. Lieutenant Leggatt piloted with great skill, and the chase was continued, both machines keeping up a heavy fire, 400 shots being fired from the British aeroplane.

The German nose-dived, and Lieutenant Leggatt followed suit, Lieutenant Howe keeping up the firing. The speed at which the British aeroplane was travelling whilst this was proceeding was about 150 miles an hour. The German pilot was wounded and his engine was damaged by fire. He was obliged to descend into the British lines, but before reaching earth his craft turned upside down. The enemy pilot and observer were taken prisoners, the former suffering from wounds.

In the first four months of 1916 the British brought down 42 enemy aeroplanes on the Western Front for a loss of 32. These figures should be borne in mind when the reader turns to the statistics of the air-fighting in 1918.

Second-Lieutenant Lord Francis Doune received the Military Cross. When on patrol with Second-Lieutenant Walker he sighted a Fokker machine 1,000 feet below them. He at once dived, and when within 60 yards Second-Lieutenant Walker opened fire. Lord Doune then headed straight for the Fokker, which had to rise steeply to avoid a collision. Second-Lieutenants Walker and Lord Doune then both opened fire and shot away one wing of the Fokker, which fell behind our lines. Lieutenant Walker also was awarded the Military Cross.

At this period the Royal Naval Air Service had a number of fighting squadrons on the left of the Allied line, besides one on the Somme. They were equipped with some of the best British machines available; indeed, they were the objects of the envy of the Royal Flying Corps, which was more limited to Government-designed aeroplanes. A few examples of the achievements of the Naval airmen are given here.

An attack was made upon Dunkirk by hostile aircraft. Several British machines went up with the object of cutting off the enemy on their return journey. One of our pilots in a Nieuport scout attacked three machines at a range of 400 yards. He opened fire on one machine and, observing another about 900 feet above him, making seawards, gave chase and fired the rest of the tray. He then reloaded, and, climbing to 10,000 feet, encountered a large two-seater, which opened fire at long range. The British pilot replied, and observed tracer bullets entering the machine, which started to smoke, and nose-dived towards the sea.

May 21st. Another R.N.A.S. pilot in a Nieuport scout, when six miles out to sea, over Zuydcoote, observed five hostile machines together and another one a little way behind. Climbing rapidly the pilot attacked the last one at close range of 100 yards. The hostile machine suddenly dived steeply, but the pilot was unable to ascertain the result as he was attacked from behind by three scouts, probably Fokker biplanes, at a range of 100 feet. The British pilot turned round to meet them, and, reloading, continued to fire. These machines, however, made good their retreat over the lines.

One of our men in a Nieuport scout followed the raiders out to sea, opening fire when off Mariakerke. He closed with three machines, one of which was seen to topple over suddenly and nose-dive out of sight. Reloading, the pilot attacked another machine which, after a few rounds, was observed to dive steeply. The third machine did not attempt to engage, but flew back over the lines. It is probable that one, and possibly two, of these machines were destroyed.

The work of the Royal Flying Corps provides almost inexhaustible material. From the official communications of the Air Board the following may be quoted:

May 4th. Second-Lieutenant C., on a de Havilland, sighted a hostile machine flying south at about 1,500 feet between Hem and Clery. He dived down and overtook the German, who also dived close to the ground, firing about 12 rounds at a range of 50 yards. The German machine tried to land, but hit a wire fence and broke up. The British pilot climbed to 200 feet, when he again dived, firing the rest of his drum at the pilot and observer, who were running across the field. One of them fell, and the other took refuge in a shed. Meanwhile Second-Lieutenant C.'s thumb switch had jammed, and he was forced to land, but the bump on landing loosened the spring, and he got off again, crossing the lines at about 500 feet under heavy fire.

May 16th. Twenty-seven fights in the air took place. Lieutenant D. and Corporal S. on an F.E. attacked an Albatross when approaching Lille. Half a drum of ammunition was fired, and the hostile machine spiralled rapidly down, firing occasionally. Later, the same machine was observed climbing again over Lille, and, following in the F.E. at about 50 yards, Lieutenant D. wheeled sharply, and opened fire at close range. The Albatross sheered away to the right, followed by the F.E. still firing at close range. The hostile machine then went down rapidly, and was seen to strike the ground at a cross-roads south of Lille. Smoke rose from the spot, and only one wing was visible. The F.E. was then attacked by a Fokker monoplane, which was driven off.

May 21st. Second-Lieutenant T., on a Martinsyde, flying at 12,500 feet, saw an Albatross over Fromelles at about 9,000 feet. He dived at it, reserving his fire till within close range. Both machines were diving at high speed with engines on. Second-Lieutenant T. having expended one drum, changed, and continued the attack. The enemy endeavoured to manoeuvre out of fire, turning in all directions, but Second-Lieutenant T. manoeuvred his Martinsyde, and managed to keep the enemy under fire at intervals. At about 4,000 feet over the S.W. corner of Lille the machines were so close that they nearly collided, but the enemy, after descending in a vertical dive, recovered himself, and escaped.

On June 29th one of our machines was attacked by three hostile aeroplanes which appeared out of a cloud. The pilot was wounded in the back and lost consciousness, but his observer, climbing out of his seat, roused him, and the pilot landed his machine safely in his own aerodrome. The observer made use of his wireless during the descent to summon a doctor.

One of the first of the French "Aces" was Nungesser, an aviator who had a remarkable career. When the war broke out he was a Hussar, aged 22 years. On September 3rd, during the retreat from Charleroi, he was mentioned in dispatches for having captured a German motorcar, put the German officers occupying it *hors de combat*, brought back the car and valuable papers which it contained under enemy fire, and, finally, placed his commanding officer, who was wounded, under shelter. The car was a French Mors, stolen by the Germans; and after that Nungesser used to be called the Mors Hussar.

On one occasion, driving the same car, he passed some old soldiers who said, "Why is this youth a mere motor-driver, while we are in the trenches?" Thereupon Nungesser refused to be a motorist any more. He became an aviator. He took part in 53 bombardments, and was thrice, as aviator, mentioned in dispatches. By the end of July, 1916, Nungesser had brought down 15 enemy machines. He is said to be the first airman to use a mirror as in motorcars to see behind him.

The famous German "Ace," Immelmann, met his conqueror in Lieutenant G. R. McCubbin, who was awarded the D.S.O. On one occasion Lieut. McCubbin seeing one of our machines about to engage two Fokkers, entered the fight, and his observer shot down one Fokker, which crashed to the ground. Returning from a bombing raid, he saw one of our machines being followed by a Fokker. He recrossed the lines to the attack, and his observer shot down the Fokker. Although very badly wounded in the arm, he successfully landed his machine well behind our lines. It was in the second of these encounters that McCubbin shot and killed Immelmann. The following account of the incident was given by the Air Board:—

On June 18th one of our F.E. aeroplanes whilst patrolling over Annay, at about 9 p.m., attacked three Fokkers. One immediately retired, whilst the other two turned towards Lens and proceeded to attack another F.E., which was then approaching from that direction. The first-mentioned F.E. (pilot, Lieutenant McC.; observer, Corporal W.) followed and joined in the fray, and, diving steeply on one of the attacking Fokkers, caused it to plunge perpendicularly to the ground. It was seen to fall to earth by one of our anti-aircraft batteries. A subsequent report from another machine in the neighbourhood states that the Fokker went to pieces in the air, and both wings broke off. Extracts from the German newspapers relating to the death of Lieutenant Immelmann make it clear that the pilot received his death as outlined above.

One day in July, a British pilot flying near Arras sighted six enemy machines approaching the British lines, and after them three other machines. He approached, and the formation scattered. At the same moment two more British machines attacked from above. The first-mentioned engaged the nearest machine, which for some reason unknown sheered off and dived, whilst a second enemy machine attacked from above. The Englishman, however, stuck to his first quarry, and, after considerable manoeuvring, got behind his tail within 30 yards and fired with such effect that the enemy crashed to earth.

Royal Aero Club rules of the road were ignored at the Front. By them it was ordained that machines, whether meeting or overtaking, shall give a clearance of at least 100 metres. At the Front pilots did not, as a rule, spend ammunition until within 30 yards of the enemy, and there were many occasions when they have flown alongside each other, only 10 yards between wing tip and wing tip, keeping up a hot fire. But it is on record that a Frenchman once brought a German machine down at a range of 200 yards.

We now begin to hear of a British pilot who was destined to become famous among the "Aces." On July 28th it was announced that the D.C.M. had been awarded to Second-Lieutenant A. Ball for conspicuous skill and gallantry on many occasions, notably when, after failing to destroy an enemy kite-balloon with bombs, he returned for a fresh supply, went back and brought it down in flames. He did great execution among enemy aeroplanes. On one occasion he attacked six in one flight, forced down two and drove the others off. This occurred several miles over the enemy's lines.

The French Air Service was doing badly in 1916 on account of administrative defects. Afterwards it made an ample recovery. The

German Fokker having been outmatched, it became the turn of the British. At the battle of the Somme in 1916 the enemy were practically driven from the skies. Indeed, at no subsequent period was our ascendancy so overwhelming, although it was never in doubt. The Germans made strenuous efforts, by reorganizing their Air Service, to apply the lesson we had taught them at the Somme.

We made at least equal progress, although there was still much amiss with regard to the ordering and delivering of new types. Over and over again if official processes had been quicker and, one might say, had everyone concerned worked solely for his country and not to advance personal interests, we could have been from 6 to 12 months earlier in the field with important new machines. The results would have been immeasurably important. Thus, in 1916, if the De Havilland, the Sopwith 1½ strutter, the Sopwith Camel, and the Handley-Page big bomber had been ordered, as they might have been, in quantities, the effect on the war would have been profound.

The French Government actually ordered Sopwith 1½ strutters on December 20, 1915. Our Government did not order any till about the following March. There were only two squadrons with this much-needed machine at the Somme even as late as September, 18 months after it had been brought out. Manufacturers were still busy making obsolete types, or at any rate inferior machines.

Dealing with the Somme operations, the *Times* military correspondent on July 25th wrote:—

The enemy continues to increase his artillery against our right, in the region by and beyond Flers, and, has evidently now massed there a great number of guns, which will have to be reckoned with in our further advance. ... In getting up his new guns he has been favoured by bad visibility. It is seven days since any rain fell, which, of course, has been advantageous to our troop movements. At the same time, the atmosphere has been continuously thick and hazy, and the denseness is increased by the dust from the dry ground, and the battle smoke. Aeroplane observation has been very difficult, for which the Germans have cause to be thankful. That is a condition which operates against us only, for the enemy has practically no observation from the air now under any conditions.

It is true that in the last few days a few of his aeroplanes have ventured in the thick air on hurried incursions across the lines, but they have amounted to nothing. It remains as true as it was when this battle began, that we have complete mastery in the air. Not only do we rule the skies above the lines, but we hold the enemy terrorized far into his own territory. Over his aerodromes our machines keep constant guard, so that his aviators can hardly rise, except under cover of the dark or in very thick weather.

A British reconnaissance was attacked on May 31st by three Fokkers when in the neighbourhood of Cambrai. The enemy were first seen diving at our machines from the rear, with the sun behind them. Our machines, which were heavily fired at, retaliated as occasion offered. Soon after the fight began one of the Fokkers was seen to turn half a loop, sideslip badly, and nose-dive. It was seen nose-diving, having apparently been hit by our fire. One of our machines was last seen soon after the commencement of the fight; but owing to the fact that all were busily engaged in the running fight, which was of a persistent nature, its fate was not observed. About the same time, however, a pilot of one of our machines reported that a machine, apparently out of control, dived over him, almost touching his top plane, and disappeared, no more being seen of it.

Two of our officers in an R.E.8, when on artillery duty, saw a Fokker flying over the enemy's trenches. They followed the German for about 1½ miles in the direction of Lille, where he turned to attack. Our officers opened fire at a range of about 50 yards. When level with the tail of our machine the enemy turned sharply and dived, and was further fired at as he turned. He dived more steeply, and was observed by Lieutenant K. to crash to earth in a field near Haubourdin.

In September, 1916, the D.S.C. was awarded in the following cases to Flight Sub-Lieutenant R. S. Dallas and to Sub-Lieutenant C. B. Oxley. The former, in addition to performing consistently good work in reconnaissances and fighting patrols since December, 1915, had been brought to notice by the Vice-Admiral, Dover Patrol, for the specially gallant manner in which he carried out his duties. Amongst other exploits is the following:

On May 21, 1916, he sighted at least 12 hostile machines, which had been bombing Dunkirk. He attacked one at 7,000 feet, and then attacked a second machine close to him. After reloading he climbed to 10,000, and attacked a large hostile two-seater machine off Westende. The machine took fire and nose-dived seawards. Another enemy machine then appeared, which he engaged, and chased to the shore, but had to abandon owing to having used all his ammunition.

Sub-Lieutenant Oxley was acting as observer with Flight-Lieutenant Edward H. Dunning, D.S.C., as pilot, on escort and reconnaissance patrol for a flight of bombing machines on the Bulgarian coast, on June 20, 1916. Two enemy machines were engaged at close range and forced to retire, and as our machine withdrew Flight-Lieutenant Dunning was hit in the left leg and the machine itself was badly damaged. Sub-Lieutenant Oxley, having first improvised a tourniquet which he gave to Lieutenant Dunning, took control of the machine while the latter put on the tourniquet. The pilot was obliged to keep his thumb over a hole in the lower part of the petrol tank in order to keep enough fuel to return to the aerodrome, where he made a good landing.

Two of our pilots, while on an offensive patrol on September 15th encountered 17 German aeroplanes at varying heights. They dived into the middle of the hostile formation and attacked. One pilot got to very close quarters with a hostile machine, which burst into flames and was seen to plunge to earth. He then attacked a second machine, which was driven down and fell in a field. A third machine went down vertically and was seen to crash.

Boelcke, a famous German "Ace," was killed in a collision in the air on October 28, 1916. A wreath was sent by British prisoners of war, and it bore the inscription, "From the British officers who are prisoners of war at Osnabruck. October 28, 1916."

Boelcke's was the first "travelling circus"; that is, a squadron of pilots selected on account of individual prowess, and moving as a complete unit by specially fitted railway trains from one part of the Front to another, as required.

On August 11th, during a reconnaissance in Egypt, a British machine was attacked by two of the enemy. A bullet broke the British pilot's jaw, another pierced his shoulder, a third found a resting-place in his left leg, and his left hand was also wounded. He fainted, regaining consciousness when only 500 feet above the earth. He was over his own lines. He brought his machine safely to land, and then found that his observer was wounded in the chest and shoulder. With difficulty he made his report, fainted and died.

A British aeroplane was soaring 11,000 feet above German territory on reconnoitring duty. Suddenly a shell burst near it, killing the pilot instantly, severely damaging the machine, but not injuring the observer, Lieutenant Howey, in any way. The aeroplane tipped nose downwards and fell 6,000 feet, Howey during this terrific fall performing a veritable gymnastic feat. He succeeded in slipping from his place to that of his comrade, unclasped his dead hands, sat upon his knees, and, in spite of the appalling situation, seized the control lever and in a miraculous manner righted his machine just at the moment it reached the earth after a veritable plunge to death. Howey was taken prisoner.

Major L.W. Brabazon Rees was awarded the V.C. on December 16, 1916. While on flying duty he sighted what he took to be a bombing party of our own machines returning home. He went up to escort them, but on getting nearer discovered that they were a party of 10 enemy machines. He was immediately attacked by one, and after a short encounter it disappeared behind the enemy's lines in a damaged condition. Five other machines then attacked him at long range, but these he dispersed on coming to close quarters, after seriously damaging two others. Seeing two others going westwards he gave chase, but on getting nearer he was wounded in the thigh, which caused him temporarily to lose control of his machine. He quickly righted it, however, and closed with the enemy, firing at a range of only a few yards until his ammunition was used up. He then returned and succeeded in landing in the British lines.

Sergeant Thomas Mottershead was posthumously awarded the V.C., and the story of his heroic flight was told in the *Gazette* as follows:—

When attacked at an altitude of 9,000 feet the petrol tank was pierced, and the machine set on fire. Enveloped in flames, which his observer, Lieutenant Gower, was unable to subdue, this very gallant soldier succeeded in bringing his aeroplane back to our lines, and though he made a successful landing the machine collapsed on touching the ground, pinning him beneath the wreckage, from which he was subsequently rescued.

Though suffering extreme torture from burns, Sergeant Mottershead showed most conspicuous presence of mind in the careful selection of a landing-place, and his wonderful endurance and fortitude undoubtedly saved the life of his observer. He has since died from his injuries.

Remarkable feats performed by Lieutenant Albert Ball, D.S.O., were described in the *London Gazette*, issued on September 26, 1916. In recognition of one action Lieutenant Ball received the D.S.O., and for another he was awarded a bar to the order. The first is thus described:—

Observing seven enemy machines in formation, he immediately attacked one of them and shot it down at 15 yards' range. The remaining machines retired. Immediately afterwards, seeing five more hostile machines, he attacked one at about 10 yards' range and shot it down, flames coming out of the fuselage. He then attacked another of the machines which had been firing at him, and shot it down into a village, when it landed on the top of a house. He then went to the nearest aerodrome for more ammunition, and, returning, attacked three more machines, causing them to dive under control. Being then short of petrol he came home. His own machine was badly shot about in these fights.

Lieutenant Ball's bar was won by the following performance:—

When on escort duty to a bombing raid he saw four enemy machines in formation. He dived on to them and broke up their formation, and then shot down the nearest one, which fell on its nose. He came down to about 500 feet to make certain it was wrecked. On another occasion, observing 12 enemy machines in formation, he dived in amongst them, and fired a drum into the nearest machine, which went down out of control. Several more hostile machines then approached, and he fired three more drums at them, driving down another out of control. He then returned, crossing the lines at a low altitude, with his machine very much damaged.

By the end of September Ball, now a Captain, had brought down 29 German aeroplanes and one kite-balloon, and he had destroyed three enemy aeroplanes in one morning. Earlier records of individual scores are not to be trusted. Thus, the Germans included destroyed kite-balloons with their successes. And some of the French and British totals included aeroplanes about whose total destruction there was some doubt. Later, however, a victory was not admitted by the British authorities until fully confirmed.

Second-Lieutenant Norman Brearley was awarded the Military Cross:—

He went out to attack an enemy kite-balloon and managed to get immediately above his objective. He then pretended that he had been hit by anti-aircraft fire and side-slipped down to 1,500 feet, when he suddenly dived at the balloon, which was being hauled down, and fired into it until he almost touched it. When at 300 feet from the ground the balloon burst into flames, and was entirely destroyed. He then returned.

Guynemer was now one of the famous French "Aces." When the war broke out he was at school in France preparing for an engineering career. Previously he had been at Westminster School. Indeed, he was of partly English extraction. His first fight was on July 19, 1915. He was up in a two-seater with an observer when he met a German aeroplane over Soissons, and there over the centre of the city, in view of hundreds of his compatriots, fought his first duel in the air.

It lasted ten minutes. Guynemer took his machine to within 50 feet of his rival to give his observer practically point-blank range, and the machine-gun fired 115 bullets. Then the observer was wounded in the hand, and Guynemer took control of the machine-gun as well as of the aeroplane. Finally the German pilot was struck, and immediately afterwards the enemy machine caught fire.

One of his duels was one of the most dramatic air episodes of the war. Guynemer, flying at an altitude of over 13,000 feet and at a distance of over 50 miles behind the German lines, sighted a German squadron of two observation aeroplanes with an escort of two fighting machines heading for the French lines. He took refuge behind some clouds until the German squadron should pass ahead of him, and then started the pursuit from behind.

The German machine nearest him chanced to be an observation aeroplane, and he opened his machine-gun fire at an altitude of just two miles. He killed the observer with his third bullet, and with the tenth the pilot was shot out from the machine, which at the same time began its whirling course down.

Although the machine was the second one Guynemer had brought down that day, he at once started after the other three, but they had all disappeared.

On one occasion at a height of about 10,000 feet a shell burst close to his aeroplane. The left wing was completely cut to bits, and the canvas fluttered in the wind, making the rents still worse. In a few seconds there was nothing left on the frame but a piece of canvas the size of a pocket-handkerchief. The machine fell, and Guynemer gave himself up for lost.

"At 4,800 feet," he says, "I determined to make a fight for it, all the same. The wind had brought me back into our own lines. I was almost happy. I was already thinking of my funeral, with sorrowing friends walking behind my last remains. I had nothing more to fear from the Pickelhauben."

He tried to manoeuvre the machine, but it would not respond. Finally he crashed to earth and by a miracle, although stunned, no bones were broken.

Major Hawker was brought down by von Richthofen on November 23, 1916. Von Richthofen, telling the story in *The Red Air-Fighter*, says:—

> The Englishman tried to catch me up in the rear while I tried to get behind him. So we circled round and round like madmen after one another at an altitude of about 10,000 feet. First we circled 20 times to the left, and then 30 times to the right. Each tried to get behind and above the other.
>
> Soon I discovered that I was not meeting a beginner. He had not the slightest intention to break off the fight. He was travelling in a box which turned beautifully.[1] However, my packing-case was better at climbing than his. But I succeeded at last in getting above and beyond my English waltzing partner.
>
> When we had got down to about 6,000 feet without having achieved anything particular, my opponent ought to have discovered that it was time for him to take his leave. The wind was favourable to me, for it drove us more and more towards the German position. At last we were above Bapaume, about half a mile behind the German front. The gallant fellow was full of pluck, and when we had got down to about 3,000 feet he merrily waved to me as if he would say, Well, how do you do?
>
> The circles which we made round one another were so narrow that their diameter was probably no more than 250 or 300 feet. I had time to take a good look at my opponent. I looked down into his carriage and could see every movement of his head. If he had not had his cap on I would have noticed what kind of a face he was making.
>
> My Englishman was a good sportsman, but by and by the thing became a little too hot for him. He had to decide whether he would land on German ground or whether he would fly back to the English lines. Of course he tried the latter, after endeavouring in vain to escape me by loopings and such tricks. At that time his first bullets were flying around me, for so far neither of us had been able to do any shooting.
>
> When he had come down to about 300 feet he tried to escape

1. Major Hawker was flying a de Havilland 2, a pusher, with a 100-H.P. Monosoupape Gnome engine.

by flying in a zigzag course, which makes it difficult for an observer on the ground to shoot. That was my most favourable moment. I followed him at an altitude of from 250 to 150 feet, firing all the time. The Englishman could not help falling. But the jamming of my gun nearly robbed me of my success.

My opponent fell shot through the head 150 feet behind our line. His machine-gun was dug out of the ground and it ornaments the entrance of my dwelling.

Up to the end of 1916 the biggest aerial battle was the one that took place south-east of Arras on November 10, 1916, when about 70 aeroplanes were engaged. The battle was described by the *Daily Telegraph* correspondent, from whose account a short quotation is given here.

About nine o'clock in the morning a squadron of British aeroplanes, 30 strong, rose from the ground and mustered in the air to go on a bombing expedition across the German lines. Part of the machines were bomb carriers, and the remainder were an escort, composed of 'fighting planes' and scouts. The squadron, taking their positions in the air, advanced towards the German lines.

A force comprising between 30 and 40 German aeroplanes came forward. The higher layers of the British force descended to the Germans' level, and promptly engaged them. . . .

There is now plan and method in these things, the aeroplanes co-operating so as to get the best results ' for the team.' The Germans were forced back and back, over their own ground, the English machines making steady progress all the while towards the objective which they had set out that morning to reach. And at length they reached it—the little township of Vaulx-Vraucourt, which is well over the German lines northeast of Bethune. Here, even while the air-fight was going on, the bomb-carrying machines dropped their bombs on the military points they had set out to damage. Then they calmly beat off the German squadron, inflicting upon them greater loss than they themselves sustained.

The casualties were as follows:—British: Two bombing machines and two scouting machines missing; one observer killed and two pilots wounded. The Germans lost probably six machines. Three of these six are certain losses, because they were seen actually to fall to the ground. The other three are not counted as certain, because, though seen to be hit and falling, they were not seen actually to strike the ground.

The end of this year saw the brilliant French offensive at Verdun, during which enemy airmen were practically driven out of the sky.

CHAPTER 7

Fighting in the Air in 1917

By the end of 1916 it was common to see aeroplanes patrolling at a height of about 20,000 feet. Indeed they were sometimes troubled even at that height by the "Archies," although it was rare to be hit. Between the summer of 1916 and the summer of 1917 there was an increase of average height, speed, and climb, on machines employed as fighters and bombers. The extension of aeroplane co-operation with infantry found a use for machines incapable of very fast climbing, but towards the end of the war a special type of "trench strafe" was designed. Formation flying became more general in 1917, and more accurate.

For fighting purposes aeroplanes may be classified in a few broad divisions, but each of these divisions comprises various types differing from each other in details with which it is necessary for the airman to be acquainted. The classification of fighting aeroplanes did not vary much from the time when fighting became one of their recognized functions, although within the divisions typal development was continual, and the speed and other qualities of machines were ever being improved.

There are the scouts, light machines quick on the controls. These, whether tractor or pusher, cannot fire astern, so that to attack them, it is best to approach from behind, either above or below. Attacking from below, a long burst of fire is possible. Diving down from above the speed of the attacker is so great that the burst of fire at effective range can only be brief, but the attacker gains sufficient speed to climb rapidly and get height for another attack. On the other hand, when a machine is attacked from below it is usually able to out-turn the attacker, since it can afford to lose a little height.

The weight of a machine, is an important factor to its manoeuvring qualities. The heavier it is the greater is its inertia, and the longer distance it will take to reverse direction. It is easy to turn a scout sharply without any appreciable skid, it is impossible to turn a heavy bomber without a certain amount of skidding, which enters into the calculations both of the designer and of the pilot. Another important detail is the distribution of weight; and, since the engine is the heaviest item in the load, the size and type of the engine are important considerations.

Some scouts are driven by rotary, some by stationary engines. The former have the advantage of quickness on the turn, due to the weight being concentrated at the centre of gravity. The rotating engine has a gyroscopic effect causing a tendency to climb when the machine is turned one way, and to dive when it is turned the other way; and a good pilot makes use of this peculiarity.

The two-seater fighter is a heavy machine, which can be "stunted", although this is not usually the best way to get the fullest fighting value of the two men and their machine-guns. The gunner in the rear (in the case of the tractors) being able to train his gun in almost any direction, it is desirable to rely more upon marksmanship than upon quick manoeuvring; and the chance of surprising a two-seater should be comparatively slight. As the gunner in these machines is right in the slipstream of the propeller, when stunting or diving he cannot stand up and use his gun easily, therefore the attacker should if possible compel a two-seater to stunt, and thus handicap it.

The two-seater pusher, of which the F.E. is an example, has a gunner out in front with a clear field of fire.

Bold attack is often successful, and by boldness of attack the British habitually fought better than the enemy, always of course excepting the German "Aces," between whom and our own or the French there was really nothing to choose. But on our side we had a greater proportion of air-fighters who were spirited in attack.

At no period of the war was it wise to begin firing at more than 200 yards' range; and it is curiously easy to underestimate the distance in the air. The trained fighter reserves his fire until he is sure; and the range is very small. Ultimately, no doubt, the range will increase, and someday aerial fights may begin at ranges of 1,000 yards or more, but before that is possible improvements will be necessary in sighting mechanism.

In formation flying the first principle is the triangle, the apex—the leader—in front, and two other machines slightly behind and above.

The two rear machines by diving can overtake the leader, and support him. If a rear machine is attacked the other can promptly come to his aid. Sometimes one such triangle is supported by another triangle overhead. No matter how big a formation, it is based upon the triangle or wedge.

At first, communication between individuals of a formation was chiefly by Very lights. Thus, a red light meant "Follow me," or "I am attacking, follow me." The code was extended by rocking the machines. For example, if the leader rocked his machine first to the right, then left, then right, it meant "The squadron will wheel to the right." Before the end of the war the British used wireless telephony with success for inter-communication in squadrons and for communication with the base. This meant an enormous advance, and one can at present only conjecture about aerial fighting of the future. But at the period under review signals of various kinds were used.

A formation is more difficult to hit by anti-aircraft artillery than a single machine; or rather, for the same number of hits a greater proportion of shots must be fired. This is due to the difficulty of the gun-layers and range-finders agreeing as to the particular machine laid on.

A machine flying at a lower level, with the earth for background, is more difficult to see than one higher and against the sky. And it is more difficult to observe accurately troops on the ground than for the troops to see the machine. This is the same condition as in pigeon shooting. Everyone knows that on a dull day with slight mist the man with the gun has a much better chance of getting birds, for the latter simply do not see their enemy approach until he is very near.

Most of the German fighters used to shoot too high when approaching end-on; and our men were instructed that it was a good plan directly within effective range to dive and then come up towards the enemy and fire at an angle, so that the German pilot was not protected by his engine. Again it was an axiom for scout pilots never to present their side to an enemy.

Perhaps of all the methods of attack, that by stalling right under an opponent is the most spectacular. With a gun firing through the propeller it is, of course, wise to keep the engine on all the time, for if the propeller slowed down the firing might be seriously interrupted at the critical moment.

Writing early in 1917, von Richthofen expressed the opinion that successful air-fighting depends more upon personal ability and energy than upon trick-flying. He testified to the British habit of accepting and offering battle whenever possible, and declares that the French have a different character—"They like to set traps and attack their opponents unawares." This, however, is the enemy's point of view and one, be it said, that perhaps passed through the hands of the German Censor before publication.

As a matter of fact, the specialist fighters on; the British side were not merely plucky, they studied and practised unremittingly. And especially did they practise aerial marksmanship. Some, like Captain Ball, adopted . the practice of dropping a newspaper or a petrol tin out of their machine and then circling round and firing at it; and to a large extent they were permitted to train themselves, although as early as 1916 Service manuals on aerial fighting were circulated through the squadrons, and previously to that lectures were given by experts. In the training of the fighting pilot at home, certainly from the middle of 1917, aerial gunnery was given the highest importance.

At the period with which we are now dealing it could, however, be truly said that the enemy air-fighters had fewer failures from the cause of machine-gun jamming than did ours, and this was due as much to the pains-taking character of the Germans as to anything else.

At the end of 1916 and the beginning of 1917 the famous "Storks" squadron was at work under Major Brocard. The "Ace" Guynemer was its principal star. Up to January 6th it had fought 820 duels and brought down 83 German aeroplanes and three kite-balloons.

Flight-Lieutenant E. E. Grange received the Distinguished Service Cross. On January 4, 1917, during one flight he had three separate engagements with hostile machines, all of which were driven down out of control. On January 5th he attacked three hostile machines, one of which was driven down in a nose-dive. On January 7th after having driven down one hostile machine, he observed two other enemy aircraft attacking one of our scouts. He was on the way to its assistance when he was attacked by a third hostile scout. He was hit in the shoulder by a bullet from this machine, but landed his aeroplane safely in an aerodrome on our side of the lines.

Lieutenant A. Dennison, on January 24th, although severely wounded in the arm, continued his fight with two enemy machines of which he brought down one, only breaking off the engagement through lack of ammunition.

Second-Lieutenant S. G. Kingsley was attacked by three enemy machines and shot down. Although wounded he did not choose the easiest landing-place, which would have made his machine an enemy capture, but deliberately went out to sea, alighted, and swam ashore. In those days British airmen captured by the enemy were well treated.

Captain Albert Ball, V.C., D.S.O., fought his last fight on May 7th, having then about 50 German machines to his score. He ascended with 10 others on the evening of that day, and was last seen as late as 8 o'clock. He failed to return. Von Richthofen purports to tell the story of the fight in his book, attributing the victory to his younger brother, Lothar. But the machine brought down by him was a triplane; and we know that Ball was not flying a triplane.

Captain Ball had many air-fights in the two previous days, bringing down three enemy machines and putting others to flight. On May 5th he sighted two hostile craft, and as he was low, he flew away from them, climbing steadily. When the German aeroplanes were quite near his tail Captain Ball swerved sharply, slid underneath one of his opponents, and turned on his machine-gun. The German fell out of control.

Captain Ball then manoeuvred in order to attack the second enemy machine, but it flew straight at him, firing steadily. Captain Ball returned the fire as the German came full tilt at him, and a collision seemed inevitable, when the hostile machine suddenly went down. Captain Ball's machine was hit in many places. During his return journey he fell in with two other hostile aircraft, but his ammunition was exhausted and his sights covered with oil, so he "put his nose down" and returned to the aerodrome.

With regard to the machines in use in the Spring of 1917, von Richthofen admits that the Albatross scout was outclimbed by the best British machines, Camels and S.E.'s. The aerial fighting had become much more strenuous.

Some of the Royal Naval Air Service fighting squadrons working in France, and almost without exception flying Sopwith "Camels," did good work, as the Honours lists show.

Flight Sub-Lieutenant J. J. Malone was awarded the D.S.O. in May, 1917, for successfully attacking and bringing down hostile aircraft on numerous occasions. On April 23rd he attacked a hostile scout and drove it down under control. He then attacked a second scout, which, after the pilot had been hit, turned over on its back and went down through the clouds. A third scout, attacked by him from a distance of about 20 yards, descended completely out of control. While engaging a fourth machine he ran out of ammunition, so returned to the advanced landing-ground, replenished his supply, and at once returned and attacked another hostile formation, one of which he forced down out of control. On the following day he engaged a hostile two-seater machine and, after badly wounding the observer, forced it to land on our side of the lines.

Flight-Lieutenant L. S. Breadner was given the D.S.C. He brought down three hostile machines and forced several others to land. On April 6, 1917, he drove down a hostile machine which was wrecked while attempting to land in a ploughed field. On April 11th he destroyed a hostile machine, which fell in flames, brought down another in a spinning nose-dive with one wing folded up, and forced a third to land.

One member of a naval fighting squadron was attacked by two Albatrosses and a Halberstadt fighter. He soon accounted for the latter by getting several hits on its engine. But now three more red Albatrosses flew on to the scene, and one of them he downed by killing the pilot. He afterwards related how delighted he was to see the head of this pilot exactly fill the ring of his machine-gun sight. But all this fighting had meant a steady loss of altitude, and he found himself close to the ground behind the German lines. The other enemy machines had disappeared. Possibly they believed he was wrecked: but in any case it is difficult to see a machine far below you.

On his way home he fired at some German cavalry; and soon after he was attacked by an Albatross. He rocked his machine until close to his opponent and then looped over him, and opening fire saw the bullets go into the pilot's back. Before he returned he fired at some Germans in their trenches.

One naval airman visited a German flying school and spread confusion and death among the pupils. The story goes that this was to avenge his brother, who was shot at and killed by a German aviator whilst descending in a parachute to safety from the burning kite-balloon in which he had been observing.

Flight Sub-Lieutenant W. E. Flett returning from a bombing raid was engaged with three enemy machines. His gun-layer, Air Mechanic R. G. Kimberley, was slightly wounded in the wrist, which numbed his hand. Not-withstanding this he succeeded in bringing down two of the enemy machines, being again wounded by an explosive bullet in the ankle. The machine was riddled with bullets, and, owing to the damage, navigation was most difficult, and the return journey was very slow. Consequently he was again attacked, but although the gun-layer was twice wounded, the enemy machine was driven off.

On other fronts the Air Services were doing good work. Thus, on the Salonika Front, Captain Green was awarded the D.S.O. and a Serbian Order. And it should be remembered that German air activity being less than in France, and their airmen usually seeking to evade conflict, it required great determination to bring them to book and usually took the British airmen well over the lines. Three German aeroplanes were brought down in two days by Captain Green, who had already accounted for four enemy machines single-handed, and another one in which he shared the honours with a brother-airman. On another occasion Captain Green flew into the midst of a squadron of six bombing aeroplanes and brought two of them down. One fell between the lines and the other in flames behind the enemy's trenches.

Squadron-Commander Roderick S. Dallas (killed in July, 1918), appointed a Squadron Commander in the R.N.A.S. in June, 1917, was the hero of many adventures, some of which are mentioned in the last chapter. Roderick Dallas was a pilot of quite extraordinary skill, and, by the way, a black and white artist of unusual ability.

Among his exploits was the following. Having "lost his engine" at some 15,000 feet, he was proceeding to glide home, when two Huns attacked him. Dallas shot them both, and reached home safely.

Much aerial fighting was due to the necessity to protect our artillery observation and photographing aeroplanes. Flight-Commander C. D. Booker on April 26, 1917, went to the assistance of some of our photographic machines, which were about to be attacked by 12 Albatross scouts. One of these he fired on at close range, and brought it down out of control. On May 24th, whilst on patrol, he went to the assistance of a formation of our machines which was being attacked by nine hostile scouts. He attacked one of the latter, which was driven down in flames and crashed. Later in the same day he attacked and drove down out of control another hostile machine. On numerous other occasions he attacked enemy machines and drove them down out of control.

Flight-Lieutenant R. A. Little, D.S.C., destroyed an Aviatik on April 28th. Next day he shot down a hostile scout, which crashed. On April 30th, with three other aeroplanes, he went up after enemy machines—and saw a big fight going on between fighter escorts and hostile aircraft. Flight-Lieutenant Little attacked one at 60 yards' range, and brought it down out of control. A few minutes later he attacked a red scout with a larger machine than the rest. This machine was handled with great skill, but by clever manoeuvring Flight-Lieutenant Little got into a good position and shot it down out of control.

On July 16, 1917, he observed two Aviatiks flying low over the lines. He dived on the nearest one, firing a long burst at very close range. The enemy machine dived straight away, and Flight-Lieutenant Little followed him closely down to 500 feet, the enemy machine falling out of control. On July 20th he attacked a D.F.W. After a short fight, the enemy machine dived vertically. Its tail plane seemed to crumple up, and it was completely wrecked. On July 22nd he attacked a D.F.W. Aviatik and brought it down completely out of control. On July 27th, in company with another pilot, he attacked an Aviatik. After each had fired about 20 rounds the enemy machine began to spin downwards. Lieutenant Little got close to it, and observed both the occupants lying back in the cockpits, as if dead. The machine fell behind the enemy's lines, and was wrecked. Flight-Lieutenant Little always showed remarkable courage and boldness in attacking enemy machines.

About this time the enemy painted their machines in glaring colours and apparently for some particular purpose, and not, as some supposed, because of the vanity of individual flyers, or, as one special correspondent surmised, after the manner of a savage who hopes to frighten his foe to death.

One British aviator who went out to search for trouble found it with a red body and wings that were green on top and blue underneath. One German squadron encountered was composed of machines painted white, red, and green, and one of khaki colour with greenish grey wings. Individual flyers have included a green aeroplane with a yellow nose, another with a red body, green wings, and yellow stripes, another with scarlet body, brown tail, and reddish-brown wings, with white crosses on a bright green background, another with yellow body and red wings, with light blue tips, a black machine with white markings, a machine with one green and one white wing, and others with silver discs, yellow noses and blue tails.

The colouring of aeroplanes, airships, and observation balloons had for long received attention, not so much with a view to "invisibility" in the air, which is probably impossible to achieve in a craft essentially opaque and usually seen against the sky, but in order to render them inconspicuous when on the ground or between the observer and the ground. The usual method was to smear them with confusing patches of dull brown and green. The new German method might be of some small assistance in confusing anti-aircraft gunners; but it might also be an experiment with a view to rendering manoeuvres in aerial battle more difficult to comprehend to an aerial enemy. Everyone must have noticed how difficult it is sometimes to see which way an aeroplane is turning, whether to starboard with left wing up, or to port with left wing down.

An artifice by which the various parts of the craft, instead of being of uniform colour, are of different colours, the more glaring the better, and especially when throughout a squadron no two machines are coloured alike, might well help to confuse an enemy even at close range. In the excitement of battle, when the aviator has so many things to look after, this might make all the difference in situations where decisions have to be made in tenths of a second. Such a scheme could, of course, only be worked provided it were completely legible to aircraft acting in concert, else it would defeat its own ends. And like many other ingenious devices used in the war, its success would depend largely upon novelty.

Experiments were made in the British Air Service in camouflaging scout aeroplanes with a view to perplexing the enemy as to direction of movement, after the manner in which merchant ships were camouflaged; but, so far as the author is aware, there were no satisfactory results.

In the fighting for Messines Ridge the British Air Service beat the Germans. On the front of General Plumer's army our aviators between June 1st and June 6th crashed 24 machines and drove down as many to an unknown fate.

An excellent description of this phase of the war in the air appeared in the *Daily Express* on June 21st from the pen of Mr. Percival Philips who, before the war gave him his opportunity as a War Correspondent, was familiar with aerodrome doings in England and abroad.

The German airmen have been making a desperate attempt to recover some of the prestige lost by their complete subjugation during the battle of Messines. When the British infantry took the ridge their comrades overhead completely 'smothered' the enemy aircraft, and prevented them from taking any part in the battle.

Since then the Germans have been roaming the skies in large formations behind their own lines. British pilots, who continually fly into the enemy's country, report that they seldom meet Germans in squadrons of fewer than 15 machines, while occasionally a flock of as many as 40 Aviatiks and Albatrosses was encountered.

These hostile craft, painted in all the colours of the rainbow, present a curious spectacle to our observers as they sail across the clouds, swinging together like a covey of frightened birds whenever British patrols turn in their direction.

On one occasion recently nine enemy aeroplanes attacked one of ours, but immediately another British machine came to its assistance the Germans flew away, firing a few futile volleys from their machine-guns.

There have been many individual feats of daring by the British pilots. Here is a brief outline of one intricate battle which was fought in the Ypres area recently. One of our offensive patrols engaged nine Albatross scouts which were trying to interfere with British flyers. Lieutenant X. peppered one of them at close range. He saw the German's left wing break off, and the wreck crashed to the ground. He then turned and fired into another hostile aeroplane only 60 yards away, and this machine staggered and lost a wing in the same way and went whirling earthwards. Later the same officer engaged four more enemy machines and drove down two of them, one being forced to land.

Lieutenant Z., of the same squadron, dived at one of four German planes which were painted like a prism, and it fell completely out of control. He then joined in the battle between the 15 Germans and the British squadron, but one of the German scouts obtained a favourable position 'on his tail,' and he spun 4,000 feet or so and shook off his adversary. Then he attacked a black and white Albatross from underneath, and it turned completely over and crashed down in a field."

Raids on England were the occasion of some desperate air-battles. Captain John Palethorpe was awarded the Military Cross in July, 1917.

On the occasion referred to Captain Palethorpe, with Air Mechanic J. O. Jessop as gunner, was engaged in an endurance trial from a testing squadron. When about three miles from the coast a formation of 17 enemy aeroplanes was sighted. Captain Palethorpe at once attacked under very heavy fire, till the gunner was killed. He then landed, and having procured another gunner endeavoured to renew the attack.

The story of a fight with raiders is told by an eyewitness in a letter to the father of Second-Lieutenant J. E. R. Young, who with his observer were killed early in July, 1917. The letter was published in the *Daily Chronicle*. Here is a brief extract from it:—

Your son, as you know, had only been in my squadron for a short time, but quite long enough for me to realize what a very efficient and gallant officer he was, and what a tremendous loss he is to me. He had absolutely the heart of a lion, and was a very good pilot. Your son has been up on every raid of late, and has always managed to get in contact with the enemy machines.

The last raid, which unfortunately resulted in his death, shows what a very gallant officer we have lost. Almost single-handed he flew straight into the middle of the 22 machines, and both himself and his observer at once opened fire. All the enemy machines opened fire also, so he was horribly outnumbered.

The volume of fire to which he was subjected was too awful for words. To give you a rough idea, there were 22 machines; each machine had four guns; each gun was firing about 400 rounds a minute.

Your son never hesitated in the slightest. He flew straight on until, as I should imagine, he must have been riddled with bullets. The machine then put its nose right up in the air and fell over, and went spinning down into the sea from 14,000 feet. I unfortunately had to witness the whole affair.

The machine sank so quickly that it was, I regret, impossible to save your son's body, as he was so badly entangled in the wires, etc. H.M.S. —— rushed to the spot as soon as possible, but only arrived in time to pick up your son's observer, who, I regret to state, is also dead.

Squadron-Commander Ch. H. Butler, D.S.C., was awarded the D.S.O. for gallantry on June 5th, when he fought single-handed two engagements with a number of powerful enemy machines. He attacked six aeroplanes together over the Thames Estuary, and later attacked two off Ostend. On each occasion his individual opponent was compelled to dive.

Lieutenant M. A. E. Cremetti, D.C.M., on the occasion of the big aeroplane raid on London on July 7th, twice charged through the raiding squadron and broke up its formation. Following up his success, he chased two of the raiders towards the Channel, and succeeded in bringing one down over the mouth of the Thames.

Lieutenant Cremetti, on leaving Harrow School, entered a motor works. When the call for dispatch-riders came, he enlisted, and went to France with our original Expeditionary Force. He did good work during the retreat from Mons, and at the Battle of the Marne, where he received the Distinguished Conduct Medal. He was also mentioned in dispatches for distinguished work at Wytschaete, and came home a few weeks later to a commission in the Royal Scots Fusiliers. Wounds prevented him being of use to the infantry, and he transferred to the Royal Flying Corps. On one occasion he saved the life of his observer and himself when shot down from a height of 8,000 feet by throwing out the Lewis gun and landing in No Man's Land. Both officers were badly shaken, and Lieutenant Cremetti, after being in hospital, was put on to the duty of testing new machines.

Names of "Aces" now crowd into the pages. Flight-Commander T. N. Gerrard, who on one occasion, flying on a triplane, lost nearly the whole of the top plane through the enemy's fire, and returned on what was virtually a biplane. He was awarded the D.S.C. in July, 1917, for a fight against from 15 to 20 aeroplanes, and alone had 10 encounters with them. Into one he fired 50 rounds at point-blank range. The enemy machine rolled over and over for 3,000 feet, and then fell out of control. He then attacked another machine which had dived on to one of our machines from behind, and, with the help of a scout, shot it down, the enemy being seen to crash to the ground.

Another scout was then attacked end-on, and received a long burst, the machine going down in a spin, but apparently was righted lower down. During these flights Gerrard's machine was riddled with bullets, but by fine piloting he landed safely.

There was a Lieutenant Vickers who three times came home with his machine hanging together by a miracle. Then he was sent home for a rest. Another pilot once returned with the bottom wing of his Nieuport missing.

Now, too, we hear of Collishaw, a Canadian in the R.N.A.S., whose name also will be found in another chapter. He received the D.S.C. for services on various occasions, especially the following, in June, 1917: 1st, Shot down an Albatross scout in flames. 3rd, Shot dawn an Albatross scout in flames. 5th, Shot down a two-seater Albatross in flames. 6th, Shot down two Albatross scouts in flames, and killed the pilot in the third.

A few weeks later Collishaw's name again appeared, this time as a recipient of the D.S.O. States the record:—

Since June 10, 1917, Flight-Lieutenant Collishaw has himself brought down four machines completely out of control, and driven down two others with their planes shot away. Whilst on an offensive patrol on the morning of June 15th, he forced down a hostile scout in a nose-dive. Later, on the same day, he drove down one hostile two-seater machine completely out of control, one hostile scout in a spin, and a third machine with two of its planes shot away. On June 24th, he engaged four enemy scouts, driving one down in a spin and another with two of its planes shot away; the latter machine was seen to crash.

Captain W. A. Bishop, another Canadian, one day in July saw three enemy machines below him near Vis-en-Artois. He took up position above a cloud and then dived through and opened fire. They did not return it, so he suspected a trap and zoomed up through the cloud and found three other enemy diving to attack him. He opened fire at the nearest, which crashed.

This pilot was awarded the V.C. in August, 1917, and the record in official language is as follows:—

For most conspicuous bravery, determination, and skill. Captain Bishop, who had been sent out to work independently, flew first of all to an enemy aerodrome; finding no machine about, he flew on to another aerodrome, about three miles southeast, which was at least twelve miles the other side of the line. Seven machines, some with their engines running, were on the ground. He attacked these from about 50 feet, and a mechanic, who was starting one of the engines, was seen to fall. One of the machines got off the ground, but at a height of 60 feet Captain Bishop fired 15 rounds into it at a very close range, and it crashed to the ground.

A second machine got off the ground, into which he fired 30 rounds at 150 yards range, and it fell into a tree.

Two more machines then rose from the aerodrome. One of these he engaged at the height of 1,000 feet, emptying the rest of his drum of ammunition. This machine crashed 300 yards from the aerodrome, after which Captain Bishop emptied a whole drum into the fourth hostile machine, and then flew back to his station.

Four hostile scouts were about 1,000 feet above him for about a mile of his return journey, but they would not attack. His machine was very badly shot about by machine-gun fire from the ground.

Captain Bishop was about 22 years of age. Educated for a military career, he came to England with the Canadian Mounted Rifles, but transferred to the R.F.C., and went to France at the beginning of 1916. He was awarded a bar to the D.S.O. for "conspicuous gallantry and devotion to duty." The official account of his services for which this decoration was awarded is as follows:—

> His consistent dash and great fearlessness have set a magnificent example to the pilots of his squadron. He has destroyed no fewer than 45 hostile machines within the last five months, frequently attacking enemy formations single-handed, and on all occasions displaying a fighting spirit and determination to get to close quarters with his opponents which have earned the admiration of all in contact with him.

In his book *Winged Warfare* Bishop remarks:—

> I belong to the steady flyers' class, but someday soon I am really going to learn to fly, to do aerial acrobatics, and everything.

Bishop was known to "Wing Adjutant," who in his book *Plane Tales from the Skies*, (also published by Leonaur,) wrote:—

> Whilst the writer was at Netheravon in the latter part of 1915, Bishop was sent down to train as an observer. He at once acquired a certain amount of local celebrity by reason of his indignation at not being allowed to become a pilot. Someone in authority had decided that he had not the requisite qualities to fly; either his nerves were not quite good enough, or he had not enough 'go' in him, or some other fault was found.
>
> The observer's course, with its hours of wireless and photography, bored him; the only hours which aroused his enthusiasm were those devoted to gunnery. All his spare time was spent on the ranges or in the gun-room, and by the time he had finished his course he was probably the best aerial shot on the station.
>
> Eventually he left for overseas with his squadron, still breathing out curses on those who condemned him to go as a passenger instead of piloting his own machine. He intended to apply again for permission to take his ticket and graduate as a pilot, and he amused us all by telling how, when his chance arrived, he would show them the mistake they had made. Even in those days he was fully confident of winning the V.C. when the time

came.

It is highly probable that those days overseas as an observer were of great use to Bishop afterwards. He was able to perfect his gunnery and observe the habits and tactics of the Huns. This knowledge he afterwards turned to good account, being, in addition to a finished pilot, skilled in all the tricks of the air, a marvellous shot, who reserved his fire until sure of hitting the target and securing a victim.

The following three entries in the Honours List of September 17, 1917, give us glimpses of the aerial fighting of the period.

Second-Lieutenant A. P. F. Rhys-Davids "has destroyed four enemy aircraft, and driven down many others out of control. In all his combats his gallantry and skill have been most marked, and on one occasion he shot down an enemy pilot who had accounted for 29 Allied machines."

Captain G. H. Bowman took part in many offensive patrols, which he led on 20 occasions, in the course of which four enemy aircraft were destroyed and twelve others driven down out of control. Although outnumbered by five to one on one occasion, he handled his patrol of four machines with such skill and gallantry that after a very severe fight he was able to withdraw them without loss, having destroyed at least two enemy machines and driven down one out of control.

Early in September a patrol of S.E.'s met 15 enemy machines in three groups near Moorslede. F.E.'s and Bristols came up and the enemy were attacked. Second-Lieutenant A. P. Rhys-Davids got one at close range and shot it down. He then pulled his Lewis gun down and fired both guns at a red machine above him. It dived steeply and Rhys-Davids followed and continued firing till 'the enemy broke to pieces. He and Maybery then made for home. On the way Rhys-Davids saw an enemy machine under some F.E.'s and engaged it. The German fought well, but was out-manoeuvred; he put his machine into a roll, then a nose-dive, but before he could recover Rhys-Davids opened fire and crashed him into a wood. Maybery engaged a black and white machine and shot him down out of control.

The action in which Voss, one of the principal German "Aces," was brought down was one in which McCudden also took part. Captain J. McCudden attacked a two-seater which he destroyed. He then saw an S.E.5 fighting a Fokker triplane, so with others dived at it, and for the next 10 minutes the enemy fought the five S.E.'s with great skill and determination. It was destroyed by Second-Lieutenant A. Rhys-Davids, who had previously driven down a two-seater out of control.

In his own account Rhys-Davids said the Albatross and the triplane were very skilfully flown. He got in several bursts on the triplane and had to put new drums into his machine-guns frequently. Once he got over the triplane and fired two complete drums into it, and the enemy not attempting to get out of the way, the two machines nearly collided. The enemy began to descend, the British machine following and firing and reloading. At 1,000 feet the British machine shot past the German, being a superior diver, and when Rhys-Davids zoomed back the enemy was nowhere in sight.

Then he met the red-nosed Albatross and opened action at about 80 yards. The enemy closed, and Rhys-Davids got some good bursts in from both guns at 20 yards' range, and the enemy spiralled down and crashed. The triplane fell in our lines, and the pilot was identified as Voss.

On the first day Rhys-Davids went up at the front something made him turn round, and to his astonishment he saw a Hun on his tail. If he had not glanced round at that moment, he would have been killed. Worse still, his gun jammed, and for ten minutes he had to get out of this machine's way by rolling and turning. Then suddenly, to his amazement, the Hun turned tail and went home.

He had very often been in big fights of 25 on each side, and after describing such battles he said:—

All you can think of is pumping lead into any machine you see and looking out and avoiding collisions, just missing each other by perhaps a couple of feet.

This young British pilot, an Etonian, who was killed at the age of 20, brought down in all 22 German aeroplanes and drove many others down out of control, possibly to crash.

About this period eight Bristol fighters fought a number of Albatross scouts near Douai. The Germans appear to have been one of the star squadrons, for they fought very skilfully. All were hit or driven down before it was over. We lost three machines.

Lieutenant O. L. McMaking and Captain Fender crossed the lines in the evening of August 11th over Deulemont. While passing under a gap in some clouds two Albatross scouts dived at them, firing continuously. Lieutenant McMaking's observer shot down one enemy scout, which burst into flames at 2,000 feet from the ground, and crashed on the canal.

The second enemy attacked Captain Fender's machine from the side and fired so effectually that the petrol tank was hit and Fender struck in the back. Observer Pioneer Smith fired at the enemy at close quarters and the German crashed near the first machine. Captain Fender fainted, his machine spinning. The observer climbed out and forward, and found the pilot's lever wedged between his legs. He pulled the pilot back, and pushed the stick forward, with the result that the machine righted. Captain Fender recovered consciousness and flew the machine home. Just before landing Smith was overheard shouting, "Pull her up, sir," as they were about to crash into hop poles. The pilot did pull her up, and landed on the other side with very little damage.

Captain Guynemer was killed on September 11th near Poelcapelle. He had 55 German aeroplanes on his score. One of Guynemer's last feats was to force a German airman to land and surrender behind the French lines, although the Frenchman had not a single cartridge left! He accomplished this feat by sheer mastery of flying and terrorizing his enemy. He flew over and under the German, heedless of the bullets, and forced him to drop, repeating those performances until the amazed German gave up and landed. The German never suspected until he was told that the reason his adversary did not fire his machine-gun was that he had not a cartridge left. Each time Guynemer passed over him he expected to be riddled with bullets.

One day in August Captain A. W. Keen, in a scout action near Nieuport, looped in order to get into a good firing position, and opened fire during the last quarter of the loop, with such effect that the German machine broke up and crashed.

How inconclusive was much of the air-fighting is shown by this incident. Flight-Commander Le Mesurier with Gunlayer Jackson in a D.H.4 on September 21st, seeing an enemy machine on the tail of another D.H.4, dived to his assistance, and fired tracers from the rear gun. Swinging round they brought the front gun into action and the German went down but still in control. The same pilot then had a running fight with five enemy aeroplanes, firing about 200 rounds from the rear gun, and tracers were seen to enter some of the enemy, one of which dived away. Close to the lines, Flight-Commander Le Mesurier turned on one of the enemy, firing and driving it off to the east. Afterwards a large two-seater enemy machine was observed; he dived to within a very short range, and Gunlayer Jackson fired into it from the rear gun. The enemy dived away steeply, but apparently under control.

All the fighting was not on scouts and two-seaters. Sometimes the heavy bombers had to fight their way. Thus on the night of September 29-30, 1917, one of our Handley-Pages, carrying eight bombs, five machine-guns, and a crew of five, was sent out to patrol at 10,000 feet near Ostend. During this patrol the Handley-Page sighted a Gotha silhouetted against the moon, and she was brought to action. The German machine went down after a few bursts had been fired into her, and disappeared in a steep spiral.

Numerous squadron actions occurred. For example, a formation of six British two-seaters engaged on photographic duties fought with 25 Albatross scouts and actually dispersed them, destroying two and driving two others down out of control.

The D.S.O. was awarded to Acting Flight-Commander Philip S. Fisher, D.S.C. During a hard fight which took place between eight machines of his squadron and about 20 Albatross scouts, he fought at least six combats single-handed, shooting down one of his opponents out of control. On another occasion, when he was acting as leader of a flight of five machines detailed for an offensive patrol, a general action took place with a number of Albatross scouts, in the course of which Acting Flight-Commander Fisher was wounded whilst fighting with great gallantry.

Here is another example of the airman's work at the front. Second-Lieutenant C. W. Warman during two clays, whilst operating under very difficult conditions in high wind and against strong hostile opposition, destroyed three enemy machines and a balloon. He displayed the greatest dash and fearlessness in attacking an enemy aerodrome, and on one occasion, when separated from his patrol, and surrounded by 20 hostile machines, he fought his way through, although his machine-gun was useless, by attacking them with his "Very" pistol, eventually regaining his own aerodrome with his machine much shot about.

Flight-Lieutenant A. Brandon, who had been flying continuously in France, bombing and fighting for upwards of eighteen months, was engaged during the Gotha raid of August 22nd. His report runs:—

When at 11,000 feet I saw 10 Gothas coming inland, I climbed up to them, and engaged one on the right of the formation about three miles out to sea at something over 12,000 feet. Fired 100 rounds from straight behind his tail at 100 yards' range. Bullets were seen to enter the Gotha's fuselage. Machine started into a slow spin. I followed and fired about 25 more into him to make sure. My gun then jammed, and in trying to clear I got into a very fast spin with my engines on. Got out of this just in time to see the enemy crash into the sea.

I then landed, had my gun jam cleared, and went up after the remaining eight Gothas—one had been shot down in flames— and caught up with them at 14,000 feet, and engaged them in turn from both above and below. Then devoted all my attention to one Gotha, and after firing 200 rounds into him silenced both his guns. I think both German gunners must have been hit, as I was able to get within 60 feet of him without being fired at. I finally ran out of ammunition.

At Mudros, one day in September, 1917, occurred a breezy engagement in which a trio of Sopwiths of different types played a noteworthy part. Warning had been received of the approach of three enemy seaplanes, whereupon Flight-Lieutenant J. W. Alcock[1] on a "Camel," Flight-Lieutenant H. T. Mellings, D.S.C., on a Sopwith triplane, and another pilot on a "Pup," went up.

Two of the enemy were single-seater "Bluebirds" of an estimated speed of 105 miles per hour, the other was a two-seater of about 97 miles per hour. The triplane got into touch with the enemy, who were then in V-formation, at a height of 12,000 feet. It got the upper berth and attacked the two-seater from in front, and was in turn attacked by one of the "Bluebirds" diving on to his tail. The triplane shook the latter off and attacked its fellow. The enemy then re-formed. The "Camel" joined in the attack, diving under the tail of the rearmost "Bluebird" and stalling within 50 yards, firing from both guns. This is always a picturesque and effective manoeuvre, and in this instance was completely successful, for smoke was seen to come from the enemy, who dived away.

The triplane then circled in behind the other "Bluebird" and opened fire at 100 yards, closing to 50 yards. The enemy dived, but flattened out close to the water, when the triplane shot off the extension of the top left wing and wounded the pilot in the back. The enemy was then travelling down wind and struck the water at great

---

1. The pilot who flew the Atlantic on June 14, 1919.

speed, breaking into small pieces.

The triplane climbed again and attacked the two-seater at 3,000 feet altitude, and the "Camel" engaged the remaining "Bluebird" and headed it off towards Imbros firing until both guns jammed. It then turned back towards the triplane, which it found clearing a jam under heavy fire from the enemy two-seater. The "Camel" hereupon, although the guns were out of action, pretended to attack, and so embarrassed the enemy, until the triplane had cleared its gun and was able to take part.

The remaining "Bluebird" had meanwhile descended, and in alighting sheared off both floats. The "Camel," having a broken inlet valve, returned. But the triplane continued fighting with the two-seater, closing to 20 yards from the front, when Flight-Lieutenant Fowler, coming up on a Sop with "Pup," wounded the enemy's observer. By this time the action was being fought close to the water up the Dardanelles, near the forts, and was accordingly broken off. A British warship subsequently took prisoner the wounded pilot of the damaged "Bluebird."

In December the fighting on the Italian front gave many opportunities for our airmen. It opened with an encounter in which the British were successful.

Four of our machines crossed the Piave on a first reconnaissance over the enemy. They were promptly attacked by five enemy scouts, one of which went down but recovered control.

"After 20 minutes of continual manoeuvring and occasional bursts of fire," writes a war correspondent, "another of the enemy was driven down. His British antagonist followed him in his dive, and as the German flattened out again the English pilot got a burst of 80 rounds into him at close range. The right wing of the German machine crumpled up. The Albatross turned over and fell to earth."

By this time the enemy had been reinforced, but another of their aeroplanes was driven down out of control. Then the four British returned, having encountered 12 German machines, of which they had destroyed one and damaged two.

CHAPTER 8

Fighting in the Air in 1918

The last year of the war opened on a situation apparently all in favour of the enemy. The defection of Russia released armies for use on the Western Front; it also released air squadrons, and prevented the diffusion of German resources over many wide fronts. But a decision had to be made in the West, and it was known that Germany intended a breakthrough with a view to Paris or the Channel Ports. The moment of the offensive was anxiously awaited.

The date of it was determined by Germany's preparedness, and by the necessity to win a decisive battle before the arrival of American armies in sufficient strength to turn the scales overwhelmingly in favour of the Allies. And there were economic reasons why the date of the offensive had to be fixed very early in the year.

As regards fighting in the air, the British Service was at this period better equipped than at any previous time. There had been much inquiry and public questioning, and there had in the past been sufficient ground for criticism to awaken the authorities to the need for special effort. Thus, the establishment of the Air Board had effected economy, and even more important improvements in the supply and distribution of material, as well as in the running of the technical departments. Now, at the most critical period of the whole war, a complete revolution in the Air Services was imminent; namely, the fusion of the Royal Naval Air Service and the Royal Flying Corps into one great "Third Arm," to be called the Royal Air Force, administratively under a new Department of State, with a Secretary having equal status to that of the First Lord of the Admiralty or the Secretary of State for War. When one contemplates the magnitude and meaning of this great innovation one entertains a new respect for British energy.

For fighting in the air we had at the beginning of the year a large number of squadrons equipped with Sopwith "Camels" or with S.E.5's. (Speed of 117 miles per hour at 15,000 feet). There were Spads and Nieuports (123 miles per hour). Shortly, the "Dolphin "was to appear on the scenes, an improvement on the "Camel"; and later in the summer the "Dolphin" (128 miles per hour at 10,000 feet) was improved upon by the "Snipe," a complete surprise for the enemy. The battle for the skies had to be waged between sides not unevenly matched as regards type of apparatus, but with the French and British numerically stronger, and with the Americans just beginning to take part.

The enemy were making great use of a new Fokker scout and a triplane. A Fokker monoplane, and a Junker monoplane, 220-h.p. Benz engine, late in the year were seen, and the speed attributed to them was about 150 miles per hour. The Fokker monoplane somewhat resembled the Morane "Parasol." A Halberstadt two-seater fighter was a good machine, almost as manoeuvrable as a scout.

An improved Albatross was another of their fighting machines. From prisoners and captured machines there was obtained plenty of evidence that the enemy were leaving nothing undone that could improve their equipment. There was continual improvement in engines, and a recognition of the need for big-power scouts. Un-questionably they were feeling a deficiency in certain materials; and in the summer of 1917 it had been noticed that the durability of German machines was inferior to ours: it took fewer lesions to bring about total collapse in the air.

German engines were perhaps on the whole more easily managed; or rather, considered together with the whole policy of training, they were calculated to give less trouble. For one thing, German aviators probably flew their machines "full out" less than British and French pilots. Some of the British engines, while perfectly wonderful as to performance, demanded from the pilot an under-standing of their slightest variations and their numerous subtleties. The great range of altitude at which machines were now flying created carburation difficulties in some cases only overcome by complications which, if not mastered by the pilot, were very apt to betray him with serious results.

The American "Liberty" engine, about which so much discussion revolved, is to be considered as part of a policy. It was an engine that at first gave out less than its nominal power, whereas many British engines gave out more. But it was designed for a quick life, and being producible in great quantities, it was intended after 65 or 70 hours of actual flying to be taken down and replaced. That was a policy that could have been pursued in the case of scarcely any British engine. It was probably a policy that would have paid handsomely if the war had continued for another year. But, as events fell out, this engine made but a limited entrance into the field before the war ended.

In the matter of navigation and other flight instruments the Germans were behind the British, who during the war achieved a technical ascendancy in nearly every department of aeronautics, and in wireless telegraphy and telephony employed in aircraft.

Before coming to the great German offensive a few aerial fights that occurred just previously may be mentioned.

Among the earliest mentions in the Honours Lists in 1918 were Flight-Commander R. J. O. Compston, R.N.A.S., awarded the Second Bar to the D.S.C. "for ability and determination when leading offensive patrols, in which he displayed entire disregard of personal danger." On January 1st he observed a new type twin-tailed two-seater enemy machine, which he attacked, firing a good many rounds at point-blank range. The enemy machine dived, but was again attacked and went down vertically with his engine full on. The wings came off, and the machine was observed to crash. Later in the day, Flight-Commander Compston observed two formations of ten and five Albatross scouts respectively. He attacked one of the enemy machines, and sent it down in a flat spin, falling over sideways completely out of control. On numerous other occasions Flight-Commander Compston had destroyed or driven down enemy machines out of control, and had frequently more than one successful engagement in the same day."

The brothers, Captain James Byford McCudden and Lieutenant Jack McCudden, both "Aces," were much heard of at this period. The former was awarded the V.C. in April. His flying service up to that date is briefly summarized here. He had accounted for 54 enemy aeroplanes. Of these 42 were definitely destroyed, 19 of them on our side of the lines. The remaining twelve were driven down out of control. On two occasions he totally destroyed four two-seater enemy aeroplanes on the same day, and on the last occasion all four machines were destroyed in the space of 1 hour 30 minutes. He had participated in 78 offensive patrols, and in nearly every case had been the leader. On at least 30 other occasions, whilst with the same squadron, he crossed the lines alone, either in pursuit or in quest of enemy aeroplanes.

On December 17, 1917, when leading his patrol, eight enemy aeroplanes were attacked between 2.30 p.m. and 3.50 p.m. Of these two were shot down by Captain McCudden in our lines. On the morning of the same day he left the ground at 10.50 and encountered four enemy aeroplanes; of these he shot two down.

On January 30th he, single-handed, attacked five enemy scouts, as a result of which two were destroyed. He only returned home when the enemy scouts had been driven far east; his Lewis gun ammunition was all finished and the belt of his Vickers gun had broken.

One day in February, after crossing the lines over Bantouzelle, at 16,000 feet he saw some enemy aircraft scouts. He tackled a Rumpler, securing a good position and firing a long burst with both guns. The enemy went down in a vertical dive, and all four wings fell off and the wreckage fell near Caudry. A little later he saw a D.F.W. south of Bois de Vaucelles at about 15,000 feet. He secured a firing position at 100 yards' range, and after firing a long burst from both guns the enemy went down in flames. He and another pilot attacked an L.V.G. which went down damaged.

On three occasions he fought against Immelmann, but inconclusively. As a patrol leader he showed the utmost gallantry and skill in the way he protected the newer members of his flight, thus keeping down their casualties to a minimum. Captain McCudden went to France as a mechanic with the original Expeditionary Force. As a sergeant he became an observer. He was the son of a soldier, and was born in barracks.

When Captain McCudden received the V.C. from the King he had just heard that his younger brother had been reported missing. Lieutenant Jack McCudden at that date had been credited with having brought down 11 enemy machines. He was awarded the Military Cross.

Another brilliant "scout" record was achieved by Captain Fullard, M.C., D.S.O., who, by January, 1918, had brought down 42 enemy machines and 3 balloons. In one day he brought down four German aeroplanes. Before breakfast one morning he and a brother officer brought down seven machines, of which he was responsible for three. His squadron up till October had brought down 200 machines, and their bag was about 250 up to January, 1918. For three months he worked with a flight of six pilots without a single casualty, and during that period they brought down more machines than any other flight in France. His goggles were shot away in a fight with a two-seater, and he brought his burning machine back safely.

General Mark Kerr told the following story of an officer of the

A SQUADRON OF FIGHTING PLANES

Royal Air Force:—

One of our fighting aeroplanes was returning, after having exhausted all its ammunition in a series of nine fights, when a tenth enemy machine was met. The British observer had only his pistol left, and with this he engaged in an unequal fight. The tank of the British machine was riddled, and as it swept by the German aeroplane to return to its own lines the observer flung the now empty pistol at the enemy, and the weapon fell in the fuselage. As he planed down to his own lines the German machine followed, and, hovering over the ground, dropped the pistol with the note, 'As air reprisals are the order of the day, I return the pistol as I received it.'

Returning from a raid with Handley-Page bombers on February 18th, Flight-Lieutenant Barker, D.S.C. met an enemy machine and attacked it from 50 feet behind and 20 yards above, firing a burst of ten rounds, and bullets were seen to penetrate the front portion of the fuselage of the German near the pilot's seat. The enemy machine stalled; and another ten rounds were fired, when it nose-dived until lost to sight. Probably the pilot was badly wounded or killed, and the machine crashed.

One of the last entries referring to the Royal Naval Air Service before its absorption into the Royal Air Force on April 1st, relates to the bestowal of the Bar to the D.S.C. on Flight-Commander C. P. 0. Bartlett. On March 28th, he carried out three bombing raids. Whilst returning from one of these missions he was attacked at a height of about 2,500 feet by three enemy triplanes, and five other scouts. One of these he drove down, attacking it with his front guns, whilst his observer shot down a second out of control. Observing that two of the triplanes were diving on him and converging, he side-slipped his machine away, with the result that the two enemy machines collided and fell to the ground together, where they burst into flames.

Intense air-fighting preceded the German offensive, for the Allies were fully alive to the fact that if they could seriously interfere with the enemy's reconnaissance, photography, and artillery observation, the effect would be to gain time. They were on the defensive, and could play no other role, at any rate until the German effort was spent. In its proper place the bombing operations of this period are referred to; and they also played an important part in delaying the programme of the German advance. Some idea of the amount of aerial fighting will be gathered from this list which includes only the heavier days.

March 8-9th.—44 enemy brought down.

March 24th.—45 enemy destroyed, 22 driven down; 10 of ours missing.

In March the British destroyed 372 German aeroplanes and drove down 205 others.

April 12th.—40 enemy destroyed, 20 driven down; 12 of ours missing.

In April the British destroyed 172 German aeroplanes apart from 75 driven down out of control.

In May the British destroyed 398 German aeroplanes, 100 were driven down out of control, and 20 shot down by artillery.

August 8th.—48 enemy destroyed, 17 driven down; 50 of ours missing.

In one week—July 27th to August 3rd—we destroyed 101 German aeroplanes and brought down 14 others; 29 of ours were missing.

After August the number of enemy aeroplanes destroyed in a day's aerial fighting declined, and seldom exceeded 40. This was due to the decreased activity and a more frequent avoidance of conflict on the part of enemy airmen. In the four weeks from August 8th, 465 enemy machines were destroyed, excluding those brought down by artillery. 200 others were driven down to an unascertained fate. 61 German balloons were fired. In that period 262 of our machines failed to return.

In September the British accounted for 537 enemy machines on the Western Front, and brought down 11 others by artillery. They also destroyed 59 observation balloons.

In one week in October 280 enemy machines were destroyed, our missing machines numbering 67.

On March 24th (the third day of the great battle) Captain J. L. Trollope brought down six enemy machines, thus creating a new record, the previous best being five held by Captain Ball and one or two other "Aces." Captain Trollope, between January 17th and March 28th, when he was killed, destroyed 18 enemy machines. His bag of six in one day was secured in the following manner, as described by the *Times* War Correspondent.

Captain Trollope was out with a formation when they saw four

101

German fighting aeroplanes trying to interfere with some of our observing machines. Captain Trollope attacked one of the enemy and fired into it from close range, when the German aeroplane fell all to bits in the air. The other three Germans scattered and got away; so, going on, Trollope soon espied two more enemy two-seaters below him, close to the ground. He dived at them and engaged them one after another, and both went down and crashed, the fighting being so low that in each case their striking the earth was clearly visible. Captain Trollope then climbed up to rejoin his formation, which was again engaged with another party of the enemy. He entered the *mêlée*, and used up what ammunition he had left, and came home for more.

Having replenished, Trollope started out again and met a party of three of the enemy trying to cross the battle line. He went for one of them, but his gun jammed, and he had to draw off till his gun got going again. Then he turned and attacked another of the enemy, who was nearer than his original antagonist, fired into him at point-blank range, and the enemy went down spinning and broke into pieces. Turning from his last victim, Captain Trollope then went after the third of the enemy party, caught it up, attacked it, and the German broke into flames in the air. This made five of the enemy shot down in a single day, and Trollope turned for home. But on the way he saw another enemy scout attacking one of our slower machines. He went to the rescue and tackled the enemy, who went down spinning, and the other pilot saw it crash.

Captain J. Gilmour was an "Ace" who by May had destroyed 23 German machines. While leading a patrol of five one day, he shot down one enemy and drove another down to a fate unascertained. Then the patrol attacked 40 Germans. Of these he alone destroyed two and sent another down out of control.

A squadron fight that was typical of many occurred one day in April between a patrol of "Camels" and an equal number of German fighting scouts. One of our pilots occupied with one of the enemy was attacked by three others who took him in the rear. He dodged these and climbed, out-distancing his pursuers; but at 12,000 feet he encountered a flight of 12 enemy scouts against which he put up a splendid fight. One of the enemy diving at him, he stalled his machine at the psychological moment so that the German swept past. Then our man turned sharply, fired a short burst, and saw his opponent go down out of control.

Meanwhile the British pilot was completely separated from his own flight, and he spent ten minutes in desperate manoeuvring to avoid the swarm of Huns. He succeeded, and by a final spin reached our lines fighting all the way. He had forced at least two others of his opponents to retire. The other members of the British patrol between them destroyed a two-seater and two scouts. And we sustained no casualties, although our machines were repeatedly struck.

Five of our scouts of the same type attacked 10 Fokker biplanes, and the leader of our flight promptly sent the enemy leader down in flames, and within a few minutes got another victim. Then with his small force he encountered a swarm of 40 scouts, Fokker, Albatross and Pfalz types. One of the Albatross scouts was taken while it was crossing his bows, and down it went. A Pfalz immediately afterwards was driven down out of control by the same pilot. After that, by performing every conceivable stunt, he outflew the enemy and succeeded in getting another victim before his ammunition was entirely spent. In the afternoon this pilot bagged five Germans; and these were not the only scores made by his flight.

A cloudland surprise occurred one day when one of our fighting scouts, enveloped in the fog, almost collided with a two-seater. In an instant our man had his hand on his two guns and fired bursts from both so close that he could see the enemy observer jump up evidently struck. The two-seater began side-slipping and the British pilot got in another stream of bullets with such deadly effect that the enemy caught fire and fell.

The first V.C.'s awarded to airmen as members of the newly constituted Royal Air Force were announced in the *London Gazette* issued May 1st.

Lieutenant Alan Jerrard when on patrol with two other officers attacked five enemy aeroplanes and shot one down in flames, following it down to within 100 feet of the ground. He then attacked an enemy aerodrome from a height of only 50 feet from the ground, and engaging single-handed some 19 machines, which were either landing or attempting to take off, succeeded in destroying one of them, which crashed on the aerodrome. A large number of machines then attacked him, and whilst thus fully occupied he observed that one of the pilots of his patrol was in difficulties. He went immediately to his assistance, regardless of his own personal safety, and destroyed a third enemy machine.

Fresh enemy aeroplanes continued to rise from the aerodrome, and he attacked them one after the other, and only retreated, still engaged with five enemy machines, when ordered to do so by his patrol leader. Although wounded, this very gallant officer turned repeatedly and attacked single-handed the pursuing machines, until he was eventually overwhelmed by numbers and driven to the ground.

Lieutenant Jerrard had greatly distinguished himself on four previous occasions, within a period of twenty-three days, in destroying enemy machines, displaying bravery and ability of the highest order.

Second-Lieutenant A. A. McLeod, whilst flying with his observer (Lieutenant A. W. Hammond, M.C.) attacking hostile formations by bombs and machine-gun fire, was assailed at a height of 5,000 feet by eight enemy triplanes, which dived at him from all directions. By skilled manoeuvring he enabled his observer to fire bursts at each machine in turn, shooting three of them down out of control. By this time Lieutenant McLeod had received five wounds, and whilst continuing the engagement a bullet penetrated his petrol tank and set the machine on fire. He then climbed out on to the left bottom plane, controlling his machine from the side of the fuselage, and by sideslipping steeply kept the flames to one side, thus enabling the observer to continue firing until the ground was reached.

The observer had been wounded six times when the machine crashed in 'No Man's Land,' and Second-Lieutenant McLeod, notwithstanding his own wounds, dragged him away from the burning wreckage at great personal risk from heavy machine-gun fire from the enemy's lines. This gallant pilot was again wounded by a bomb whilst engaged in this act of rescue, but he persevered until he had placed Lieutenant Hammond in comparative safety, before falling himself from exhaustion and loss of blood. The observer, Lieutenant A. W. Hammond was awarded a bar to his M.C.

Some of the great French fighters were vying with our D'Artagnans of the air at this period, and like ours they paid heavy toll.

Lieutenant Fonck, on May 9th, equalled Captain Trollope's feat, already described, of destroying six enemy machines in one day. While on patrol with other pilots he encountered three German two-seaters. He got the upper berth, and opened fire at short range. Within a few seconds two of the two-seaters were falling down to crash. The third he sent down in flames. The whole thing was over in less than two minutes. In the afternoon, flying near Montdidier, he met nine Germans—four Pfalz scouts, and five Albatrosses. Fonck single-handed brought down two of the scouts and an Albatross two-seater.

This remarkable success was achieved at an expenditure of a total of 52 rounds of ammunition, which is evidence of wonderful shooting; but more extraordinary still is the fact that up to this time Fonck had never received a wound in aerial fighting, nor had his machine been hit, a fact that is only accounted for by phenomenal manoeuvring skill.

The Distinguished Service Medal was awarded to Sydney F. Anderson, a leading mechanic in the Royal Air Force for an act of cool courage that could scarcely be beaten. His job was to look after the aft gun. The machine he was in had been flying behind the German lines with other British machines when they met a German squadron, which divided the British force, driving the two-seater in which Anderson was flying on the German side and away from our lines. A gale of wind was blowing in the wrong direction for the British machine, which had been hit in the petrol tank.

Anderson shouted down the tube, "Slow down, and I'll run along and tie her up." With his tools in hand he climbed out on to the lower plane, and for over an hour and a half, poised aloft, travelling all the time, he did his job. Then he crawled back, got into his seat, and the British lines were reached in safety, and Anderson had saved his pilot's life and his machine.

In 1918 night fighting in the air became fairly common, although only a year before few experts thought it was ever likely to be so. In this connection several entries in the Honours Lists tell their own tale.

Major C. F. A. Portal had a wonderful record. During a period of four months, says the official chronicler, chiefly under adverse weather conditions, he repeatedly carried out successful raids by day and night, his ingenuity and daring enabling him to drop many tons of bombs on important enemy posts. One night he crossed the lines five times, only landing between each flight to replenish with bombs. Another day he took on, single-handed, five enemy machines, and drove down three of them—a most gallant and splendid feat. On another day, despite thick mist, he registered one of our batteries on an enemy battery, causing the destruction of one pit and obtaining one fire and two explosions; and another day, flying 5½ hours, he carried out two very successful counter-battery shoots, observing 350 rounds.

Captain H. J. Burden, D.S.O., from the time he joined his squadron in February to the end of October, accounted for 17 enemy machines—12 crashed, two driven down out of control, and three destroyed in flames on the ground during an attack on an aerodrome. On the morning of August 10th he led his patrol in three attacks, and himself destroyed three enemy machines. In the evening of the same day he destroyed two more. Two days later he attacked a large number of Fokkers, seven of which were destroyed, accounting for three himself.

A few pages back an adventure in which Lieutenant McLeod rode home on one of the wings was recorded. On one occasion in July, Second-Lieutenant T. B. Dodwell was acting as observer in a two-seater, when in diving to the assistance of another machine, his own machine commenced to fall out of control. Despite this, he continued to engage three enemy machines that were attacking him, and eventually drove them off, an operation that called for great coolness and skill, as the shooting platform was most unsteady. Realizing that the machine was out of control owing to the loss of lift in the tail plane, half of this being shot away, he left his cockpit, and, climbing along the wing past the pilot, he lay down along the cowling in front enabling the pilot to obtain partial control of the machine and head for home. When nearing the ground he climbed back into his cockpit to allow the nose to rise, and the pilot succeeded in safely landing. This undoubtedly saved the machine and both lives. Second-Lieutenant Dodwell was awarded the D.S.O.

A parallel instance was afforded by an airman on a big bomber flying near Ostend. A shell from an "Archie" struck the tail, and the impact turned the machine upside down, out of control, and the pilot was thrown out of his seat. He clambered on to the fuselage, rode it like a horse, moved his legs and body backwards, forwards, and sideways, maintaining balance, steadily glided down over the German lines amid a fusillade from the anti-aircraft guns, and finally crashed to the ground and was injured.

Captain C. Joseph led a formation of scouts under a large force of enemy aircraft, with a view to inducing them to descend to attack him. In this ruse he was successful, and in accordance with arrangements previously made, another formation of our machines then appeared on the scene, and a combined attack was made on the enemy, resulting in the destruction of four aeroplanes and three more being brought down completely out of control. Our patrol leader was wounded.

A British airman was attacked by three enemies, who were in such a hurry to settle him that two of them came into collision. The wings of one broke off, and it went down, while the other started downwards in a slow spiral. Our pilot went after it and opened fire, with the result that it burst into flames.

A British patrol sighted six German scouts and effected a surprise attack, our patrol leader picking out the third enemy machine, which went down vertically to crash. Our man then attacked the second in the line and shot that down, and in falling the enemy hit the German leader and both went to earth together in one jumbled mass. The other three got away, but a German two-seater came along, and again our patrol leader attacked and sent it down.

The German machines met were as often as not painted in various colours. Some were brilliant red, after the von Richthofen fashion; some blue with a white band; some salmon pink; some slate grey; some yellow and blue; and so on. Doubtless there was little in this beyond a means of recognition in the air, or to suit individual pilot's whims. British pilots, too, had their little vanities, but these seldom went beyond the carrying of mascots or small discs painted on the machine. Certain squadrons were known by a distinct badge. Thus, one squadron had all its motor transport, aerial and road, adorned with a picture of a lean dog peering into an empty cupboard. The name of the Squadron Commander was Hubbard.

In the Parish Magazine of Hughenden, Bucks, is the record of an adventure that befell the son of the Vicar, Captain G. H. P. Whitfeld. The account reads:—

It may interest some to hear the details of Captain G. H. P. Whitfield's adventure on the day (August 8th) when he was taken prisoner: 'Captain P——l and I went off to bomb a certain place, and the clouds were only 1,500 to 2,000 feet, so we blew through them, getting glimpses of the ground. We were nearly at the objective when I saw a hostile machine below us. The clouds, however, hid him at once, but I was quite ready for him, when he suddenly appeared behind. We fired at each other hard, but his first burst did a lot of damage, cutting the ailerons controls. His second burst hit my hand, smashed my gun, also breaking the main tank and magneto, besides hitting P——l in the foot. We then went down in a spin completely out of control, but somehow, by a miracle, P——l got it out at 100 feet from the ground, and we did a perfect landing. I must say the pilot of the German machine was a sportsman, for he stopped firing when he saw we were out of control.'

The British Service lost about this time Major Edward Mannock, a Londoner, who succeeded to the command of Major Bishop's squadron when the great Canadian air-fighter returned to the Dominions. Major Mannock was an "Ace," with 58 victims up to July 1st. But he had other successes afterwards.

On the very day, October 6th, on which Garros, the brilliant French pioneer and war pilot was killed, Fonck, his countryman, already referred to in this chapter, brought down four Germans in an engagement that lasted twenty minutes, bringing his official bag up to 70. Garros, who might have retired with honour after his long and bitter captivity from April 18, 1915, to the Spring of 1918, preferred to fight the enemy, and having made some practice flights on modern high-speed scouts, he soon left his mark on the Huns.

There was a big encounter on September 3rd between a Royal Air Force squadron working with the Navy and seven Fokker biplanes. The squadron met the enemy formation over Lille. Diving on the lowest of the formation one of our Flight-Lieutenants fired some 300 rounds from his machine-gun at 50 yards' range. The enemy turned to avoid conflict, but tracer bullets were seen to enter his cockpit, after which he sideslipped and crashed. The remainder of the enemy were engaged over Roulers at a height of about 6,000 feet. The leader of the British formation attacked one Fokker at close range, raking him with machine-gun bullets, which pierced the petrol tanks, so that he burst into flames and crashed. The rear enemy machine was also put out of action. Another Fokker, although piloted with great skill, was unable to escape, and was shot down.

An escort squadron, co-operating with a squadron of bombers, met 14 Fokker biplanes near Zeebrugge. Four of them were destroyed, two falling to the bag of one of our pilots. Two other machines were driven down out of control. Of the four destroyed machines, two fell into the sea and went under.

A large formation of enemy machines was encountered one evening over Menin at a height of over 10,000 feet. There was a fierce struggle, in the course of which one Pfalz scout broke in two. Five other enemy machines were destroyed, and seven driven down out of control to an unascertained fate.

The Distinguished Flying Cross was awarded to Second-Lieutenant S. L. Dunlop. The machine in which this officer was acting as observer met a flight of Germans. He shot one of these down in flames, and shortly afterwards another. During the second fight his pilot was severely wounded and lost consciousness. Second-Lieutenant Dunlop leaned over the fuselage to support his pilot, kept the machine in control, and from time to time fired at the enemy aircraft as they closed on him. He succeeded in reaching our lines and, with the help of the pilot who had recovered consciousness, landed safely.

On September 16th, Captain R. L. Manuel, one of a patrol of 11 machines, engaged 15 hostiles. By skilful manoeuvring he completely defeated the enemy in a fight of 20 minutes, by which time only four German machines remained aloft, and these retired. Six of the enemy machines almost certainly crashed.

Here are two more night-flying adventures. Captain D. V. Armstrong had specialized on this, and had been responsible for the training of a large number of our night-flyers. On the night of September 10th, learning that an enemy machine had passed over our lines he volunteered to go up. The weather was so bad that flying was almost impossible. There was a 50-mile wind accompanied by driving rainstorms. In spite of this, Captain Armstrong patrolled the air for over an hour, although his machine at times almost got out of hand.

On the night of September 15th Captain C. J. Brand fought an enemy machine which he met at an altitude of 8,000 feet. It was a two-engine bomber. Major Brand's fire took effect, and burst the sump of one of his opponent's engines, and the oil from it covered the British machine in a black spray. In spite of this, he continued the engagement driving the enemy down to 200 feet, at which height he was under such intense machine-gun fire from the ground that he had to break off the combat.

The same officer a few weeks later encountered another two-engine machine. Firing two bursts of twenty rounds each, he put the enemy's starboard engine out of action. Closing to a range of 25 yards, he got three more bursts in, and the enemy caught fire and went down in flames. He was so close to the enemy that the flames almost scorched his face.

In Italy meanwhile the British Third Arm was adding to its laurels. Early in September two of our machines encountered six enemy at a height of 17,000 feet. After manoeuvring for position, one of ours attacked and sent down three of the enemy in quick succession. His companion brought down two others. During the fight, which occupied 15 minutes, the medley of machines descended to within 2,000 feet of the ground. All the Austrians fell within our lines, and four of the pilots were dead and the fifth wounded.

A patrol of Sop with "Camels" on the same front went for a big crowd of Fokker biplanes and triplanes. While one of ours was engaged with one of the biplanes the pilot observed that one of our machines was being hard pressed by a triplane. He at once came to the rescue, and his attack caused the Austrian to turn so sharply that the wings of his aeroplane collapsed. The same pilot immediately after got another victim.

Later in the day he led his patrol against a formation of 17 Fokker biplanes. Getting in a short burst at one of the enemy he saw the tail of the Fokker break away, whereupon the machine fell out of control. Meanwhile a Fokker was hanging on his tail, but swinging suddenly round he got in a good burst and the enemy went down. Others of our patrol also were successful.

Early in the war a subject much discussed was the reported determination of French airmen to ram Zeppelins or enemy aeroplanes, if all other methods failed, deliberately sacrificing their lives for the certainty of bringing an enemy down. Under conceivable circumstances such a sacrifice would no doubt have been justifiable; but there are no fully verified instances of its occurrence. In fighting, collisions were not infrequent, but whether this was due to deliberate ramming or to accident could only be established by the pilots who never survived. It is by no means improbable that some of these collisions were the despairing last resource. Thus, Major Barker, whose remarkable fight against odds is about to be described, twice during that action charged opponents, and in each case was saved unexpectedly by his enemy swerving off in the nick of time.

One possibly authentic incident was recorded in the French *communiqué* of July 30, 1916:——

On the morning of July 27th a French aeroplane piloted by Quartermaster de Terline attacked a German machine over Chalons. The French pilot had just opened fire when his gun jammed. The enemy was in flight. Two of our machines then saw Quartermaster de Terline swoop upon his adversary, in a manner that left no room for doubt that he did it on purpose, crash into him and fall with him to the ground. The French pilot and the two German airmen fell in our lines and were killed.

On the morning of October 27th Major W. G. Barker, D.S.O., won the Victoria Cross for the following service. Flying on a Sopwith "Snipe" over the Forêt de Mormal he attacked a two-seater at a height of 21,000 feet, and after a short burst it broke up in the air. At the same time a Fokker biplane attacked him, and he was wounded in the right thigh, but managed, despite this, to shoot down the enemy aeroplane in flames. He then found himself in the middle of a large formation of Fokkers, who attacked him from all directions, and was again severely wounded in the left thigh, but succeeded by hard fighting and rapid manoeuvring in driving down two of the enemy in a spin. He lost consciousness after this, and his machine fell out of control. On recovery he found himself being again attacked by a large formation, and singling out one machine, he deliberately charged and drove it down in flames.

During this fight Major Barker's left elbow was shattered and he again fainted, and on regaining consciousness he found himself still being attacked; but, notwithstanding that he was now severely wounded in both legs and his left arm shattered, he dived on the nearest machine and shot it down in flames.

Being greatly exhausted, he tried to break off the fight and regain our lines, but was met by another formation which attacked and endeavoured to cut him off; but after a hard fight he succeeded in breaking up this formation and reached our lines, where he crashed on landing. This combat, in which Major Barker destroyed four enemy machines (three of them in flames) and drove down six others, brought his total successes up to 50 enemy machines destroyed. The engagement lasted about 40 minutes.

Major Barker was awarded the Military Cross on January 10, 1917; first Bar on July 18, 1917; the Distinguished Service Order on February 18, 1918; second Bar to Military Cross on September 16, 1918; and Bar to D.S.O. on November 2, 1918.

The reader may well wonder how a man with bad wounds in the thigh and arm could not only control an aeroplane but could "fight his ship." Normally, it is true, a pilot uses both legs and hands; the legs for rudder control, the hands for manoeuvring the machine and controlling the engine and the firing lever. The "Snipe," however, like other well-designed machines, even of the fast scout division, does not get out of hand if the pilot leaves it to its own devices for a time. Moreover, a clever pilot can do a certain amount of manoeuvring by alternative control, in much the same way as a fiddler can play a tune on one string. Major Barker's action, however, stands out as an example of dogged pluck in spite of great pain and loss of blood. Before the end he had become desperate, and, hemmed in by enemies, he twice charged intending to ram. But each time he fired as he charged, and each time, when only a few feet off, his opponent swerved down bursting into flames.

The end of this Homeric fight was witnessed from the ground, for the British pilot was seeking a haven. Experts watching said it was the finest exhibition of brilliant "stunting" ever witnessed. Two at least of the enemy were sent down before, seeing his chance, he broke through the circle of Germans. With only one hand to use and almost exhausted he could not properly control the machine, but landed at high speed, crashing into a hedge and stripping the under-carriage off the machine. Then he fainted.

Another V.C. was won by Captain A. W. Beauchamp-Proctor, who had previously won great distinction and many honours, and who between August 8th and October 8th proved himself victor in 26 decisive combats, destroying 12 enemy kite-balloons, 10 enemy aircraft, and driving down four other enemy aircraft completely out of control. Between October 1st and October 5th he destroyed two enemy scouts, burnt three enemy kite-balloons, and drove down one hostile scout completely out of control. On October 8th while flying home at a low altitude, after destroying an enemy two-seater near Maretz, he was painfully wounded in the arm by machine-gun fire, but, continuing, he landed safely at his aerodrome, and after making his report was admitted to hospital.

CHAPTER 9

Zeppelins and the Defence

For many months after war broke out the threatened raids by airships on England were not made. It is difficult to believe that the reason was any other than that of unreadiness either of ships, men, or organization; and it is certain that the Germans had fewer airships than was popularly supposed. If raids could at that period have been made by ten or a dozen airships they would have effected a great deal of moral damage unhindered. They could have safely travelled at low altitudes, and thus secured something like accuracy of aim. The delay gave the Admiralty time to organize our anti-aircraft defences, this being one of several novel undertakings of the Sea Service which seemed rather to belong to the domain of the War Office.

The general public were so preoccupied by the greater events of the war, and by the fever of voluntary recruiting, that the menace of the Zeppelins was not seriously entertained. For one thing, the prophets who foretold invasions by 50 of these huge vessels were so hopelessly discredited that, pendulum-like, opinion swung over to the opposite extreme of belittling the enemy's aerial preparations. Then, as always, a small body of sound knowledge and opinion existed, guided by experts who preferred truth to sensationalism. But it was a small body: it was aware almost to the day when the first Zeppelin attempt would be made; it refused to be driven by that prospect into a state of panic. It was persuaded that the Zeppelins would enjoy a very small measure of success, and that they would soon find our defences too formidable. And events proved them right.

For some of the wrong impressions that prevailed the authorities were to blame. During the vote-catching days of peace a responsible Minister had solemnly declared that we had an effective defence against attack from aircraft; and when the first few Zeppelins visited us, and the invaders, although they did little harm, enjoyed almost complete immunity, there was a certain amount of quite natural complaining. Few of the general public were soundly instructed, or knew anything of the technicalities of the subject; but all realized that promises had been lightly made, and that they had been trifled with.

Month after month passed. London was attacked in the night, and at diminishing intervals. The casualty total, at first entirely civilian, mounted up. The Anti-Aircraft department was overhauled or completely changed two or three times. Then, one night, in full view of tens of thousands of sleepless Londoners, a great airship was brought blazing down. Our "bag" was soon enlarged; and ere long it could be boasted that the Zeppelins that came to London suffered 100 per cent, casualties. Then, better still, Zeppelins that avoided London, and went to the Northern counties and the North-East Coast, suffered the same fate. Let us see how our airmen and our gunners managed to bring about the defeat of the *Kaiser's* airship fleet, and let us try to understand the difficulties that had to be surmounted by this entirely unprepared land of ours.

For their early failures our anti-aircraft defenders quite undeservedly lost the confidence of a section of the public. Our defences, as a matter of fact, were ludicrously inadequate. Old Martini rifles adapted to fire explosive bullets to a maximum height of 1,500 or 2,000 feet, for months constituted part of London's armament! Much stupidity of a like character could be recalled, if it were worthwhile, and if it would not be unfair to recall it without at the same time fully describing the sound measures that at the cost of heavy and prolonged labour were being taken.

The only airships with which Germany could hope to raid this country were of the rigid division; airships, that is, having their gas-envelope or envelopes encased in one protective sheath of metal or wood. They were chiefly Zeppelins, but there were a few of the rather less capable smaller Schütte Lanz type, of which the airship brought down by Lieutenant W. Leefe Robinson was a representative. Of the airship fleet that existed at the outbreak of war some were comparatively small vessels incapable of a sufficiently prolonged voyage, combined with speed, altitude, and bomb-carrying capacity. Perhaps eight or ten vessels capable of raids on England were in existence. The best of these had a speed of about 60 miles per hour independent of wind; but this speed, being the maximum, and very uneconomical of fuel, their average speed was about 40 miles per hour. They could attain by the lift of their gas a maximum height of about 15,000 feet; but this only by the sacrifice of some of the war load. They were usually manned by a crew numbering from 22 to 28.

Their hydrogen gas was carried in 16 to 20 compartments partitioned from each other transversely in the long cylindrical hull, of which the bow was hemispherical while the stern was tapered off The outside of this hull consisted of a sheath of aluminium built up as a trellis girder, the whole compacted by a fabric covering.

The ships varied in length from 520 to 560 feet, and had a gross lifting capacity of 28 to 38 tons. Larger vessels were produced later in the war.

Taking the LZ77 brought down by French guns at Revigny in February, 1916, a sufficiently representative type, the following are the important characteristics. In place of a number of small parallel rudders and elevators of former types there was a compact empennage not unlike that of a tractor aeroplane. Rudder and elevator were "flaps" hinged to the vertical and horizontal fins respectively. This vessel was driven by five Maybach engines each of 180-200 H.P. Early Zeppelins had three of these motors driving four screws, two port and two starboard. An intermediate type had four engines and four screws. The LZ77 had a fifth engine driving a screw just behind the stern car.

This addition of power not only increased the horizontal speed, it increased the climbing speed; and it enabled the vessel, with inclined elevator, to ascend above the level it could attain by the mere discharge of ballast. Indeed, nearly all modern airships are a combination of dirigible balloon with static buoyancy, and aeroplane with dynamic lift.

The 1914 type carried about a ton of bombs a distance of about 450 miles. The LZ77 carried 20 projectiles of an aggregate weight of about 1½ tons. Each bomb was carried in a bomb-dropper formed of a hook which the weight of the bomb opened when the hook was freed by electricity controlled from the cabin. For defence, the airship carried six machine-guns——two on the top, two in the forward car, two in the stern car.

Whereas earlier Zeppelins carried 1½ tons of water ballast, and usually navigated at less than 6,000 feet altitude (their maximum being about 9,000 feet) the LZ77 and its contemporaries often travelled at 10,000 feet. The water ballast is expendable load carried for the purpose of adjusting the lift to various conditions and altitudes. Apart from deliberate ascent by its discharge to increased heights, there are various causes compelling its steady waste; thus, there is a continual leakage of gas through the envelope, and any reduction of temperature or deposit of moisture would cause the ship to descend if ballast were not expended. On the other hand, the steady consumption of fuel of the engines gradually diminishes the load, and saves the water ballast; and the discharge of bombs acts in like manner. The latter has a very useful side to it, for it enables the ship to climb to its maximum height, or thereabouts, just at the time when it is most necessary to evade pursuit or shell-fire.

What became known as the "super-Zeppelin" had a gas-capacity of about 2,000,000 cubic feet giving a gross lift of about 60 tons, and was driven by six engines. In all the later Zeppelins intended for raiding England some of the petrol tanks and guns were fitted so that they could be instantly jettisoned.

The wireless outfit included an aerial of 500 feet of stranded copper cable at the forward end.

The following summary of typal characteristics may be useful for reference.

(1) The airships destroyed by Flight Sub-Lieutenant R. A. J. Warneford and Flight-Commander Bigsworth were 621 feet in length, and had a capacity of 953,000 cubic feet. They had a gross lift of 29 7 tons, with a "useful load" of 8 tons. There were 18 gas-bags. The power was four 210-H.P. Maybach motors. The maximum speed was 50 miles per hour. The height attained was 8,250 feet. These ships were armed with four machine-guns, and carried 1¼ tons of explosives.

(2) The next type was 544 feet in length, and had a capacity of 1,060,000 cubic feet. Lift——gross 33 tons, useful, 14 tons. Gas-bags, 17. Motors, four 240-H.P. Maybach. Maximum speed 53 miles per hour. Fuel for 26 hours. Armament, 5 maxim guns and 1¼ tons of bombs.

(3) The L15 destroyed by Lieutenant A. de Bathe Brandon, and the L19 destroyed in the North Sea had the same dimensions as the previous type, but with a useful load of only 10 tons. These vessels, however, carried five motors, each of 240 H.P., and had an altitude capacity of 11,500 feet. There were five maxim guns, including one on top, and two tons of bombs.

(4) A later type was 560 feet long and of 1,235,000 cubic feet capacity; gross weight 38¼ tons; useful lift 13 tons; 19 gas-bags; six

210-H.P. Maybach engines; speed 59 miles per hour; fuel for 30 hours; altitude 13,200 feet; armament, two large-bore machine-guns on top, and six maxims, and 2¼ tons of bombs.

(5) The airship (L31) brought down at Potters Bar, in Essex, on October 1, 1916; and the L32 and L33 were 680 feet long, and had a capacity of 1,906,000 cubic feet; gross lift about 56 tons; useful load 19 tons; speed 65 miles per hour; fuel for 32 hours; six 250-H.P. Maybach motors driving five propellers; altitude 16,500 feet; armament two large-bore machine-guns on top, one at bow and one at stern, and six maxim guns.

(6) The last Zeppelin type had a length of 775 feet; capacity 2,472,000 cubic feet; speed 77 miles per hour; fuel for 28 hours; seven 250-H.P. Maybach motors; gross lift about 65 tons; useful load 40 tons; maximum altitude 18,000 feet; armament four large-bore machine-guns on top and six maxims, and four tons of bombs.

By maximum altitude the reader will understand the height attainable under the most favourable circumstances, and not a height to which the navigators could ascend whenever and as often as they pleased.

In most of the later Zeppelins the captain's cabin was forward. It contained the three control wheels. Close by was the wireless room enclosed in a casing of cotton-wool to ensure silence.

Any value of the big airship lies in its capability for long-distance voyages (and with engines stopped, of course, airships can still remain aloft), and for night operations, the latter being more or less hazardous for heavier-than-air-craft which, in the event of engine-failure or exhaustion of fuel, must land. So far as distance alone was concerned, London was within range of the enemy's aeroplanes, but not until the end of 1917 did these come by night, although more than once the Kentish coast had previously been reached on bright moonlight nights and by day.

The Zeppelin, on account of its size, made a good mark for anti-aircraft guns, and when our defences were put into order hits were easily secured, in one case a direct hit being obtained with the first shot at a height of over 10,000 feet.

Another drawback to the Zeppelin was its vulnerability to incendiary bullets, a very few of which would be almost sure to include the fatal one. Indeed, one hit of a small shell such as can be fired from a machine-gun might be sufficient to destroy the "Dreadnought of the

Skies." It followed naturally that the very small relative improvement in the duration and reliability of aeroplanes, involving greater safety in night-flying, would make the Zeppelin obsolete as regards war purposes; and that situation arose before the end of the war. A practicable method of rendering the airship almost immune from the fire danger by employing helium instead of hydrogen gas is now suggested.

For months after war broke out we had no range-finding system of the slightest use against a target moving swiftly in two dimensions of space, visible for only a few seconds at a time, and that might or might not be picked up by a searchlight and held for a few seconds. And seldom did a hostile airship remain over London for more than 15 to 20 minutes; for having dropped its bombs, its chief concern was to hurry homewards evading gunfire or pursuit. Due credit having been given to the enemy for producing the Zeppelin airship, while certain British aeronautical experts were ridiculing all "gas-bags," and while the Government was assuring the public that we had nothing to fear; and to the crews of the airships for a fine combination of aeronautical skill and pluck; to the British undoubtedly belongs the credit for the discovery of measures that proved an effective antidote and involved the exercise of far greater intelligence, skill, and pluck than the enemy's.

Take the question of the guns. We had no anti-aircraft guns worth mentioning even on the Western Front. We had no trained gunners for such weapons. All these deficiencies had to be remedied. That, in all the circumstances, it took us two years to put this side of our anti-aircraft defences on a sound basis is no occasion for surprise. No nation that had purred so contentedly to the strokings of "leaders" who were ever at pains to avoid recognizing the possibility of war themselves, and even sought to turn the mind of the people from anything that might help them to prepare, could expect to do any better.

From the technical point of view the difficulties were great. Take, for example, the searchlight. Nothing looked to the lay mind so simple as the provision of numerous powerful searchlights, and their ranging of the skies until the hostile airship was detected; and nothing seemed easier than to keep the raider in the field of vision until either shell-fire from below or from one of our aeroplanes destroyed him. The author heard one virtuous British citizen after a Zeppelin raid loudly complaining in a railway carriage to the tune that he paid a heavy income tax; and, by G—d, he was not getting the value for his money!

The difficulty was very much greater than that of observing marine craft in narrow seas at night. To escape the beam an airship can move in two dimensions: it can quickly change altitude as well as direction; and once out of the slender beam of light the latter must ply the immensity of the sky on the chance of picking it up again. If the observer with the light stood directly behind it, he could see nothing. He had to stand at a distance, and direct the light from that distance. Experience showed that verbal control—commands spoken to the searchlight operator, was far too slow. Wire control was an obvious possibility, but the wire soon got slack, and it was difficult to secure a control that was not jerky. Yet the movement of the searchlight directing its range on a distant but moving small object must be smooth and delicate. A rigid bar control with some strong yet nicely adjusted smooth-working mechanism was one direction in which experiments were made. For many months no success attended our searchlights and anti-aircraft guns.

The target, in the case of a Zeppelin 500 feet in length, it at a height of 6,000 feet, appeared in the searchlight as a slender silver pencil one inch in length held at a distance of 12 inches from the eye. It was often travelling at a speed of about 20 yards a second, so that it took 10 seconds to pass a given point. The shell would take about three seconds to reach the target, if the gunner was lucky enough to get a direct hit. The airship, as a rule, pursued a zigzag path when under fire.

The enemy were credited with the intention of coating their airships dull black in order to render them less conspicuous in the searchlight. It may be doubted, however, whether this device would avail, since the envelope of an airship is usually covered with moisture, or rime, which in the beam of light would render it sufficiently visible.

The high explosives (shrapnel was used very seldom) first employed were afterwards supplemented by incendiary shells bursting into a sheet of flame calculated to ignite any leakage of gas in the airship.

Our aeroplanes, provided they were of sufficient speed and altitude capacity, were a deadlier weapon than the guns; and it became clear that a big provision of searchlights and plenty of aeroplanes were the surest defence, as distinct from preventive measures.

From aeroplane machine-guns it was sometimes the practice to fire a stream of projectiles consisting of ordinary bullets and "tracers," or incendiary bullets, alternately. Contrary to the usually accepted reports, the ordinary "tracer" bullet was successfully used in September, 1916, when it was the means by which Captain Robinson brought down his great quarry. A "drum" of a Lewis machine-gun contained about 50 projectiles, and the stream of bullets was visible by day or night, as smoke or flame, thus facilitating marksmanship.

As our experience and means increased, listening posts were established all round London; and these, in conjunction with the barrage, ensured that in whatever direction raiders approached they would promptly be confronted by a line of shells bursting at various heights. Then the "apron" was devised, to aircraft a sufficiently dangerous and invisible obstruction which caused raiders to maintain a certain minimum altitude, and thus gave our aviators a smaller region to cover.

We tried to baffle the Zeppelins by obscuring localities as much as possible by drastic no-lights orders, and undoubtedly succeeded to a considerable extent, although even on slightly misty nights London itself was visible to raiders partly on account of the Thames and partly by its artificial light. Everything points to the conclusion that Zeppelin navigators were only enabled to pick up a general idea of locality by following the Thames, or some other river, and that as regards London they had little idea as to which of its 200 square miles they were directly over. In the last year of the war wireless direction control was used; but of this, more anon.

There were 51 airship raids on Great Britain (aeroplane raids are dealt with in a separate chapter); but this number takes no account of three or four occasions when Zeppelins approached our coasts but were driven away. The first raid was on April 14, 1915. London was first visited on May 31, 1915. The raiders almost invariably chose moonless nights.

On January 31, 1916, raiders travelled over 100 miles inland, in one case 180 miles. It is reckoned that 365 bombs were dropped on that occasion, when Burton-on-Trent was bombed. On the return journey the L19, running short of petrol, alighted on the North Sea. A British trawler came alongside, but, although offered money, the skipper refused to take the crew on board, as he was outnumbered by two to one, and feared he would be overpowered. Soon afterwards the airship broke up, the crew perishing.

The raid of March 5, 1916, was in snowy weather, and one of the raiders passed from Spurn Head over the Eastern Counties to Deal, dodging snow-storms and lighting his way by throwing out flares which lit the countryside for miles around.

CHAPTER 10

Night-Flying Conditions and Dangers

Their fellow-airmen's testimony that the first aviators who went up after Zeppelins at night, and either succeeded, or did not succeed in bringing one down, were plucky fellows, should be good enough for the layman. Their fellow-airmen knew the circumstances; and their judgment, which in this case accorded so well with the view of the general public, is unquestionably right.

Aviators sent up to attack Zeppelins at night in the early days of the war ran tremendous risks, quite apart from the possibility of being shot down by the enemy. And no matter how successful the airman might be in the performance of his task, he had always the landing to make afterwards. In the first 18 months of the war the facilities for night-landings were primitive, and in practising night work, and during Zeppelin raids, there were numerous fatalities. At one time, without indicating the actual number of the losses sustained in this manner, it was admitted officially that 30 *per cent,* of night flights terminated fatally, 50 *per cent,* in serious injuries, and 70 *per cent,* in wrecked machines.

Practising night landings, Flight-Lieutenant Gates was killed at Hendon. The first fatality in actual war operations of the kind was that of Flight-Lieutenant Lord whilst attempting to land on a fast scout in the dark. Early in 1915 Lieutenant Hilliard was killed whilst landing a Caudron biplane in the dark, his load of bombs exploding. The list, given in full, would, indeed, be a long one. Our airmen were called upon in those days to face unfair odds. Night work was done often on "parasol" monoplanes, and on fast scouts, at a time when only a few illuminated aerodromes were available; whilst the lighting arrangements of these were of the crudest.

Machines carried quite ineffective devices for lighting up the ground for landing. Enforced landings due to engine failure in open country meant probable death. One is amazed now at the neglect of the most obvious precautions to minimize the dangers of this work, and only the stress of a sudden great emergency can account for it. It would be a simple matter to expatiate at length on methods of securing safety in night-flying. As the war lengthened out matters improved; but at first our airmen were sacrificed to the general unpreparedness of the nation, which of course was reflected in a lack of efficiency in every department. They actually flew Blériot "parasols" and the early B.E.2C on this duty.

There were some remarkable escapes. A night-pilot landed on a Caudron, and his bombs blew up. Investigation showed where his skids struck the ground. About 25 yards farther on was the wreck of the machine burned by flaming petrol. And about 20 yards farther still was the place where the pilot had been thrown. The first shock had released the firing mechanism. The second shock had exploded them and had blown the pilot out of the machine into some grass, where he fell without being stunned, and was able to roll over and over till he put the flames out. His worst injury was a badly burned hand.

In the course of a protracted search for enemy airships it was only too easy for aviators to lose their way. Before the war Germany had an elaborate system of illuminated aerodromes for night-landings, and of lights for guiding aerial navigators at night. In April, 1914, twenty-one beacons were in operation. Three examples of the system employed will suffice for illustration.

(1) Belgern-on-the-Elbe, Prussian Saxony: a revolving electric light flashing once in every 1-5 seconds, 72 metres above ground, 150 millimetres focal distance, 7,000 candle-power. Gave warning of high-tension cables.

(2) Bernkastel-Kues: a revolving electric light giving two flashes, 425 metres above sea-level, 150 millimetres focal distance, 250,000 candle-power. Showed position of aerodrome.

(3) Bonn: a fixed electric light with Fresnel lens or circular disc of stepped prisms, 25 metres above ground, 8,500 candle power. Gave, by a series of flashes, the number of the station.

Navigation lights would, of course, be of assistance to the enemy, and might have to be turned off, but there was very little excuse for the lack of provision of landing aids, which can easily be arranged only to be turned on when the incoming aircraft displays a signal. This was done later in the war with complete success. In Germany the beacons were sunk in the ground of the aerodrome, and covered with glass of sufficient strength. Also, there were illuminated indications of the direction of the wind. A white light in the centre of the field and four red lights at distances of 100 yards from it served to indicate the points of the compass. By this means the direction of the wind at any time could be signalled.

By comparison with the mere flying risks, an encounter with one of the earlier Zeppelins was regarded as sport; and flights that terminated without sighting the enemy as failures. Visibility was all in favour of the aeroplane. Vulnerability was all against the airship. Meanwhile, the night-flyers were honoured almost exclusively with respect to their success in bringing down enemy airships: and in that luck played a very big part.

Recognition was given, however, in other cases; thus, in June, 1916, the following officers were recommended to the Army Council in connection with their services against air-raiders. Major F. V. Holt, D.S.O.; Major T. C. R. Higgins; Second-Lieutenant A. de B. Brandon; and Second-Lieutenant C. A. Ridley. These officers had shown "great bravery and readiness to take risks of all sorts, going up and landing at night in all weathers, more often than not under most dangerous conditions." Second-Lieutenant Brandon was the first pilot to succeed in dropping bombs on a Zeppelin at night.

It would be easy to pick out the names of a dozen aviators who deserved the Victoria Cross as much as any of its recipients. No one knows what they did except their own comrades. Cases of unrewarded heroism, of course, are not peculiar to the Flying Services; indeed, we may be sure that if all the deserving received the V.C. and the D.S.O. the number of these decorations would be multiplied threefold. Our admiration of those whose bravery was witnessed by responsible officers, or achieved its object, is not in the least diminished by the knowledge that there are many whose equally brave deeds have not been officially recognized. In the course of the war, too, as everyone knows, decorations had varying values. In some cases as time wore on they became more difficult to win; in others, their value to the holder diminished.

An instance of unsuccessful and unrewarded courage was that of a friend of the author stationed on the East Coast who was sent up to attack a Zeppelin. He was flying a B.E.2C in the days when this type of machine was underpowered. He could neither climb high nor fly fast. Knowing perfectly well that only a fluke could bring success, such a fluke, for example, as that the Zeppelin should have engine trouble, he obeyed orders and ascended from the flare-illuminated aerodrome.

He sighted the Zeppelin and tried to close with it, but when still 2,000 feet below his quarry he found that he could not get another foot of altitude out of his machine. He continued the chase, however, while the Zeppelin shaped its course for home; and he found that he could just keep pace with it. The situation was quite hopeless, save for the possibility that the enemy not perceiving him, might descend to within range, but with bull-dog persistence he determined to "hang on" until compelled to return for lack of petrol.

Also, he dropped his bombs to lighten his machine, and this had the effect of increasing his altitude, and he was able to climb to within 500 feet of the chase, which was now perfectly visible against a "false dawn" in the eastern sky. To reach this height he had sacrificed his one means of attack, and he was still below the Zeppelin, whilst the latter could at will have risen a further 1,000 or 2,000 feet. Not even a desperate attack by ramming was open to him, and his petrol was nearly at an end. He turned back.

Behold him, then, over the sea, with no land visible, and with only the compass to guide him; knowing well that if he went out of his course he would have to alight on the water with the scantiest chance of being rescued. He had risked all that the successful destroyer of a Zeppelin risks, and had failed through no fault of his own. That no other machine was available, or even the same machine with a more powerful engine, was due to the remissness of the authorities, and to ignorance which was proof against the warnings of men who had made a study of aerial warfare.

Certainly the B.E.2C was a machine much preferred by pilots for night-flying to the Blériot "parasol," which some were condemned to use; but in the emergency of landing without lights it was no safer than most other types.

Our man arrived safely at his aerodrome, cold, hungry, and dispirited. Scores of similar incidents occurred during the raid season.

Most of the apparatus used was of the crudest description. Night-flyers took care in those days not to bring their unexpended bombs home with them for fear of a bumpy landing. There were practically no safe-guards. In one case an airman who thought he was comfortably over the waters of the Thames Estuary dropped six bombs, and discovered after he arrived at his aerodrome that he had dropped them on a town; fortunately without doing any harm.

CHAPTER 11

The Zeppelin Beaten

On the 17th of May, 1915, a Zeppelin airship returning from a raid on England, chased by our defending aeroplanes, was intercepted by a squadron from Dunkirk, three of which got to close range. Flight-Commander Bigsworth dropped some 60-lb. bombs and secured hits: and one of the after compartments of the airship was seen to emit dense clouds of black smoke. The airship was evidently disabled, but apparently she just managed to get home, although at the time it was rumoured that this vessel was destroyed. This was the first serious brush between airship and aeroplanes in the air, and the latter suffered no casualties.

A few weeks later occurred the first fight to a finish between airship and aeroplane. On June 7th, at 2.30 a.m. Flight Sub-Lieutenants Wilson and Mills flew on separate machines on a raid to Brussels. They destroyed a Zeppelin shed and the airship in it at Evere. At the same time two other airmen started for another airship harbour. Flight Sub-Lieutenant R. A. J. Warneford, flying a Morane monoplane, at 3 a.m. sighted a Zeppelin returning from a raid on England. It was the long-desired opportunity. Alone in the sky, and with nothing to rely upon save the frail aeroplane and himself, he shirked not the issue. He knew that the Zeppelin could bring rapid fire to bear upon him, and that it was extremely doubtful whether he, while controlling his machine, could make any effective reply. Filled with a single purpose, and putting aside all thought of personal safety, he planned his manoeuvres and method of attack, with what success we all know.

Living in tense moments, his mind under discipline through almost unimaginably distracting events, he flew close enough to his powerful enemy to drop six bombs accurately, close enough to be almost shattered by the explosion and flame that followed, and turned completely over by the whirlwind that followed the fire. He righted his machine, but was forced to land in enemy territory. Here fortune favoured him, for he was able to restart his engine and fly away. The debris of the Zeppelin fell on a convent near Ghent killing two nuns. Only one of the crew escaped death.

The same officer was on one occasion flying with an observer when they sighted an enemy aeroplane. The observer fired, but his gun jammed. Warneford took a second gun, stood up, fired, and brought the enemy down, his own machine meanwhile getting out of control and beginning to dive. He just had time to get into his seat and resume control and right it. The knowledge of what was happening and of the mere instant of time at his disposal had not paralysed action or aim. His victory over the Zeppelin was recognized by the King, who sent the following message:—

Most heartily congratulate you upon your splendid achievement of yesterday, in which you, single-handed, destroyed an enemy Zeppelin. I have much pleasure in conferring upon you the Victoria Cross for this gallant act.

George R.I.

Flight Sub-Lieutenant Warneford was born in India, but was a member of an old Yorkshire family. He had spent some years in Canada, but came to this country when the war called the sons of the Empire together. He joined the 2nd Sportsmen's Battalion. When he transferred to the R.N.A.S. he at once showed marked ability; and his trainer, Flight-Lieutenant Merriam, one of our pioneer instructors of flying, once remarked of him that he would "either break his neck or do big things." He was certainly a very fine aerial jockey; but his skill did not avail him a few days after his success against the Zeppelin, when, flying near Paris, he crashed and was instantly killed.

There was a Zeppelin raid on the East Coast on August 9, 1915, and one of the raiders was so seriously damaged by anti-aircraft guns that she only just managed to stagger to Ostend, the last part of the journey being by water, and in tow. News of this having been sent to our aircraft base at Dunkirk, Flight-Commander Smyth-Piggott went up on a B.E.2C and flew over to Ostend, where he sighted the Zeppelin about three miles off-shore and in process of being hauled in. He at once attacked, dropping three 20-lb. bombs, and then went up into the clouds and prepared for another attack. The Zeppelin was escorted by four destroyers, which opened fire on the British aeroplane whenever it came into view. The rear compartment of the airship had been damaged by one of our bombs.

From Dunkirk other machines were sent up. A Bristol scout, piloted by Flight Sub-Lieutenant Besson, caught the airship at the moment it was being towed between the harbour piers. The pilot dropped bombs from a height of about 1,000 feet, and one of them exploded near enough to damage the Zeppelin. Following Besson came Flight-Lieutenant Bettington on a Bristol scout, and he nearly fouled some kites sent up by the enemy for that purpose. He dropped several bombs but with no apparent success.

The enemy were making great efforts to haul the airship in, and the workmen engaged on this task were over and over again dispersed by our airmen. The latter in their successive reports were able to set any doubt at rest. Total destruction was not effected, but the enemy were able to save only a few pieces of the airship intact.

Sometimes the official announcements of aerial encounters need no embellishment: they convey a sufficiently vivid picture of the reality. Thus, on August 1, 1916, the Admiralty issued the following:—

At 5.15 this morning one of our aeroplanes pursued and attacked a Zeppelin 30 miles off the East Coast. The pilot had fired over two trays into the Zeppelin, when he was temporarily incapacitated by a portion of his machine-gun flying off and stunning him. The Zeppelin was nowhere to be seen when the pilot regained consciousness, and he was therefore forced to return to his station.

London will never forget the raid of September 3, 1916, when of a total force of 13 airships—four possibly five—reached the metropolis. The date is memorable for affording Londoners the unforgettable spectacle and triumph of an enemy airship descending in flames. The airship was a Schütte-Lanz, and it was brought down at Cuffley, on the northern outskirts of London, in full view of the awakened multitudes, and visible from any point of vantage within a range of 60 miles. At the instant the airship burst into flames all who saw it, no matter how far away, knew it for what it was; and scarcely a street in London's 250 square miles did not ring to the shout of exultation.

The doomed airship, so high up that it looked like a silver pencil in the concentrated rays from half a dozen searchlights, had been seen manoeuvring this way and that to escape the shells. A timely cloud gave it the opportunity it sought, and it disappeared. The gunfire ceased. Then, after a few seconds of stillness, the thin crackle of machine-gun fire was heard, and far up in the sky a ball of flame appeared. The fiery ball began to fall, enlarging and streaming out behind. A muffled explosion was heard, and the whole heavens were lit up. And so the airship crashed to earth in flames and wreckage, its crew of sixteen dead.

On the following Tuesday the *Gazette* contained the following announcement:—

> His Majesty the King has been graciously pleased to award the Victoria Cross to the undermentioned officer, Lieutenant William Leefe Robinson, Worcester-shire Regiment and R.F.C., for most conspicuous bravery. He attacked an enemy airship under circumstances of great difficulty and danger, and sent it crashing to the ground as a flaming wreck. He had been in the air for more than two hours, and had previously attacked another airship during his flight.

This was the first airship destroyed by an aeroplane's machine-gun fire, an important factor in the success having been the ordinary "tracer" bullet capable of being fired from a rifled gun. The action took place at a height of 12,000 feet, Lieutenant Leefe Robinson, although under fire from the airship's machine-guns, fired three bursts into the gas hull, when she caught fire. The commander of the airship was William Schramm.

Lieutenant Robinson had done good work in previous raids, and on one occasion had been baulked of success by engine failure. His success in the dark early hours of September 3rd, was no fluke. He had served his apprenticeship in one of the most dangerous and heart-searching tasks in the war in the air. On this occasion, flying a single-seater biplane with no great fuel capacity, he soared aloft into the black night to challenge an enemy who had inspired even for war-time an unusual degree of hatred and disgust because of a method of attack that, although aimed at a city containing troops, munition factories, and military depots and headquarters, must inevitably fall almost entirely upon civilians.

But that indeed was the avowed object, according to the German code. He flew to and fro in the cold and darkness seeking a foe that would only be made visible by the searchlight beam. Describing his adventures, he said he had been up over an hour when he saw the first Zeppelin. She was flying high, and he went up after her, climbing to get a position above. But there was rather thick fog, and she escaped after he had fired a few rounds at long range.

The next ship he saw he determined he would attack from the first position. He met her just after two o'clock at a height of about 10,000 feet, and fired. Very soon he saw flames near her forward petrol tank. The flames rapidly spread along the body, and she dipped by the nose and went down slowly. He was so pleased that he looped the loop several times.

The story falls short of completeness, for it omits any reference to the danger from our anti-aircraft shells bursting all round the airship, a risk that no method of signalling could altogether remove.

Lieutenant Robinson was born in India. He went to Sandhurst, and entered the Army in 1914. As an observer in the Royal Flying Corps he served in France, and in May, 1915, was wounded by shrapnel in the arm. In the Spring of 1917 Lieutenant Robinson was captured in the great aerial struggle that heralded the British offensive. Released after the Armistice was arranged, he came to England only to die in an illness following influenza.

During the same raid that saw the Schütte-Lanz brought down at Cuffley, three gasometers at Retford were fired by Zeppelin bombs. They flared, but did not explode. On the same night one of the raiders dropped an empty observation car that had hung suspended on a long cable, which broke.

On the 24th of the same month another big raid took place, and again the raiders paid a heavy price. So far as London was concerned this was the most striking of all the airship raids, and in its first stages no one could fail to be impressed by the apparent ease and deliberate-ness of the attack and the immunity enjoyed by the attackers, who dropped their parachute white flares to light up the districts over which they were moving, and then let their bombs fall. These, however, as usual failed to do any military damage; but two of the latest type of Zeppelins were brought down in Essex, one of them totally destroyed with its crew by one of our aviators after it had been damaged by gunfire, the other brought down damaged and its crew captured.

The successful airmen on this occasion were Second-Lieutenant F. Sowray and Second-Lieutenant Alfred de Bathe Brandon, a New Zealander.

These two officers on separate machines had an exciting search for the raiders. When at last the searchlights showed one of them Second-Lieutenant Sowray bagged it, firing inflammable bullets from his machine-gun, some of which quickly took effect, setting the airship alight. The flames spread rapidly and culminated in an explosion and general blaze, the wreck falling at Billericay.

Second-Lieutenant Brandon attacked a second raider so effectively that it was forced to land. It had been hit by shell fragments and also by machine-gun fire, but had sustained no vital damage. The crew surrendered to a village constable.

Both airmen were awarded the D.S.O.

Second-Lieutenant Brandon had previously helped to destroy a Zeppelin, the L15, which came down in the Thames Estuary in the previous April. His success over London was due to the bombs he dropped, three of which took effect. His own machine was repeatedly struck by machine-gun bullets.

The circumstances relating to the previous success are worth recalling in the words of a trawler skipper. He said, "We heard heavy firing up in the air, the firing was so heavy that our ship shook. At 6.15, one mile from the Kentish Knock lightship we saw a great commotion on the water to the westward. There were a number of destroyers and mine-sweepers clustered round a big Zeppelin which was lying disabled on the sea. I saw a German come out of the door of the Zeppelin's car, crawl down the side, and hold up his hands. Others followed him. The ship was buckled in the middle, but the warships were endeavouring to get her in tow."

Brandon was injured in an aeroplane accident in March, 1917, near Dorking. Attempting a landing in a fog he flew into a tree, and in the crash he sustained a serious fracture of the right leg.

Lieutenant Sowray, when the war broke out, was still studying. He had won mathematical scholarships and had passed the Intermediate for the B.Sc. He was about to enter the India Civil Service. Like that other Zeppelin destroyer, Lieutenant Leefe Robinson, Lieutenant Sowray had been wounded while fighting in France as an infantry officer.

Another Zeppelin was destroyed on October 1, 1916, at Potters Bar, by Lieutenant W. Tempest, who was awarded the D.S.O. Lieutenant Tempest was called to action while having dinner. After reaching a height of 10,000 feet and patrolling there for about two hours, he saw a Zeppelin in the searchlight and under heavy fire from our guns. These took effect, Lieutenant Tempest meanwhile raking it with his machine-gun, and the airship caught fire.

The commander of this airship was Heinrich Mathy, one of the most experienced in the Zeppelin fleet. And the fate of this ship, which was witnessed by some of her sister ships, had a marked effect on their crews.

Another Zeppelin action deserves a place in this record. Lieutenant C. T. Freeman was awarded the D.S.C. for a determined attack on a Zeppelin at sea. He only abandoned the attack when he had used up all his ammunition. As darkness was approaching and his chance of being picked up was remote, his courage and devotion in returning to the attack a second and a third time was, as the official chronicler puts it, "exemplary." This Zeppelin was returning from the raid of August 2nd.

A running fight across the North Sea between a Zeppelin and a British two-seater aeroplane, the latter an Army machine not adapted for oversea work, occurred on August 25, 1916. The British machine set out from an aerodrome on the south-east coast in the early morning. The airmen were successful in firing two drums of ammunition into their opponent, and it was not until the other side of the North Sea was reached that they gave up the chase. They then had to return to their base more than 100 miles away.

The raid on the Norfolk coast on November 28, 1916, ended badly for the enemy who, in their official report, admitted the existence of "extraordinarily powerful defences." In connection with the destruction of one of the raiders the following awards were granted: the D.S.O. to Flight Sub-Lieutenant E.L. Pulling and the D.S.C. to Flight-Lieutenant E. Cadbury and Flight-Lieutenant G. W. Fane. While the airship was descending in flames its crew continued to fire at the British machines.

Captain R. H. M. S. Saundby and Second-Lieutenant L. P. Watkins were given the Military Cross in recognition of their work in attacking and bringing down a Zeppelin on the morning of Sunday, June 17, 1917. The airship was attacked by the two machines and sent down in flames. Three of its crew were taken prisoners; the rest were found dead.

A great fight occurred between a Zeppelin and one of our aeroplanes, a D.H.9 which set out from Great Yarmouth on September 15, 1917, and engaged the airship for over an hour, firing 400 rounds into her, all the while under heavy fire from her guns. The action was fought at over 12,000 feet. Through engine-failure our machine descended to the sea, and one of our seaplanes rescued its occupants; but with these on board the load was so great that she had to taxi back 50 miles to the base.

So heavily were airship raiders losing in their attacks on England, that by the autumn of 1917 it became very doubtful whether any conceivable military or moral damage caused was worth the cost. It is highly probable that the enemy had at this date to some extent allowed their judgment to be upset by their passionate desire to injure England. It must be remembered that the altitude to which raiders were driven by the defences had greatly increased, and that by our "apron" defence of London the airships were confined to a region between their maximum height ("ceiling") and the top of the "apron." This enabled our aeroplanes to confine their attention to a limited zone, and it helped our anti-aircraft artillery in the same way. Our anti-aircraft weapons had been increased in number, and the method of using them had enormously improved. It is known that at this period the raiders had a great fear of London's defences, and there was a difficulty in getting crews for the work.

It was in these circumstances that the most ambitious of all the raids was attempted on October 19, 1917; when twelve of the latest and biggest airships set out to raid London and the Midlands. This was known as the "silent" raid, and it was supposed by many at the time that the engines of the airships which, it was said, were stopped in order to prevent the noise of their coming from being heard, could not be restarted owing to the great cold. It is at least as likely, however, that the engines were not stopped, and that they were merely silenced in the usual way, but that the high wind at the great altitude the airships maintained swept them away.

The raiders relied for course-keeping chiefly upon wireless direction control; and when the fate of the expedition became known it was asserted that our spies had found out the necessary particulars enabling our wireless stations to jam all the German wireless signals on the night of the raid. That, of course, would not be impossible; it would scarcely be possible to jam the German signals unless the key in use were discovered beforehand. But, as a matter of fact, the disaster can be explained much more simply.

Driven to a great height by the fear of our defences, the Zeppelins came into a stream of air moving at 90 to 100 miles per hour, just such a wind as prevailed during the ballooning Grand Prix of 1910, when some extraordinary runs were made, and nearly all the aeronauts deliberately landed in forests in order to diminish the probability of broken limbs. In the wind they were in the Zeppelin navigators may or

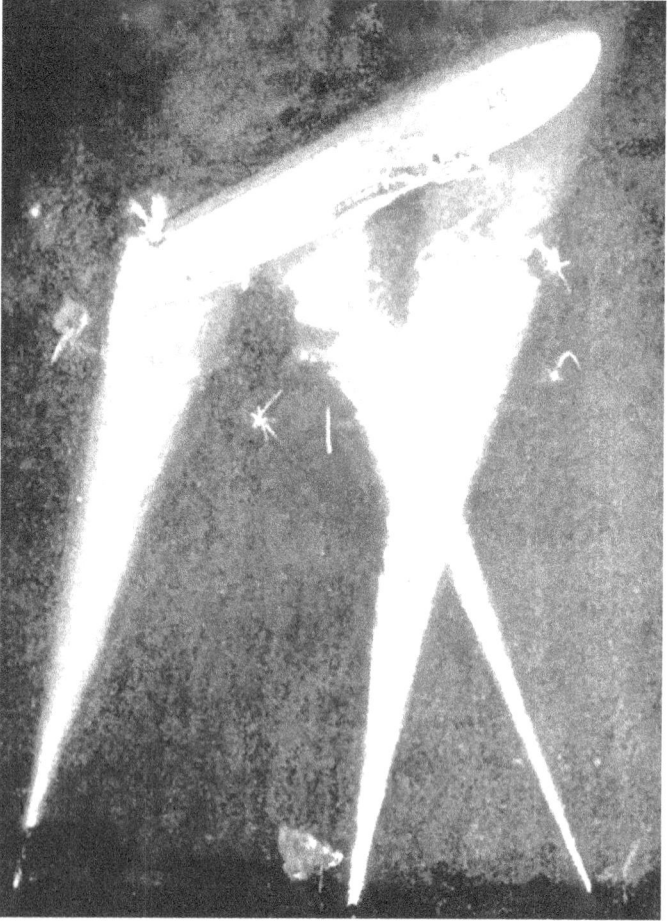

THE CRIPPLING OF ZEPPELIN "L15" OVER THE EASTERN
COUNTIES BY A TRIANGULAR BATTERY OF LAND GUNS

may not have known their position. In any case, they could not remedy it, for their maximum speed did not exceed 70 miles per hour; and the wind being something like 90 degrees to their homeward course, they simply could not "make it." Battling against this hour after hour, fuel would soon run short, and a certain amount of engine trouble due to running "full out" would be inevitable. The enemy, with their knowledge of meteorology, ought to have known what to expect. The conditions, at any rate, were perfectly familiar to British aeronauts. But the disaster was in large measure due to effective British anti-aircraft methods, compelling raiders to navigate at high altitudes.

The wireless apparatus on L49, the airship that came down at Bourbonne-les-Bains, was deranged, which, of course, merely showed that this particular vessel had a mishap, not that the wireless control for the whole fleet had broken down. Indeed, it is known that during the helpless drift across the Channel they picked up a message to the effect that a Zeppelin school-ship had broken adrift from Germany with no one on board.

Unquestionably the great height, the extreme hardships, and the poor visibility, all contributed to the disaster. The capabilities of the Zeppelin had outstripped the endurance of the crews. The cold experienced during this raid was bad enough: 30 degrees below zero Fahrenheit. Probably, in some cases, in spite of the heat from the exhausts the water ballast froze. That would be an inevitable sequel to engine-stoppage. "God blew and they were scattered."

The mere fact that some of them escaped proves nothing one way or the other. These may have seen the danger in time, and turned back before it was too late. It rather discounts the jammed wireless theory. As to the engines, the Zeppelin navigators had had a good deal of experience of work in very low temperatures; and they would have taken all the usual precautions against freezing. Bombs were dropped apparently in panic, as ballast. Of the twelve airships that set out very few returned to harbour. The fate of the others is here summarized.

L44 destroyed at St. Clement at 6.45 a.m. on Saturday, near Lunéville. All the crew perished.

L45 brought down at Mison, near Gap. Destroyed by crew, who were taken prisoners.

L49 forced down at 9.20 a.m. on Saturday, near Bourbonne-les-Bains, and captured with its crew.

An airship brought down at 4 p.m. on Saturday, between Gap and

Sisteron in the High Alps. Set on fire by the crew, who were all captured.

An airship chased by French airmen near Fréjus, and believed to have drifted out over the Mediterranean and become a wreck at sea.

L50 came down at Dammartin, Haute Manne, where she jettisoned some of her crew and one of her cars, and reascended. Fate unknown.

Two other airships; fate unknown.

In September, 1918, Major Cadbury, the same officer who has been mentioned already, was with two others awarded the D.F.C. for services during a Zeppelin raid. They destroyed one airship, and damaged another at some distance from land. This was on the night of August Bank Holiday, when five Zeppelins made the attempt. The action took place at 17,000 feet, 40 miles out at sea. It was remarkable for the occurrence that in it Commander Peter Strasser, the chief of the Zeppelin fleet who had accompanied many raids on England, was killed.

The ship he went down with was one of the latest and largest, exceeding a cubic capacity of more than 2,000,000 feet. The raiders committed the mistake of approaching quite close to our coast before they picked up their position; and before they turned back they were perceived. A squadron of British machines put out, at least four of them engaging the enemy. The engine of one aeroplane was hit, and it had to descend. A second, after a long chase, had machine-gun breakdown, and returned. The two others, each unknown to the other, were in at the death of the Zeppelin, one on each side; and each returned with a report that it had destroyed a Zeppelin. But it was then discovered that this was one and the same airship.

The great height to which Zeppelins were now driven taxed the altitude capacity of our aeroplanes to the utmost. At this period Royal Air Force units working with the fleet were relying upon seaplanes and deck aeroplanes, (types more fully considered in another chapter). Few of these could climb so quickly as the Zeppelin; and on many occasions Zeppelins were seen over the North Sea reconnoitring, and then getting away without a scrap, while our aeroplanes were laboriously climbing the last 6,000 feet. But on one occasion we were too clever for the Hun. The wily Englishman planned a little surprise. A small deck barge was sent out on patrol and, unnoticed by the enemy, who were doubtless looking out for the usual big "mother ship," a fast-climbing fighting scout went up from it. "Old Man Zep," expecting his customary immunity, was cruising about at 19,000 feet, and he did not realize that the tiny aeroplane seen only when it was too late to escape, was his master. Up it came, and the airship's usual tactics availed not. The aeroplane soon got level, and began firing, and to such purpose that the airship caught fire and suffered the fate that is inevitable when pitted against an up-to-date aeroplane.

Other actions with Zeppelins than those recorded in this chapter took place in connection with naval operations, and a reference to some of these comes into the chapter on Sea Aircraft.

Count von Zeppelin, whose remarkable career is no doubt known to the reader, lived to see his great airships obsolete as fighting or bombing craft capable of being employed against a well-equipped enemy. And it is difficult to see how this verdict can be reversed until some means be found of rendering an airship non-inflammable. Even then it would be handicapped by its great size making it a good target. Moreover the big aeroplane more and more approaches it in the matter of reliability, duration, and carrying capacity, besides having the advantage of greater weather worthiness, ease of landing, and requiring fewer men on the ground to take it in. Count von Zeppelin died on March 8, 1917, at the age of seventy-eight.

CHAPTER 12

Aeroplane Raids on England

Between Christmas Day, 1914, when a German aeroplane flew over Sheerness, and the end of the war there were 62 German aeroplane raids on England (airship raids are the subject of a separate chapter). Most of these raids were quite trivial and harmless, but at one period they threatened to become formidable.

The enemy first sent aeroplanes by night on January 23, 1916, during a bright moon. Not until November 28th of that year did a German aviator drop bombs on London. He did very little damage, and was brought down during his return journey.

Aeroplane raids assumed a serious aspect in May, 1917, the enemy still choosing moonlight nights. The bombs killed and wounded many civilians, but seldom effected damage of importance. As many as 20 machines, on some occasions, visited London and the South-East of England; and during good weather and favourable phases of the moon parties came on four or five successive nights. The first "dark night" raid was on March 8, 1918; but it is probable that the light from a fine display of the Aurora Borealis was good enough to enable the raiders to pick up the Thames Estuary. At that period, moreover, the Germans were using wireless direction control, which enabled them to find their general position without the aid of landmarks.

There was a brief period of daylight raids in the middle of 1917, and Londoners will not soon forget the spectacle of the two large formations of big bombing machines which flew over the city on the morning of Saturday, July 7th, or their feeling of impotence when, in spite of the heavy firing of our batteries, not a Hun was hit, nor the steadiness of the formations apparently disturbed. As a matter of fact, the enemy were flying at a great height, and the light mist—suffused brightness—was all against our gunners; and it is known that by our fire and by the fear of our aviators climbing up to attack, the enemy's plans were considerably upset. After that month, however, the raiders enjoyed steadily diminishing success, and suffered heavier and heavier losses.

In raiding by daylight one advantage of formation flying is that it is best for defence against aeroplanes, which can seldom do effective work unless they can cut out single members of the formation. We have yet to see a battle-royal between big well-armed formations, although in the fighting on the Western Front, and as regards fighting scouts, matters at times reached that point. But formation flying on a bombing raid is advisable, also, for the reason that it confuses the anti-aircraft batteries which, in ranging, have to take simultaneous observations from two bases on one machine; and it is extremely difficult-practically impossible—to do this by agreement on one machine of a group, the members of which, although apparently near each other, are in reality separated by considerable distances. The aeroplanes are usually at such a great height as to appear little more than specks in the sky.

Raiding by night, on the other hand, speaking generally, is done with least loss when single machines, or groups of two or three, set out at intervals of a few minutes. This ensures the greatest demand on the enemy's batteries and defending aeroplanes, and creates a deeper moral effect.

Some of the problems that our defence had to solve have already been indicated in the chapter on Zeppelin raids. There were others peculiar to "Gotha nights." Searchlights, as an aid to anti-aircraft artillery, towards the end of the war suffered a certain depreciation. This was partly due to the success obtained with sound-ranging. The enemy's aeroplanes could not come in absolute silence—unless we except Zeppelins drifting on a favourable wind—and the noise of the motors, whether "silenced" or not, enabled our listening posts to locate them with sufficient accuracy to direct the barrage fire. Nor could the enemy know when he was in this way being located. On the other hand, the searchlights, terrifying though they were to an airman, enabled him to dodge and zigzag and change altitude, besides giving him in many cases a clue as to his whereabouts. Against the sound-ranging was the handicap that in a city the babel of other sounds interfered with the clearness of the results.

The barrage, as regards London, was not put up with a view to obtaining direct hits so much as to fend off the intruders. The idea of the defence system in London towards the end of the war was, first, to keep raiders away from populous or important regions; secondly, to render their casualties too heavy for them to persist. The latter object was achieved by the barrage fire and "apron" defence playing up to our fighting aeroplanes; and it was considered that direct hits or disablement due to the fire of our batteries would be a matter of luck.

The balloon "aprons," which were first employed towards the end of 1917, were useful not so much for entrapping enemy raiders as in compelling them to approach London at an altitude of not less than 9,000 or 10,000 feet. This gave our airmen and artillery a limited zone of the sky to look after. The net idea, of course, is almost as old as the hills; and it was applied to marine warfare certainly as soon as mines, torpedoes, and submarines came into use. Large numbers of people suggested it to the Admiralty and the War Office directly air raids were threatened; and the newspapers, in attributing its invention to any particular officer in charge of the defences, went very wide of the mark. Nevertheless, a good deal of credit attaches to the ingenious minds of officers of subordinate rank that made the "apron" possible after early failures and disasters due to technically unsound experiments.

Among these was Mr. E. T. Willows, one of our airship pioneers. The balloons employed were the familiar kite-balloons without the baskets. The wires were quite slender ones of high tensile steel, although at the top it was necessary to employ stouter stuff to carry the weight suspended on it. Without going into technicalities, it may be said that the "aprons" consisted of a large number of loose wires hanging vertically from a horizontal cable which was sustained aloft by the buoyancy of balloons. There were three balloons to about 1,000 yards, and the "apron" extended downward to about a mile from the ground. But the enemy did not know where the clear space was either below the "apron" or between the cables by which the balloons were moored; nor did they know how many of these "aprons" were distributed around London, nor where they were. A still later improvement concerning the balloons was the subject of successful experiments in one of the countries of the Alliance, the British authorities thinking little of it at first. It is an invention that will probably have a marked influence on the future of free ballooning.

Experiments with the "aprons" were not always conducted without accidents; and in one case disaster attended them, and two lives were sacrificed through a technical blunder. But out of this good came; for the enemy getting hold of a distorted version of the incident, came to the erroneous conclusion that the "aprons" were mobile, and thereupon entertained a deeper dread of them than ever. This is known from captured orders instructing raiders to be especially cautious of the "aprons," and not only to give them a wide berth overhead, but also to act on the assumption that they might be found wandering about at any part of the country.

One of the Gothas brought down in January, 1918, damaged an "apron," and was damaged by it; but the virtue of this defence was of the passive order: it compelled the Huns to fly at such a height that they could not tell which particular part of London was under them, and were obliged to drop bombs haphazard.

There is on record the narrative of his experiences written by one of the German raiders in June, 1916, quoted by the *Daily Telegraph* from the *Frankfurter Zeiting*.

At ten o'clock the commander shoots from his machine a rocket, which is the sign for the start. He goes up first, then all the big well-loaded birds rise and take their course towards London. The Belgian coast is soon reached. On the left hand we can see the front. Nieuport, with the great flooded area, Ostend, Zeebrugge, and, farther to the right, Holland. We make signs one to another. A feeling of complete security and confidence in absolute success are with us all. The leading machine turns slightly to the left. We are now over the sea, the coast slowly disappears, and the barometer shows increasing height. Then, before us, appears a bank of clouds; behind it, veiled in mist, is the English coast. Now we are past the clouds, and under us are the English outpost ships. Then we see the mouth of the Thames as if it were approaching us. Sheerness knows us well.

Now it is a straight course for London. The first shots of the anti-aircraft guns reach our height, but don't disturb us. The firing having been passed, our squadron closes up. On the left is the Thames, whose bends we follow carefully on the map. Closer we approach our objective. I look with some anxiety at a cloudbank lying ahead. Curse it, are we going to have bad luck again this time! Five minutes pass. I look around for my comrades. They are all there in close phalanx. Then, at last, behind the clouds, is the city of the Thames. The first English chaser planes appear ahead, but much below us. Now, cousins, which of us will have to pay today? Still they do not disturb us; we are above the clouds.

THE "APRON"—A SECRET OF OUR ANTI-AIRCRAFT DEFENCE

At last, surprisingly clear and distinct, so that everything can be recognized, London's sea of houses beneath us. Our first greetings drop in quick succession—more, still more. Then we proceed, coolly and calmly, passing over the suburbs, for it is the centre we must hit. We regard nothing but that one object. There are the Tower, Liverpool Street Station, the Bank of England, Admiralty, ships on the Thames—all are absolutely clear. Everything is below us.

Now is the moment. I press the bomb-release handle, and follow intently the course of the greetings of the German people to the English. They are plentiful, blow after blow bursting bombs in the heart of England. A wonderfully impressive sight. Over the centre of London, high up between us, the bursting shells of batteries; down below, exploding bombs, clouds of smoke, and fires. Over us all, the smiling sky. The squadron turns. A last glance at the city—*auf Wiedersehen!*

This account may be compared with descriptions by British aviators of bombing raids in the next chapter.

The nature of the work of the German raiders became so desperate by the end of 1917, that only desperate men were employed; the "bad boys" of the Service. The terrible London barrage, and the dread of the "aprons" unnerved them, and by the spring of 1918 the losses had reached prohibitive point.

The Gotha bombers, considered quite dispassionately and after the war, were nothing to be proud of from the technical point of view. They owed something to British designs, and were a compromise of the enemy's "giant aeroplane" experiments with points taken from a Handley Page bomber captured early in 1917. The first two-engine Gotha with which we are concerned in this chapter differed from the first Handley Page bomber in the important respect that its propellers were behind the main planes, whereas those of the British machine were tractor.

The Gotha appears to have given a good deal of trouble to pilots; and we know for a fact that many accidents occurred in taking off and in landing.

The first Gothas to visit England were driven by two 260-H.P. Mercedes engines. The bomb load was 800 lbs.; and they could fly at about 74 miles per hour for six hours. Their "ceiling" was about 12,000 feet. A later type had four 260-H.P. Mercedes engines, and could fly for nine hours at 80 miles per hour. Its maximum height when loaded was only 10,000 feet. Returning, they climbed to about 15,000 feet, at which they considered themselves fairly safe from "Archies." The last type used against England had five Maybach engines, each of 260 H.P. They carried over 4,000 pounds of bombs, at least two of these weighing 600 lbs. each; and one of these was dropped on a London suburb. The airmen were kept warm by electrically-heated clothing which, of course, was also used in the British Service.

On a Bristol fighter Captain R. Baker and Lieutenant G. R. Spencer destroyed a Gotha near Ostend on July 21, 1917.

Flight-Lieutenant H. S. Kerby encountered eight Gothas on August 12, 1917, 30 miles out at sea, and attacked without result. Subsequently he saw a single Gotha in the water, and he threw his life-belt down to its crew. On the same day a Sopwith triplane attacked a Gotha five times between the North Foreland and the mouth of the Scheldt, firing 350 rounds and scoring many hits. He was then attacked by a formation of eight enemy scouts who fired small shot at him.

On August 22, 1917, during a German aeroplane raid, Flight-Commander Hervey on a Sopwith fighting machine attacked ten Gothas off the North Foreland, selecting a machine on the right of the formation for his attention. He fired two drums of ammunition into this machine, which fell into the sea near Margate. Flight-Lieutenant Kerby drove another of the enemy down into the sea in the same region. In this affair Squadron-Commander Butler, D.S.O., in a fight with the enemy, had the wires controlling the firing of his machine-guns cut by a bullet. Nevertheless, he got the guns at work by pressing the levers, and attacked a machine over Dover; but he was pressed hard by several enemy machines and compelled to return to his aerodrome by the partial disablement of his aeroplane, of which the aileron control wire was almost severed and the engine had been repeatedly struck. He went up on another machine and, attacking a Gotha, wounded the stern gunner.

Flight Sub-Lieutenant Drake set one of the enemy machines on fire, but did not see its ultimate fate; and Flight-Lieutenant A. F. Brandon, who happened to be up on a first practice flight on a Sopwith "Camel," attacked a Gotha and sent it down in flames. Lieutenant Brandon then returned, and obtaining another mount resumed the pursuit of the enemy.

From the Honours Lists the following are selected to illustrate the nature of the work of our defending airmen. The Second Bar to the Military Cross was awarded to Captain Gilbert Ware M. Green,

D.S.O., who, whilst flying at night on patrol duty, encountered an enemy aeroplane, which he attacked with great determination and skill. Although there was very little light, he succeeded in hitting one of the engines of the machine, which, by reason of the damage, was forced to come down in the sea off a South Coast port, and two of the airmen were made prisoners. In the early evening raid on London by 16 to 20 aeroplanes on December 18, 1917, one of the raiders was hit by gunfire, and finally came down in the sea off the Kent coast, two of the crew of three being captured alive.

The Distinguished Flying Cross was awarded to Lieutenant E. E. Turner who, whilst piloting his machine during a hostile air raid, displayed great determination and skill in manoeuvring at a height of 11,000 feet under heavy enemy fire, which enabled his observer to bring effective fire on the enemy, resulting in its being driven to the ground. Lieutenant H. B. Barwise received the same decoration. Whilst acting as observer to Lieutenant E. E. Turner on patrol duty, during an air raid, he showed great courage and ability. Although exposed to severe fire from the enemy he took prompt advantage of the skilful piloting of the machine, which enabled him to bring effective fire on his antagonist, as a result of which the enemy aeroplane was badly damaged and forced to land.

CHAPTER 13

Bombing the Germans

British air raids on Germany began on September 23, 1914, when two of our airmen left their cards at Düsseldorf , but it was not until three years later that the serious business of bombing Germany began, our Air Services, in the meantime, being occupied almost entirely with work nearer at hand. Nor did the enemy do much more than we did, despite the fact that before the war they had given a good deal of attention to bomb-dropping. In October, 1914, the Germans made about a dozen raids into France, and lost eight of their machines without doing any damage. French airmen, on October 30, 1914, bombed the headquarters of the Duke of Wurtemberg, near Dixemude, and did a lot of damage to buildings and motor-cars. The Staff fled into the woods.

The first few weeks of the war, while the Germans were overrunning Belgium and France, called for all our fortitude. Any little ray of light in the gloom was welcome. One of the first cheerful items of news was the Admiralty announcement that on September 23rd, British naval aeroplanes bombed the Zeppelin shed at Dusseldorf.

"The conditions were rendered very difficult by the misty weather, but Flight-Lieutenant G. H. Collet dropped three bombs on the Zeppelin shed, approaching within 400 feet. The extent of the damage done is not known. Flight-Lieutenant Collet's machine was struck by one projectile, but all the machines returned safely to their point of departure."

From an advanced base that had been very smartly organized the airmen set out at dawn. At the base they divided into two parties, one bound for Düsseldorf, the other for Cologne. The weather was misty; and the Cologne party, on reaching the city, found it enveloped in thick fog. They flew around for over an hour, afraid to drop bombs at random for fear of killing civilians. Finally, they turned back without discharging any bombs. The Düsseldorf party also encountered misty weather, but were able to see the town; and Flight-Lieutenant Collet, coming down very low, dropped all his bombs on the Zeppelin shed. He saw flames break out, but could not ascertain the extent of the damage done. His bombs were fitted with time fuses, intended to delay the explosion until the aeroplane had flown clear, and he believed that, owing to the low altitude, some of his bombs did not explode at all.

Flight-Lieutenant Collet was killed in an aeroplane accident in the Dardanelles a year later.

On October 8th Squadron-Commander C. A. Spencer Grey and Lieutenants R. L. Marix and S. V. Sippe bombed the Zeppelin shed at Düsseldorf with complete success. The first two were on Sopwith scouts, and Lieutenant Sippe flew a B.E. They started from Antwerp, but Sippe's engine failed and he had to return. The others got into thick weather, and did not see the ground for long periods. Lieutenant Marix once came down to find out where he was, and nearly ran into trees. On reaching Düsseldorf he came down to 500 feet, and dropped his bombs while under heavy fire from guns and rifles. The shed was set on fire, and the airship in it destroyed. Squadron-Commander Grey went as far as Cologne, and dropped his bombs on the railway station. He then returned to Antwerp and found Marix there. These three pioneers of Rhineland bombing only got away from Antwerp just in time, and had to sacrifice their machines.

A similar raid was made, as related in the Admiralty dispatch published November 24th—

On Saturday a flight of aeroplanes under the command of Squadron-Commander E. F. Briggs, of the R.N.A.S., with Flight-Commander J. T. Babington and Flight-Lieu tenant S. V. Sippe as pilots, flew from French territory to the Zeppelin airship factory at Friedrichshafen. All three pilots in succession flew down to close range under a heavy fire from guns, *mittrailleuses*, and rifles, and launched their bombs according to instructions. Commander Briggs is reported to have been shot down wounded, and taken to hospital as a prisoner. Both the other officers have returned safely to French territory, though their machines were damaged by gunfire. They report positively that all the bombs reached their objective, and that serious damage was done to the Zeppelin factory.

This flight of 250 miles, which penetrated 120 miles into Germany, across mountainous country in difficult weather conditions, constitutes with the attack a fine feat of arms.

The machines flown were Avros. The total time occupied during the flight was four hours. One enemy airship was destroyed in its shed, another shed was damaged and the hydrogen-making plant was demolished. The *Lokalanzeiger* gave the following account of the raid:—

Two airmen were signalled at noon from Constance, flying in the direction of Friedrichshafen. The military authorities were at once informed. At 12.30 the aeroplanes appeared over the town. The balloon gun-detachment opened fire with shrapnel and machine-guns. One of the aeroplanes glided down to within 1,000 feet of the airship shed, and dropped bombs, but without doing any damage. The aeroplane's petrol tank was pierced, and the pilot forced to land in the Zeppelin yard near the shed. He was taken out of his machine, and removed to the prisoners' quarters in the hospital, having a slight wound in the head. The other machine dropped bombs near the town and the station, and damaged three houses. He then came over the Zeppelin works, and threw bombs without causing damage.

Only small bombs were used, and the appliances generally were of the crudest. Bomb-sights were at this period in use, and it was the practice to release a bomb while gliding, or flying, as slowly as possible, first levelling the bomb-sight by spirit-level. Only by descending very low was there any likelihood of hitting the target; but there was little danger to the bomber from the effects of the explosion. Later in the war, when very heavy bombs were used, there was a high minimum safe altitude, over 5,000 feet in some cases; and delay-action fuses were used, giving as much as 15 seconds' interval before the explosion. Voisin biplanes and Blériot and Morane monoplanes were among the types of machines at first used in bombing. And, flying comparatively slow machines low over the target, the danger from anti-aircraft guns was serious enough. The guns fired shrapnel and high explosive. A small shell contains 360 bullets, so that heavy shrapnel fire filled the air with a screech of missiles, and it is no wonder that the average height at which flying over hostile country was done soon increased.

Bruges and other places in Belgium, and the enemy's rear positions in France, were frequently bombed during the winter 1914-1915, and in his dispatch covering the operations from February to April, 1915, Sir John French stated—

> In addition to the work of reconnaissance and observation of artillery fire, the Royal Flying Corps was charged with the special duty of hampering the enemy's movements by destroying various points on his communications. The railways at Menin, Courtrai, Don, and Douai were attacked; and it is known that very extensive damage was effected at certain of these places. Part of a troop train was hit by a bomb, a wireless installation near Lille is believed to have been effectively destroyed, and a house in which the enemy had installed one of his headquarters was set on fire. These afford other in-stances of successful operations of this character. Most of the objectives mentioned were attacked at a height of only 100 to 150 feet. In one case the pilot descended to about 50 feet above the point he was attacking. Certain new and important forms of activity, which it is undesirable to specify, have been initiated and pushed forward with much vigour and success.

The French were engaged in the same way. By way of reprisal for the bombardment of Nancy by a Zeppelin, one of their aeroplanes threw five bombs on the German headquarters. The projectiles all fell on the buildings in which the Imperial Staff was installed at Mezieres-Charleville. They also bombarded the station of Freiburg, in Breisgau. Finally, a flying squadron of 15 machines dropped bombs, with complete success, on the German military buildings of Ostend. The aeroplanes were violently cannonaded, but all returned safely.

The enemy had set up an aeroplane base at Ghistelles, near Bruges, and that remained there until early in 1918, when so persistent had the attentions of our bombers become that it had to be definitely abandoned. The first bombing raid on Ghistelles took place on January 19, 1915.

On March 2nd a Frenchman bombed the explosives factory at Rottweil. The French official account of the bombing of this powder factory, "one of the most important in Germany," stated that the aviator descended as low as 1650 feet over the works in order to throw his bombs with the greater accuracy. He dropped four 3½-inch melinite shells, the first on acid tanks, the other three on the works. From the acid tanks blue smoke shot up, which the aviator at first supposed was the smoke of an anti-aircraft gun. But a huge flame then arose from the same spot, with dense clouds of smoke which reached as high as the aeroplane.

A British machine accompanied a French flight early in April to Tullingen and Haltingen, and dropped five bombs on the station at the latter place destroying some coaches. The bombs smashed the gas conduits, and a gas tank took fire. The flames could be seen from places 50 miles away. The British machine dropped more bombs on the junction of the line for Bale and Freiburg, but was struck by a shell fragment and was compelled to land at Burgfelden. The two occupants were wounded.

"Eyewitness" reported that on April 19th a British aviator attacked the German airship base near Ghent. Carrying three heavy bombs besides small ones, he arrived near his objective about five o'clock in the evening and, after reconnoitring, he dropped a bomb on the airship shed. He was being fired at all the time from the ground and from the car of a kite-balloon. He got into position directly over the latter, so that its occupants could not shoot at him, and continued to drop bombs. He then planed down to a position between the balloon and the ground, so that he could not conveniently be fired at from either. Having dropped his last bomb he returned unscathed. In connection with this raid Lieutenant L. G. Hawker was awarded the D.S.O.

The French frequently sent bombing parties to the Rhine, notably on June 15th, when they penetrated as far as Ludwigshafen, and damaged important factories. These raids are merely mentioned here; but an idea of their extent may be obtained from the fact that on July 26th, 31 French airmen raided a Rhine manufacturing centre; on July 31st, 45 machines set out on one objective; and on August 27th, 62 aeroplanes took part in a raid.

The Victoria Cross was awarded to Squadron-Commander R. B. Davies and the D.S.O. to Flight Sub-Lieutenant G. F. Smylie, who, on November 19, 1915, carried out an air raid on Ferrijik junction on the Salonike-Constantinople railway. Sub-Lieutenant Smylie's machine was brought down by shell fire. The pilot, keeping it in control and releasing all his bombs except one, succeeded in hitting the station with them. On alighting he set fire to his machine, leaving the unexploded bomb to ensure its destruction. He then perceived Squadron-Commander Davies descending, and fearing that he would land near the burning machine, and thus risk destruction from the bomb, he exploded the bomb by means of a pistol bullet. Squadron-Commander Davies landed, took up Sub-Lieutenant Smylie in spite of a party of the enemy who were approaching, and returned to the aerodrome.

The Military Cross was awarded to Captain J. E. Tennant. One night he bombed the sheds of an enemy aerodrome from a height of only 30 feet. He shut off his engine in order to avoid giving warning, despite the risk of not being able to start it again. His machine was damaged by the explosion of his own bombs at so low an altitude. On his return he asked for permission to take another machine and repeat the operation.

For services in March, 1916, the D.S.O. was given Second-Lieutenant Henry Yates. He was instructed to bomb an enemy water-works. On arrival he found the place defended by anti-aircraft guns, and infantry lying on their backs, firing heavily. He descended to 600 feet, and dropped a bomb which almost completely destroyed the water-works machinery. He then attacked a machine-gun detachment, firing at it with his own machine-gun, and driving it from its position.

In Egypt our airmen were living up to their high reputation under particularly trying conditions. The official narrative of an incident that occurred on June 18, 1915, needs no embellishment. Eleven of our machines set out for El Arish. The objective was an enemy aerodrome. The attack was a complete surprise. When the first of our aeroplanes arrived at 8 a.m. two enemy machines had been run out of their sheds, and in one of them the pilot and observer were already seated ready to ascend, while a party of seven or eight mechanics were holding on to the wings or standing near the machine. They and the machine were blown to pieces by the first bomb, which was dropped on them from a height of 100 feet.

Our aeroplanes arrived at close intervals and attacked both the hangars and the camp with bombs and machine-gun fire at a low altitude, while two escorting machines remained at observation at a great height. Our aeroplanes were under heavy fire. The raid lasted over an hour, and an open hangar containing an aeroplane was hit and set on fire, and another hangar was fired. Hits were obtained on other buildings, and it could be seen that the soldiers in the aerodrome suffered several casualties. A machine in the open was almost completely destroyed. Bombs were also dropped on the town of El Arish.

One of our pilots was forced to descend in the *Wadi*. After he landed his machine was seen to be ablaze, and it is supposed that he set it on fire himself to prevent its capture. Another pilot was forced to land some miles to the west of El Arish, but one of the escorting aeroplanes landed near him and, after destroying his machine, managed to carry its pilot and passenger home. Several unsuccessful attempts were made to ascend before they got away.

On July 2nd, Sir Douglas Haig reported:—

Yesterday, in spite of the high wind, a large amount of successful work was done in the air. An important railway depot was attacked with powerful bombs, and a large number of other bombs were dropped on depots, railway junctions, batteries, trenches, and other points of military importance in the enemy's lines. Our machines attacked a railway train on the line between Douai and Cambrai. One of our airmen descended to below 900 feet, and succeeded in dropping a bomb on a truck which exploded. Other pilots saw the whole train in flames and heard further explosions.

This was during the battle of the Somme. Night bombing by the summer of 1916 was a regular practice. On the night of August 8-9, a French aeroplane dropped bombs on the powder factory at Rottweil, on the Neckar; 320 lbs. of explosives were dropped on the buildings, where two great fires and several explosions were observed. This raid occupied 3½ hours and covered a distance of 219 miles over particularly dangerous country. A great number of similar bombing raids are recorded in the French officials.

French, British, and Belgian airmen, 60 strong, bombed Houthoulst Wood, where a German base was concealed. The airmen passed through a heavy barrage, but reached their objective and dropped 9,000 lbs of bombs, setting fire to the wood and exploding the ammunition and destroying buildings.

On September 25, 1916, a big attack was made at Libercourt with the object of interrupting traffic on the Lille-Douai railway. The point of attack was 40 miles behind the German Somme front. At Libercourt a branch line from Lens joins the main line from the west, and a similar branch line from the same direction comes in a few miles lower down. This was a most important centre of movement for the enemy's troops. Within four miles were three German aerodromes. At one of them, Provin, a big shed was destroyed; and at Phalempin a fire was started. The aerodromes were deluged with bombs. While this was going on, attacking squadrons with other aeroplanes in escort crossed overhead, waiting for the opportune moment.

The first train was seen to leave Libercourt at 1.40 p.m. The second train was arriving on the line between Heninlietart and Ostricourt, where it joins the main line. One of our machines descended to about 800 feet over the first train near Ostricourt, and dropped six bombs. The engine was hit, and it jumped the rails, and three coaches were telescoped. The soldiers got out and ran for cover, but the machine came down lower and fired at them, leaving many dead and wounded on the ground. The second train was blocked by the wreck.

Another of our machines carried out a similar manoeuvre. Three bombs fell on the train. The German troops seeking to escape were heavily fired at by our aeroplane's machine-gun. While this was going on some of our machines bombed Libercourt Station, blowing up buildings, and doing much damage to the permanent way. The raids on Essen are memorable for their moral effect rather than the material damage. They were by French aviators mounted on British machines. Lieutenant Daucourt, the famous pre-war pilot, and Captain R. de Beauchamp set out on September 23, 1916, and covered a total distance of 500 miles in a raid on Essen. A few months later, July 7, 1917, Sergeant Major Gallois performed a similar feat.

On November 17, 1916, Captain de Beauchamp, leaving Nancy at eight o'clock in the morning, dropped bombs on Munich at noon, and landed safely in Italy. He was in a Nieuport biplane. He flew over Colmar and the Black Forest at a great height, experiencing very low temperatures. The total distance covered was 438 miles.

On November 12th an enemy aerodrome at Kut el Amara was bombarded, and much damaged; and on the following day an enemy camp at Al Ain was heavily attacked. On the night of December 14-15 our aero-planes flying by moonlight bombed the pontoon bridge on the Tigris while it was being towed upstream. The material was blown up and scattered. In connection with the latter operation, Captain J. H. Herring was awarded the D.S.O. He was flying continuously for six hours under heavy fire; and he brought back valuable information on another occasion.

On January 27, 1917, Flight Sub-Lieutenant Smith with Captain Wedgwood Benn on a Short, and Commander Samson, Flight-Lieutenant Clemson and Flight-Lieutenant Brock on Sopwiths, set out to bomb Chilkedere Bridge on the Bagdad railway. The first pilot dropped bombs at the bridge, but they failed to explode. He dropped more bombs on the defences south of the bridge, and did some damage; and he then descended to a low altitude and fired at the troops on guard. The other airmen also dropped bombs on the bridge, which was put out of use for some time.

The D.S.C. was given to Flight Sub-Lieutenant H. E. P. Wiggles worth "for conspicuous gallantry and enterprise on January 23, 1917, during a bomb attack by aircraft, when considerable damage was done to enemy blast furnaces at Burbach. During this flight he fought five engagements with enemy aeroplanes in formations of three, four, and five at a time."

In the, summer of 1917 our first big bombing squadron was established in France close to Dunkirk. Bombing entered upon a new phase on account of the greater range and carrying capacity of these craft. Here, therefore, it will be well to glance at the organization that was set up and the methods employed.

The Handley Page bomber of this period was driven by two Rolls Royce engines, each of 250 H.P. It could carry from ¾ to a ton of bombs. Each bomb was slung on its dropper; and one could see the vertical steel rods and their intricate connections making a bewildering mass of machinery in the floor of the machine. Pilot and "gun-layer" at side by side, and from their "office" the machine-gun man forward crawled out to the bows through a small door. Steering on the ground was effected by means of the propellers, the engines being controlled by one big throttle lever, by pulling which forward or back both throttles were opened or closed. By turning the lever round, one engine or the other was accelerated, and its opposite slowed down, causing the machine to turn.

The pilot could telephone to the operator astern any such message as, "We are going to land. Wind up your aerial." The bomber could signal to the pilot which way he desired him to turn by means of red and green lamps. Thus one red meant a point to port; two green lights, two points to starboard.

The machines were loaded up by day. Then, at the appointed hour, the C.O. and the ground officer took their places on the "bandstand," as the searchlight station was called, where they had ready to hand Very pistols, the telephone, flash-lamps, and other apparatus. The crews of the first and second machines prepared first, and tried their engines. Across the aerodrome the row of landing lights could be seen. At the back, the outlines of one of the sheds could at will be picked out in the darkness by some scores of electric lights that could be instantly switched on. These, however, were only used to guide returning pilots.

If all appeared favourable, the ground officer turned a searchlight on to No. 1 machine. That was the signal to be ready. Shortly after, he waved the searchlight; and at that the engines were opened out, and the machine swept forward into the field, taxying up to one end, turning round, and driving forward for the ascent. Each machine carried a red Port and a green Starboard light just under the leading edge of the bottom plane; also a white stern light. The pilot could turn on a great white light below the machine forward, to land by.

The first machine climbed in great circles to find out whether the visibility was good. If favourable, a red Very light was fired from the machine, which at once set out on its raid. Four minutes later the second machine started, and thereafter the others at four minutes' intervals. Only the first one reported as to the visibility.

As they approached the lines, any one of them that happened to be caught in an English searchlight fired a Very light of a colour determined and advised at the last moment, as a signal for the day. It was their "Pass friend. All's well."

One after another of the machines having gone, everything remained at "attention," ready to receive any returning ones. On their approach each of these fired a white Very light. At 10 seconds' interval this was answered by a light from the ground, if all was well. If there was no such reply, the machine circled about, its navigation lights on. When the answering signal was received the landing was made by the landing lights and the white flare on the machine.

If a returning machine was compelled to land in a hurry because of engine trouble or casualties, it sent a "must" signal by wireless as it approached. Everything else was then put aside until its landing was effected.

By August, 1917, raids were nightly occurrences, sometimes as many as fourteen machines setting out from one aerodrome, individual pilots going across the lines four or five times in a week. At first there were surprisingly few casualties, and scarcely any losses through trouble with the engines. The number of expert machine men and ground mechanics was, of course, large. The aerodrome used by such big heavy machines required an exceptionally firm surface; otherwise, in wet weather the machines were apt to get bogged.

The Royal Flying Corps, meanwhile, was bombing by daylight with smaller machines, R.E.S's, D.H.4's, and F.E.'s, and, indeed, any two-seater available. The amount of bombs dropped during the autumn of 1917 usually averaged about 25 tons a week. But one squadron of Handley Pages dropped 35 tons in one week at this period.

Here is a night-bombing experience. Fourteen machines prepared to carry out a programme suggested by the Army: and the start made a stirring scene. The first machine started, and we watched anxiously for the red signal. It was long in coming, as if the pilot felt very doubtful about the conditions. But it came at last.

Waiting in the bows of one the process could be watched. A machine was just getting away, the thunder of its engines drowning the distant drone of its immediate predecessor. Then Lieutenant Barker called out "Start the starboard engine." One turn did it; and, having run it for a few seconds, the pilot called out, "Start the port engine." Soon, just astern to right and left, both the great four-bladed propellers were spinning.

A flash of white light enveloped us, and everything was made clear for our start. The light waved; and the next instant the great machine lumbered forward, turned to the right, and rolled up the field. We made a half-circle turn, the throttles were opened out, and the machine plunged forward at good speed, and in a very few seconds was off.

Below was the receding aerodrome, the row of landing lights still visible; and by turning round one could see the battle lines. Searchlights swept the sky; star shells blazed. One could pick out batteries firing at timed intervals, and could also see vertical, or almost vertical, stabs of flame as the "Archies" blazed away at our other machines ahead. From the sea to Ypres, and beyond, was a blaze of many-coloured fire.

Higher and higher we flew, still circling; then the compass steadied as we settled on an easterly course. Our navigation lights were switched off, and we got nearer to the battle. At times great smudges of cloud swept past us; or, rather, we overtook them, on a following wind.

Here was a searchlight lighting up the clouds close at hand, like a great lamp under a ground-glass floor. Every instant it seemed we must be caught in the beam, which swept to and fro seeking for the machine whose engines were so clearly audible below. Suddenly, after three or four minutes of vain seeking, the machine became a tangled mass of brilliant lights and black shadows. We were in the light; but it is extremely likely that through the cloud we were not seen.

Occasionally the boom of explosions was heard, but whether caused by shells bursting in the air near us, or heavy guns just below, or by the bombs of one of our machines ahead, it was difficult to say. As we got into the battle, at a height of 8,000 feet, shrapnel burst into red fragments in the sky at a higher altitude than we were, but a long way off. There were veritable fountains of red, yellow, and white flame; star shells here and there along the line; great red flares illuminating sections of the trenches; and the jets of flame from British and also from the German guns.

Some batteries fired in salvos, some singly. A sudden intense realization of the drama being enacted down there came over one, and a feeling of pity strong enough to check personal fear, although engine-failure might compel us to descend in German territory, or increase of wind or losing the way might mean that the dawn would find us at the mercy of a flight of Hun fighting machines, or at any moment a direct hit might settle our fate, or a shell fragment select one of us for its billet.

Right away to the left at Ostend "green onions" were shooting up. These were long chains of green fire, each of many hundreds of links, reaching a height of nearly 10,000 feet, sent up by the Huns to catch hostile aircraft and set them on fire. Our people laughed at them. It was said that one day a R.F.C. pilot brought one home on his machine. He had caught it after the flames had died out! Quite close to our right a string of these "green onions" climbed above our machine and fell gracefully away and "went out."

Our 'bus often rocked and bumped, and one seemed to feel the thud of distant explosions. Two or three times the Huns fired something which made a huge ball of red flame, that hung for some seconds before it died out. The trenches below, also, were at times lit up by a dull red glow, and not by the ordinary star shells. We could see no men, only this amazing demonstration of the war of races.

Over the German lines many searchlights were sweeping for us. Again we were caught in the beam, and it held us for a long time; but nothing hit us. We reached the dark country beyond, and changed direction two or three times, all the while dodging dangerous points and looking for Thourout, Then, suddenly, we plunged into rain and the profound blackness of clouds at night. Almost immediately we flew on a down slant, the rain cutting our faces, and the compass card spinning (for under these circumstances, at night especially, it was almost impossible to keep a straight course).

We came down through, perhaps, 4,000 feet of it, and then suddenly emerged, and right below us were brilliant lights and searchlights, and the battle lines again in view. This was Westende, a hot corner; and, sure enough, they *pom-pomed* us, the shells bursting below the machine, and the *thud, thud,* being audible above the noise of

INTO THE BARRAGE AS VIEWED FROM A BRITISH BOMBING

the engines. We went off on another tack, and almost directly came towards Ghistelles aerodrome. Here we dropped our bombs, hearing them and seeing some of them burst. The enemy was firing at us all the time, probably mystified as to the direction whence we came, and whither we were heading.

We beat back close to the coast line, and at half-past three, far ahead, could see a tiny row of lights marking the shed at Coudekerke guiding home one of our 14 machines. Nearer and nearer we approached, and our navigation lights were now switched on. We got within signal distance, and fired a Very light; but the coast not being clear, we had to make two big circuits before the answering signal to our next call was received. Lower and lower, until we swept at a low altitude over the tents of the Malays, then over shocks of cut wheat; and then the stubble of the aerodrome left of the landing lights, the grass showing silver in the light of landing flares. We touched ground without a shock, and taxyed rapidly right up to our shed's entrance, in order to be out of the way of the next arrival.

All save two of the machines that set out that night dropped their bombs. These two failed to find an objective. All machines returned safely, although two were struck by shell fragments. One of the bombs started a big fire at an ammunition dump which lasted for two hours, the fire being visible 25 miles away, and the repeated explosions audible over the battle din.

By the spring of 1918 it was no longer possible to send night raiders without escort, for the enemy's fighting machines had to be tackled. The barrage of fire grew in intensity. In flying by groups, with escort, on reaching the objective—often the Rhine towns—the leader fired a signal, and guns and bombs were got ready for instant use. Directly a searchlight picked up the formation, the sky was covered with puffs of smoke, shells shrieked through the air, and long beams flashed to and fro to aid the German gunners. Then the machines dived, each intent on keeping his proper interval, and not to get separated from the formation. The escort remained aloft to meet the enemy fighters when they arrived.

On sighting the objective, another signal was made, and then the bombs began to boom, and the red flame of burning buildings became visible. Often such a raid concluded with a terrible struggle in the air, with heavy losses on both sides.

A narrative issued by the Air Board describes a bombing expedition to a bridge 120 miles behind the German lines. There was a bright moon marking, as a silvery ribbon, the river they were seeking. They traced its bends, and picked out the villages and towns by their lights. Then, sure of their mark, they throttled down, and on almost silent machines glided over the unsuspecting town.

The bridge made but a small mark, but they were getting lower and lower, and the "gun-layer" was carefully bringing the target into the sights, directing the pilot meanwhile how he should "aim" the machine. At last he pushed the levers quickly four times, releasing as many bombs. The rattle of the releasing gear could be heard. Then long seconds of tense anxiety as they peered out at the bridge now almost immediately below the machine. Suddenly, one after the other, four bombs burst in dazzling flashes, one on the right of the bridge itself, one in the water near it. For a while nothing was visible owing to the smoke. But, turning the machine round for the home run, they could see beyond a doubt that they had achieved their purpose, a thought to cheer them during their three hours' toilsome anxious voyage. The report of the operations was something like this:—

The railway bridge at —— was successfully attacked on the night of October ——. It was put out of action. Seventeen Germans were killed. A boat was sunk, and the house near the bridge was destroyed. The Germans are searching vainly for them. All movement of troops had to be diverted.

At much-threatened places, such as Ostend and Bruges, the enemy resorted to smoke screens to prevent our airmen seeing military objectives.

In daylight raids when an escort was sent it waited till the bombers had climbed to the rendezvous height. Then the scout machines followed, rising to a few hundred feet higher still. The whole party circled round until the signal to "carry on" was laid on the ground. And when they had set out, the two-seater fighters followed to act as rear-guard during the return journey.

On September 10th Second-Lieutenant S. H. Long attacked an observation balloon shed with a 100-lb. bomb; but being heavily fired at by an anti-aircraft battery, he silenced the guns with this bomb and returned for another one, with which he attacked the balloon. He only narrowly missed it as it was being deflated. On September 23rd he attacked trains from 500 feet, breaking the rails in two places. He returned to the attack on the first train three times, and finally climbed to 1,000 feet in order to make better use of his bomb sight; on the second occasion he made most of his return journey at 1,000 feet in order to examine villages, roads, etc.

On September 25th, he attacked a train at 500 feet under heavy rifle-fire, and damaged the line. Late on the same day trains were moving at 25 miles distance, and in spite of darkness and bad weather, he volunteered to attack. Heavy rain prevented him reaching them, so he turned to attack Peronne station, descending to 500 feet under heavy anti-aircraft gunfire. This fire prevented him reaching the station, but he climbed to 1,500 feet and attacked a "Rocket" battery, silencing one of its guns.

On the 26th Lieutenant Symington from a low altitude got a direct hit on a moving troop train, wrecking it, and shortly afterwards Second-Lieutenant Learmount dropped more bombs on this train, thus preventing repairs and keeping the line blocked.

In the operations beyond Bagdad our aeroplanes did splendid service, and had many adventures. On one occasion they dropped bombs on a Turkish aerodrome at Kifri (110 miles NE. of Bagdad), doing much damage. On the return journey one of our aeroplanes was forced to land and had to be burnt, but the occupants were brought in by other machines.

The D.S.C. was given to Flight-Commander A. M. Waistell in connection with the bombing raid on Chanak on the night of October 17, 1917. In spite of the fact that there was no moon, and that the weather conditions were so adverse that other pilots were unable to reach the objective, he succeeded in reaching Chanak and dropping his bombs. On the return journey he hit the side of a mountain, being unable to see it on account of the darkness, the machine catching fire on crashing. Although severely injured about the face and knee, he was able to climb out of the machine, and eventually reached the aerodrome, having ridden ten miles over extremely rough country with a badly lacerated knee. This was the occasion of the Kaiser's visit to Constantinople and Chanak, news of which had in good time, by some mysterious means, reached our headquarters.

One of our big bombers set out for Cologne on October 28, 1917, but met bad weather and had to abandon the attempt. Finding themselves over Duren, however, the airmen dropped twelve 112-lb. bombs on the factories there. On the way home they saw no land for 2J hours, but crossed the lines at a low altitude under heavy fire from the German "Archies."

The story of the flight of a British battleplane from London to

Constantinople, and the bombing of the warship *Goeben* and of the German General Staff quarters at the Golden Horn, was told by Mr. F. Handley Page.

The machine, starting on December 14, 1917, was a Handley Page equipped with two 275-h.p. Rolls Royce engines. On board were the pilot, Commander Savory; the second pilot, Lieutenant McLaren; the engineer, Lieutenant Rawlings; and two mechanics. There were also all their luggage, beds and bedding, two tool-boxes containing the spares and tools for the engines, and an extra consignment of spares, practically equivalent to a further engine. To complete the equipment there were strapped on two 11 ft. 6 in. four-bladed propellers, covered over with a tarpaulin, the whole being securely fixed to the side of the fuselage. Complete, the machine was over 6 tons in weight, and as its weight when light was about 8,000 lbs., a useful load of no less than 6,000 lbs. was carried on this flight.

Setting out from Hendon, the company of five reached Paris, and flew through France down the Rhone valley to Lyons, and on to Marseilles. From Marseilles they flew to Pisa, and thence to Rome, where they landed.

From Rome the battleplane proceeded to Naples, and on to Otranto. Crossing the Albanian Alps, the aviators flew on to Salonika, and thence to their base to prepare for the final stages of the trip to Constantinople, which involved flying 250 miles over a hostile country.

While flying across the Albanian Alps the airmen could see the hostile Bulgarian horsemen chasing them, in the hope that their machine might be forced to descend and give the crew as prisoners into their hands. Cross winds, clouds, and all kinds of atmospheric disturbances rendered the latter portion of the voyage most difficult and perilous. The mountain-peaks ranged from 8,000 to 10,000 feet in height. Happily the engines never failed for one moment, and even with the heavy load on board there was never the slightest fear on the part of the pilots that any trouble would arise.

After a short rest at their base and careful overhauling of the machine, the airmen set out on what was the culminating achievement of their wonderful flight. The bombing of the Turkish capital was done at night. A 2½ hours' journey brought the two pilots and engineer left to man the aeroplane over the Sea of

Marmora; and straight up the Sea of Marmora they headed for the attack on the *Goeben* and the Turkish capital itself.

Constantinople was reached when flying at a height of 2,000 feet; and there, lying beneath them, could be seen the *Goeben* with all lights on and men walking on deck. Constantinople itself was brilliantly illuminated. The Golden Horn was clearly silhouetted.

Once the aeroplane flew along a line parallel with the *Goeben* in order to determine its speed and give the necessary data for bombing. Circling twice, the machine dived down to 800 feet, and four bombs were released. These missed the *Goeben*, but exploded against submarines nearby. Again the aviators flew round, and returning they hit the *Goeben* with four bombs. This seemed to disconcert the Turks, for all lights went out.

The pilots then went off towards the Golden Horn and dropped two bombs on a ship called *The General*, which was the head-quarters of the German General Staff. Finally, they visited the Turkish capital, and dropped two more bombs on the War Office, which, in the words of the Turkish *communiqué*, 'was not destroyed.' By this time Constantinople was thoroughly alarmed, and guns which had not been previously fired were now directed upon the aeroplane. The flight back down the Sea of Marmora was accompanied by a fusillade of shrapnel and high explosives, and when the machine landed it was found that it had been struck in twenty-six places. One shot had partially disabled the oiling system of one engine; and the return journey was made on one engine alone.

One of the principal causes of the delay in the opening of the German offensive early in 1918 was the disorder caused by the splendid work of the British Third Arm; and it is impossible to rate too highly the influence this had on the final result. Putting the lowest value upon it, we may be sure that but for this brilliant work of our airmen the war would have been prolonged over another winter. Bombing played a big part in these activities, and it would be an easy matter to fill this chapter with items in the Honours Lists, such as the following:—

Lieutenant F. G. Huxley dropped a bomb upon a gun which was being moved to the rear, damaging it and killing three horses; and another bomb on a wagon, which was blown over, two of the personnel and one of the horses being killed. He then engaged a body of three hundred troops marching along a road, and scattered them, causing many casualties. Later, having disorganized a large party of enemy infantry with bombs and machine-gun fire, he shot down an enemy scout.

Flight-Commander C. R. Lupton, on March 26th, carried out at low altitude four bombing raids on enemy communications. In the course of these raids he caused great damage to enemy transport, and inflicted serious casualties among their reinforcements. He had carried out many bombing raids, says the official report, and by his courage and resource instilled a spirit of confidence and daring in all those who flew with him.

Second-Lieutenant D. R. MacLaren on one occasion, when on low bombing work, bombed a long-range enemy gun over five miles behind the lines, obtaining from a height of 200 feet two direct hits on the gun truck, and two on the railway track alongside. On his way back he met an enemy two-seater, which he shot down. He then attacked a balloon and destroyed it, and wound up by destroying another two-seater aeroplane.

Captain C. J. Marchant, with two other pilots of his squadron, bombed a freight train from a height of 60 feet, derailing three trucks. On another occasion he, with five others, bombed and fired at a column of enemy transport with such good effect that three-quarters of the personnel became casualties, and most of the vehicles were destroyed. They brought down two enemy two-seaters out of control, and destroyed a third.

Second-Lieutenant A. B. Whiteside, who had already taken part in over fifty night-bombing raids, on one occasion, after having bombed a large ammunition dump and blown it up, proceeded to bomb a town which held large numbers of the enemy, also raking it with his machine-gun from a low altitude. Returning to his squadron, he obtained more bombs and ammunition, and with the same observer attacked a train. His machine was badly knocked about with enemy fire from the ground.

Lieutenant K. D. Marshall was the leader of a formation detailed to attack an enemy aerodrome. They destroyed three enemy machines and eight hangars without suffering any casualties. This officer was engaged a few days later in an attack on a great enemy war factory. Just as the bombs were falling, an enemy formation of fifteen machines appeared, and Lieutenant Marshall turned his squadron so quickly in their direction that the enemy scattered and were unable to re-form. Up to this time he had taken part in twenty-seven bombing expeditions.

One squadron went out four times in one night, and was bombing for eleven hours. In another squadron each man made six trips in one night. The Independent Air Force of the Royal Air Force, under Major-General Sir Hugh Trenchard, C.B., between June 6 and November 10, 1918, dropped 550 tons of bombs, of which 160 tons were dropped by daylight. This work, of course, was almost entirely long-distance bombing into Germany. The Independent Air Force lost 109 machines in this period; but in most cases the airmen had performed their mission. Some of their adventures are related here in the dispatch of Major General Sir H. Trenchard, from which a small portion is quoted.

On July 31st No. 99 Squadron, under the command of Captain Taylor, went out to attack Mainz. They encountered forty hostile scouts south of Saarbrücken. Fierce fighting ensued, as a result of which four of our machines were shot down. The remaining five machines of the formation reached Saarbrücken, and dropped their bombs on the station. On their way home they were again attacked by a large number of hostile scouts, and suffered the loss of three more of their number. Immediately after their return No. 104 Squadron, led by Captain E. A. Mackay and Captain Home-Hay, proceeded to attack the factories and sidings at Saarbrücken, which they successfully accomplished with no losses.

On August 11th No. 104 Squadron, under the command of Major Quinnel, attacked the station at Carlsruhe, in spite of bad weather conditions, causing a heavy explosion in the station, and scoring many direct hits on the sidings. In the course of fighting one of our machines was brought down and three of the enemy were driven down out of control.

Frankfurt was attacked for the first time on August 12th by twelve machines of No. 55 Squadron, under the command of Captains B. J. Silly and D. R. G. Mackay. Most of the bombs burst in the town east of the goods station, and all the machines returned safely, with the loss of one observer, who was killed by machine-gun fire. The formation was heavily attacked by forty scouts of various types over Mannheim on its way to the objective and throughout the return journey. Two hostile machines were destroyed, and three were driven down. The average time taken by each machine on this raid was 5 hours 30 minutes, but all machines reached their objective and returned safely, though they only just cleared the trenches on their return journey, running completely out of petrol.

On August 22nd twelve machines of No. 104 Squadron started on a raid on Mannheim. The formations were led by Captain J. B. Home-Hay and Captain E. A. Mackay. Two machines had to land under control about five miles over the lines, after driving away eight hostile machines. Immediately before the objective was reached fifteen hostile machines attacked the formation with great spirit. The formation came to 6,000 feet in following the leader, who was shot down under control. In this action three German machines were destroyed. Despite constant and determined attacks by superior numbers, ten machines dropped bombs on Mannheim, seven of them bursting on a factory, where four fires were caused. A direct hit was also obtained on a large building close to the Badische Anilin Soda Fabrik works.

On the night of August 25-26th two machines piloted by Captain Lawson and Lieutenant Purvis made an attack on these works. One pilot shut off his engine at 5,000 feet, and glided in on the target from the N.W., following the river. He was at once picked up and held in the beams of the searchlights, and an intense anti-aircraft barrage was put up. The machine continually changed its course, but could not get away from the beams, which almost blinded the pilot. At this moment the second machine glided in with its engine almost stopped, underneath the first machine, got immediately over the works below the tops of the factory chimneys, and released its bombs.

The searchlights at once turned on to this machine, when the first-comer turned, and made straight for the works and dropped its bombs. The searchlights were turned almost horizontally to the ground, and they were under heavy fire all the time. In spite of this they remained at a low altitude and swept the factories, works, guns, and searchlights with machine-gun fire. On the return journey both of these machines passed through rain and thick clouds, whilst lightning and thunder were prevalent throughout the trip.

No. 99 Squadron was attacked by six hostile machines fifteen miles over the lines. These were driven off. Ten hostiles then attacked, and were also driven off. Fifteen hostiles then attacked over the objective. After dropping bombs the formation turned towards the hostile machines, and so disconcerted them that they scattered.

On the return journey several enemy scouts kept up a running fire. One of these, attacking from the front, was driven off by the leader's observer firing over the top plane. No. 104 Squadron was attacked at long range fifteen miles over the lines, but drove the enemy off. Over the objective fifteen enemy machines attacked and followed the formation back for seventy miles. Near the lines the formation was again attacked by seven of the enemy. Over two tons of bombs were dropped at Mannheim in this raid.

On the night of September 16th-17th seven Handley Page machines were missing. Five of these, detailed for Cologne and Mannheim, were probably unable to return in the face of a strong south-westerly wind, which increased after the machines had left the ground. The missing machines undoubtedly attacked various objectives well into Germany before they had to land. It was reported that one of them landed in Holland owing to engine trouble, after having dropped its bombs on Bonn, and was interned.

The machines used in these raids were chiefly the D.H.4 with 275-H.P. Rolls Royce engine; the D.H.9 with 200-H.P. B.H.P. engine; the F.E.2B with 160 H.P. Beardmore engine; and the Handley Page with two 375-H.P. Rolls Royce engines. By November, 1918, a few D.H.9's were driven by Liberty motors.

By the spring of 1918 the casualties inflicted on our bombing machines had much increased. The enemy sometimes sent up swarms of their less experienced airmen, who hung on our flanks for great distances, fresh relays always being ready to take the places of those who dropped out. It was therefore necessary to send out strong escorts with bombing expeditions by day or by night. The numbers of the enemy engaged on this duty made up for individual lack of brilliance. They compelled our men to use up ammunition quickly.

During the tremendous battles of 1918, at times there were more than 300 of our machines up together on a front of perhaps 15 miles; and a great many of these would be engaged in bombing from low altitudes the enemy's communications and troops—an amazing spectacle.

On August 16th and 17th, raids were made on Habourdi and Lomme aerodromes, near Lille, which afford us a very good idea of some of the work our airmen had to do. In the first place our machines attacked from a height of no more than 200 feet, and two enemy machines were fought in the air and crashed. Machine-guns and anti-aircraft guns were attacked from above with our machine-guns as soon as they tried to open fire, and were silenced. Hundreds of bombs were dropped. Three large hangars, containing numbers of aeroplanes, were burned out, and several others were badly hit. Two machines on the ground outside the sheds were destroyed. Fires were caused in the officers' and men's quarters, and a building supposed to be the officers' mess was blown up. A number of outbuildings and an ammunition shed were set on fire. During the return journey a train was shot at till it stopped; a Staff motorcar was shot at in the road, and it turned over in the ditch, and it is practically certain that all the occupants of the car were killed.

In the raid on Lomme aerodrome more than 100 bombs were dropped from less than 100 feet. This was too low, and the concussion damaged some of our machines. Four sheds were set on fire, and it is believed that others were damaged. A number of outbuildings were wrecked, and the personnel running for shelter in all directions suffered many casualties. Two enemy machines were crashed. Afterwards our men attacked road transport. In this, as in the previous raid, the aerodrome was practically wiped out.

Captain A. C. H. Groom led a formation in a long-distance bombing raid on September 25th. During the operations the leader of another formation was shot down, and his formation broken up. Captain Groom rallied these machines, and kept them together, displaying marked initiative and daring, for both on the outward and return journey he was subjected to incessant attacks by enemy formations. It was largely due to his efforts that the objective was successfully bombed, and that his formation and the remaining machines of the other returned without further loss.

Captain E. J. McClaughry, of the Australian Flying Corps, Was awarded the D.S.O. for many acts of daring, notably on September 24th, when, attacking a train, he obtained a direct hit, cutting it in two, the rear portion being derailed. He then fired at the front portion until it pulled up. Sighting a German two-seater, he fought it and drove it down. On his way home he saw seven Fokker biplanes, and although he had used the greater part of his ammunition he engaged the leader. During the fight he was severely wounded by fire from a scout that attacked from behind. Nevertheless, he turned and drove it off. His ammunition being now expended, he endeavoured to drive off two of the enemy by firing Very lights at them. He lost consciousness, but recovered sufficiently to bring his machine back.

Often our airmen were called upon to do almost impossible tasks. When the German armies narrowly escaped a great disaster in the retreat from the Marne across the Vesle we sought to hamper the crossing of the river. At one point it was spanned by a wooden bridge, the destruction of which was urgently required by the army command. The enemy had posted, for the protection of this bridge, a number of powerful anti-aircraft guns, and two 12-inch howitzers, besides machine-guns, for they expected we should send our bombing squadrons to such a vital point.

Perhaps no heavy bombers were available; at any rate, large numbers of scouts, each carrying four 20-lb. bombs, were despatched on this errand, not by formations, but singly! One after another they set out, approached the bridge, and some, who were not shot down before, dropped their bombs; but these, in any case, were not big enough to do much damage. One after another they were shot down, until 37 of them had become casualties. One after another failed to return; but the stream did not cease until that number had been lost. Never once did a man hesitate to obey an order which can, perhaps, be compared to the blunder that sent the Light Brigade to destruction at Balaclava.

CHAPTER 14

Artillery Observation

Realization of the war, of the vast numbers engaged, of the heroism displayed, of the sufferings endured, is impossible to any mere human being. Day by day all the tidings their anxious countrymen were vouchsafed of the men at the front was a laconic, impersonal, colourless dispatch, seldom exceeding 200 words in length. The war correspondents tried to tell the story, but each of them had to confess the inadequacy of words and printed space. Thousands of books, and vast and elaborate official histories that will take many years to prepare must still fail, if only for the reason that no man can ever read all of them.

Take, for example, the routine of the Flying Services, one considerable part of which consisted of artillery observation during 1,700 days of war. Consider only the Western Front, from the sea to Switzerland, where hundreds of machines began with the dawn their aerial drudgery—drudgery of watching the enemy, of regularizing our "shoots," and discovering new targets, while the "Archies" sent up their firmament-splitting shells.

Flying in all weathers, save thick fog, at heights regulated more by the degree of visibility at the time than by any thought of safety, the same scene every day, until every detail of trench and dugout, of ruined village and shivered coppice, was stamped indelibly on the brain, each detail fitting into its particular square, and its section of its square on the map. The same scene every day, but varying dangers; and each day, according to the strength and direction of the wind, bringing its own course-bearing and fuel-consumption problems.

The deeds of the fighting pilot thrill us, but who can fail to feel equal admiration for the artillery observer? Out in all weathers, and enduring passively, hour after hour, exposure to the enemy's fire with seldom the thrill that fighting an aerial opponent gives, he required nerves of the steadfast order. Going up in squally weather, it was often a critical business getting away from the aerodrome, and it was not uncommon for a pilot to be compelled to land immediately, anywhere he could. Impossible to wait for weather reports in the morning, so imperative was the need to have the observers at their work directly the light was sufficient. Such high winds have been braved under these circumstances that machines have been unable to make any net progress; and have, in the teeth of the wind, travelled tail first.

In such winds, of course, the work cannot proceed; but, notwithstanding the risk, "the air must be tried." Thus, thousands of brief flights were made, the pilots performing feats of airmanship that before the war would have won them fame. Or, getting away before the dawn on misty mornings, sometimes at the imminent risk of flying into the cables of observation balloons, the balloons at the top end of the cable being out of sight. More than one man met his death in this way.

The *Manual on Artillery Observation* enjoins as the four cardinal principles, "Adequate tuning-in; Clear crisp sending from correct position and in correct altitude; Watching the gunfire, and using a stopwatch to time the shot; Accuracy in noting the fall of the shot." But to give the reader a mere idea of the training necessary to secure these things would occupy several chapters. Who can convey to the layman the toil and trouble of the "observer's course"; the grinding at Morse and wireless, the exercises in pin-pointing, the elaborate gunnery instruction, to say nothing of engines, navigation, and "rigging"?

The artillery map is one of about three inches to the mile. It is divided into squares, lettered and numbered, the final subdivisions making it possible to indicate a point within 10 yards of accuracy. A specimen identification of one of these squares is, say, M 7 *d* 8 6, which string of letters and numbers must be given in a particular order.

Setting out on his job, the observer's care is to get his aerial out safely, which he begins to do when the machine is about 500 feet off the ground; then to test the tuning, and to get it right, so that his messages may be clearly heard at the ground station. While this is being done the operator continually sends a message in code indicating the number of his machine.

The observer must be able to do everything without hesitation-to read his map, and indicate a position on it in an instant, to give a position on the "clock" system without having to pause to consider where the hour hand, at 9 o'clock, points. He must know quite a lot about gunnery, including such matters as the time taken by a shell to travel a given distance. The latter is necessary, because it enables him to attribute a given burst to a given battery. Thus, when beginning to observe a "shoot," he gets up and out towards the target. He then turns the machine towards the battery firing, and having observed the flash of a trial round, looks at his stop-watch; and if, for example, the range be five miles, he expects to see the shell burst somewhere near the target after a lapse of 30 seconds. He turns the machine, and, without any premature strain on his sight, attends to the region of the target just in time to see the burst. If he did not do everything by methods for which he is elaborately trained, he would be utterly valueless as an observer in the nerve-trying conditions in which he has to work, and he would exhaust eye and brain to no purpose.

The business is much more complicated than the sketch here given conveys, but the observer must follow it with the accuracy and quick-ness of second nature. His know-ledge of the more common code messages must be perfect, and his skill as a wireless operator sufficient, even while the "Archies" are bracketing him, or a duel between friend and foe is raging close at hand, to enable him to carry on his work unruffled. Upon the silencing of enemy batteries, no matter how carefully concealed and camouflaged they might be, upon effective counter-battery work, depended the existence of his own batteries, the lives of the infantrymen, and the fate of the transport.

Then try to imagine the strain on the observer. He is perfectly well aware of the fact that his life, apart from ordinary fighting risks, depends upon the skill of the pilot who, moreover, may at any mo-ment be incapacitated by wounds. And the pilot is also at the mercy of a care-less or inefficient observer. The latter may have responsibili-ties other than that of observing; for example, he may have to warn the pilot of a petrol leak somewhere near the magneto. Many a pilot has found on landing that his observer has failed to notice this not uncommon, but rather dangerous, mishap, and may have thanked his lucky stars whilst quietly rebuking the offender.

Communication between pilot and observer is always a difficult matter. At first the simplest signals were used, movements of the head to right or left, or touches on the shoulder or back. One way was to fix up a board on the rear edge of the top plane, with four coloured discs on it, red, green, white, and black, and perhaps also a cross, so that the pilot, merely by pointing to one of the discs, could indicate one of certain prearranged messages, such as "That's a *Boche,*" or "It is one of ours." Speaking-tubes were also used.

Any clear day, and at any point along the Western Front, the aerial spectacle to an airman flying at a height of, say, 10,000 feet was curious. If the reader has ever stood outside a big aquarium tank he may have seen on the imitation sea bottom, perhaps, a few crabs; and just above them, some deep-swimming fishes; about the middle of the tank a few leisurely good-sized fellows ranging to and fro; and, overhead, small shoals of little fishes. From an aeroplane on the British side of the lines, looking east, could be seen an aerial spectacle on a vast scale suggestive of the aquarium.

Below, the line of sausage balloons that, although two or three thousand feet high, look as if they were actually on the ground. They might be either crabs or anemones. Immediately above them, artillery observation two-seaters flying on a regular beat at no great speed. High overhead, flights of not less than four, and often as many as 20 fighting scouts looking for trouble, in other words, waiting to pounce on any enemy machine attempting to interfere with our routine. A few bunches of black smoke of slowly changing shape showed that the "Archies" were at work as usual; while some dissolved, fresh ones appeared.

The amount of routine flying almost passes belief. From August 14 to 21, 1916, our airmen helped the guns to range on 730 German batteries. Through their attention to duty, 128 gunpits were totally destroyed, whilst 321 explosions were caused among batteries. In that week they flew over 1,200 hours; they took 6,000 photo-graphs of the enemy's territory; dropped over 2,000 bombs, and fired more than 30,000 rounds at the enemy's ground forces. On October 13, 1916, on our First Army's front, the enemy's guns at 17 points were silenced, at any rate temporarily, owing to the effectiveness of our artillery observation.

In September, 1917, the Royal Flying Corps flew, in the aggregate, 4¾ years. One day in that month our guns, directed by aeroplane, silenced 73 German batteries, destroyed 21 gunpits, damaged 35 other gunpits, and caused 33 fires and explosions. Most of the observing at this period was done at a height of six to eight thousand feet, where, however, our machines were in effective range of the enemy's guns.

When the war began our airmen had practically no experience to fall back upon; they had everything to learn, their machines and general equipment were of the crudest, as also were the enemy's. In those

173

days a great deal depended upon the ability of the individual airman to make, ways and means. Artillery observation was sometimes on single-seaters. It was the work of these men that laid the foundations of artillery observation as practised later. Surprising things were done in spite of the difficulties.

Thus Captain Lewis, on a single-seater, "spotted" battery after battery, and returning because his machine was riddled by bullets, went up on another single-seater and continued his observing in spite of being slightly wounded. He returned, and again resumed his work on his first machine, which in the meantime had been patched. This officer was killed about a year later. His name is coupled with that of Captain Trevannon James, these two officers being responsible for the success of the R.F.C. wireless, having worked at this problem before the war.

On July 6, 1915, Second-Lieutenant O. D. Filley and his observer were observing for the artillery. Twice, although they were not in a special fighting machine—it was a B.E.2C,—they attacked German aeroplanes and, after driving them away, resumed their artillery work. Finally, two hostile aeroplanes came up together, and although they had only five rounds of ammunition left they at once attacked. In this encounter the observer was killed in the act of firing, and the engine damaged, but the pilot brought the machine safely back.

Engaged in this duty in an F.E. biplane, Captain Kinnear, with his observer, Lieutenant Morgan, near Hooge, sighted a German two-engine machine. They fought for about 36 minutes, circling round each other and manoeuvring for the advantage of light and position. The British machine over and over again tried to close to short range, but each time it approached nearer than about 100 yards the German sheered off.

Once, however, the enemy was not quick enough, and the British machine dived steeply down and flew under him within 50 feet. But at that moment, unluckily, the Lewis gun jammed—a trick machine-guns have, especially at high altitudes and in low temperature. The big German was accompanied by a scout, which flew over the F.E., keeping up a continuous fire. Although apparently having the British machine at their mercy, the two enemy craft broke off the fight. Our machine at that time had only half a drum of ammunition left.

It was then attacked by a third German, which fired about 30 rounds and retired. Although so short of ammunition the British machine tried to close with this new opponent, but could not do so, as the German had the advantage in speed. The British machine then continued its artillery observing. The fighting was clearly visible to our batteries below, and the feeling of relief can be imagined when one after another the enemy machines were seen to break off the fight and fly away, leaving our men in undisturbed possession of the field and returning to their job as if nothing had happened.

On June 8, 1916, one of our machines directed a battery on a train at Salome. Six direct hits were obtained, and the train was set on fire, and was seen to be burning an hour and a half later. Another ranged a battery on to a railway station. Large explosions were seen in a shed, which was demolished.

The Military Cross was awarded to Second-Lieutenant L. S. White, who, on February 6, 1917, as observer, flew over the enemy's trenches at a height of only 1,500 feet for more than an hour and a half in bad weather. He attacked the enemy in the trenches with machine-gun fire, and located 16 enemy batteries during this flight. Lieutenant W. E. Gower was given the M.C. for the following:

> When his machine was set on fire he stood up in his seat and sprayed the pilot with a fire extinguisher, thereby enabling his pilot to regain control of the machine and to make a successful landing.

In the Messines Ridge battle, in June, 1917, enemy aircraft were prevented from participating by the remark-able work of the Royal Flying Corps. Before this battle the enemy held the high ground, and he could see us while we, from the ground, could not see him. We had to rely for observation on the air; and our guns smothered the enemy's artillery. One squadron alone on one day gave reports which enabled our guns to silence 72 enemy batteries. One brigade sent in 390 calls, in response to which our guns are known to have obtained 160 direct hits.

A typical day's work (February 16, 1918) included 33 reconnaissances, eight of which were long-distance photographic flights. Eighty-three hostile batteries were successfully engaged to destruction and six neutralized. Nine gunpits were destroyed; 33 damaged; and 29 explosions and 26 fires were caused. Eighty-eight zone calls were sent down; and a total of 2,547 photographs were taken, this being a record.

CHAPTER 15

Reconnaissance and Photography

Vast armies living partially underground on fronts of many hundreds of miles, clad in "invisible" uniforms, moving along underground passages, or, chiefly at night, capable by means of railways and motor transport of swift concentration at threatened points of attack; cavalry reconnaissance useless, and commanders forced to rely solely upon the work of spies: with the creation of these problems came the solution in the shape of flying machines. They worked at first at low altitude. They were soon driven, by the fire of specially designed artillery, to altitudes at which experts had declared their work would be useless. Nevertheless, by improved photo-graphic appliances, and as the result of experience, they proved equal to the task, although often they flew low and risked heavy casualties. Higher and higher were they driven, and it became clear that the heights at which aerial observation is barely possible on the clearest of days is within range of high-angle guns.

A war correspondent, who had seen the older style of war, and was now watching the new, wrote in the *Morning Post* in March, 1915, as follows:—

Like thistledown the airmen were dropped out of the blue air. Anything less like war could not possibly be imagined, yet each carried deadly weapons at his disposal, each might bring news that would win a victory. How different from the scout of old days, dropping road-stained and exhausted from his trembling horse! The contrast indeed was greater, for the scout had really brought only himself home; his news he had thrown out into the air from the front, 30 miles away; it had been caught by the maze of delicate wires; and, long before the scout himself arrived, its purport had been discussed at headquarters, and an order had perhaps already been issued on the strength of it, setting troops in motion. Marvellous; but the romance of the thing was richer for that dripping horseman who had thrown soul and body into the scale against fate. The airman needs as high a courage and capacities more highly trained, but the exquisite mechanism he controls has come between him and the simpler forces, that naked touch of nature which of itself is a reward.

And the same writer reports one of our generals as saying: "The aeroplane finds its business harder every day."

It was soon found that the airman who was not also a soldier was of very little use except as pilot. There were, however, striking exceptions, men without previous military experience who proved instantly adaptable—born observers they. "Eyewitness" remarked upon the division of reconnaissance into strategical and tactical.

It is difficult to draw a hard-and-fast line between them, or to define exactly where one begins and the other ends, but the former may be said to be undertaken exclusively for the purpose of ascertaining the strength and dispositions of the enemy in a strictly limited area along a battle-front, by locating and examining his trenches, gun emplacements, headquarters reserves, supply parks, and railheads. Its sphere ceases at a comparatively short distance from the front of the opposing forces. All that is going on in the area far behind the enemy's line comes within the sphere of strategical reconnaissance, which is undertaken with the object of obtaining information about the enemy in a particular part of the theatre of war, and so enabling a commander to form an idea as to his opponent's designs.

While tactical reconnaissance is chiefly of value to corps or divisional commanders, to enable them to know what is in their immediate front, and to make their local dispositions accordingly, the higher leading and direction of the large masses—in a word, the plan of campaign framed by a commander-in-chief and his General Staff—depends upon the results of strategical reconnaissance.

The intelligence upon which such plans will be based is that referring to the amount of transport and rolling stock on roads and railways, the strength of columns of troops, the size and situation of bivouacs, parks and supply depots, second lines of defence, and any other fact which may afford a clue to the strength and disposition or movements of an enemy's masses, and to his intentions. To gather information of this nature by aerial reconnaissances the observer either travels above a previously selected line of country, or passes to and fro over a certain definite area, noting and recording everything of value that he sees. This latter method is the slower, and is used only when very detailed information is required.

This is not work which can be carried out by everyone. The really first-rate observer must possess extensive military knowledge in order to know what objects to look for and where to look for them; he must have very good eyesight in order to pick them up, and he must have the knack of reading a map quickly, both in order to mark correctly their positions and to find his way. To reconnoitre is not easy, even in fine weather, but in driving rain or snow, in a temperature perhaps several degrees below zero, or in a gale, when an aeroplane travelling with the wind rocks and sways like a ship in a heavy sea, and may attain a speed of 150 miles an hour, the difficulties are immense.

In these circumstances, and from the altitude at which it is necessary to fly in order to escape the projectiles of anti-aircraft guns, columns of transports or of men are easily missed. Indeed, at a first attempt an observer will see nothing which is of military value, for it is only after considerable practice that the eye becomes accustomed to scouring a great stretch of country from above, and acquires the power of distinguishing objects upon it.

Psychology also comes in, and the temperament of an observer is of the greatest importance. He must be cool, and capable of great concentration in order to keep his attention fixed upon his objective in spite of all distractions, such as, for instance, the bursts of shell close to him, or the noise of rifle bullets passing through the planes of his machine. He must withstand the temptation to make conjectures, or to think that he has seen something when he is not absolutely certain of the fact, since an error in observing, or an inaccuracy in reporting, may lead to false conclusions and cause infinite harm.

Many men are absolutely unfitted for such duty, and even trained observers vary in their powers of recon-naissance. Some have a special aptitude for strategical work, the wide field of action and the chance of gaining an insight, as it were, into the workings of the enemy's mind appealing to their imagination and to their taste for discovery. The spirit of adventure also enters, for long reconnaissances are hazardous, and before the minds of those carrying them out the prospect of being forced by engine trouble to descend in the enemy's lines cannot but frequently be present.

As in other branches, our airmen sent out on recon-naissance had to build up from the beginning. One of the first officers to fly over the German lines in the first week of the fighting was Captain (now Major-General) L. E. O. Charlton, and he was one of the first to un-der-stand the significance of German movements which many would have failed to grasp. His reports were of inestimable value to our Expeditionary Force, which in those days would certainly have been overwhelmed had it not been for our handful of devoted airmen.

A born aerial reconnaissance officer was the son of a well-known artist, who, after the battle of Neuve Chapelle, in March 1915, when the trenches were all mixed up and parties of British, French, and Germans were isolated from their fellows, memorized the position from a height of 10,000 feet, and brought back a perfectly accurate report.

Lieutenant Collishaw, who afterwards became a famous air-fighter, won one of his first distinctions by instantly perceiving the signifi-cance of a German concentration near Fort Douaumont, at Verdun; and although he had been wandering about in the sky for some time try-ing to locate his position, he flew to the nearest French headquarters and gave in a report.

A glance at the official report of the first two months of the war helps us to understand fully the conquest our airmen achieved over the difficulties inherent to flying in war. Among those difficulties was the fire directed upon them not only by the enemy but by friends, who could not distinguish German from British. A long letter to his home from one of our airmen was published in the *Daily Mail*. Here is a brief extract:—

My first reconnaissance was at Maubeuge. We ran into clouds just beyond Mons, so had to turn back. As we were coming back over the French lines I saw a movement and bustle among the troops, and then there was a noise of about a thousand rifles cracking at us. They had mistaken me for a German because my machine was different from most of the others. That was my baptism of fire, and I shall never forget it. My first sensations were of surprise, which rapidly developed into a kind of fear, which in turn changed to fascination.

It positively fascinated me to see the holes appearing in the planes as each bullet ripped its way through (although there were very few of them). I was looking at my instrument-board to see what height I was, when suddenly a bullet hit the board, and a splinter jumped up in front of me. At the same time a bullet pierced the petrol tank, and all the petrol ran out. Another one hit one of the instruments and smashed it. There was nothing for it but to come down, so I landed in the first good field I saw.

The next reconnaissance I made I had a taste of 'Archibald,' the anti-aircraft gun. We were up by Valenciennes, which was infested with Germans. Suddenly I saw five or six white puffs of smoke beneath us, which were shells bursting. The next time they made a better shot, and were on the same level, but to the left.

One airman came down near Peronne. Many helpers ran up, and found an unconscious hero with five bullet wounds; but his information was carefully written. His observer had been killed outright.

"Archibald," the nickname given first of all to one German gun, but soon applied generally to all anti-aircraft artillery, was of various kinds. At first shrapnel was much used, bursting into white smoke, whence a crowd of bullets spread fanwise. High explosive, the use of which extended enormously during the war, burst into black smoke with a terrific detonation calculated to stun the pilot, or even break a machine, more than 100 yards away. Then there was a green burst, reputed to be gas: and a great ball of red flame known as the "flaming onion." Also there was the long green linked chain described in the chapter on bombing.

Being bracketed was a terrifying experience. First the airman would see suddenly appear in the blue sky, perhaps 1,000 yards or more away, four black dots rapidly enlarging. Because of the noise of his engine he could hear nothing else. The "new hand "would scarcely believe that the black blots were messengers of death for him. But the old hand knew that in two seconds or so a second series of black blots would burst nearer: they were already on their way up through the calm air. He did not wait to see whether the Hun had accurately corrected; he pulled back his lever till the machine nearly stalled, ruddered hard to right or left, and turned over cartwheel-wise. Or perhaps he side-slipped or dived 1,000 feet.

The great thing was to occupy another spot in the sky as quickly as possible. If the enemy were watching him they could see the manoeuvre; but at that height it would appear a very small turn, and impossible accurately to measure or judge. For the moment it had baffled "Archie." But sometimes "Archie" was lucky at his first attempt.

Many years ago the author urged the desirability of taking up Staff officers as observers in aeroplanes. The war soon called for the specially trained observer, who, at first, strange to say, was esteemed less highly than the pilot, and has always been treated less generously in the matter of pay. He must have many qualities not necessary to piloting, and, as time goes on, the distinction between him and the pilot will be more and more marked, for his training will be increasingly specialized.

In the early days of the war there were occasions when Staff officers wholly unused to the air were taken up; and the experiences of a trained cavalry reconnaissance officer of middle age on his first flight gives us an idea of the work. At first he was deeply interested in watching the pilot's doings. Then he became completely absorbed in his own work. There was the battlefield below him; the trenches, the railways, the villages, the woods. He became so busy detailing the changes he had been sent up to observe, with comparing what he saw with the notes on his Staff map, that he quite forgot that he was two miles above solid earth. The pilot was fully occupied with the difficulties of route-keeping and the care of his machine, the passage of time and the ever-diminishing fuel. Neither had a thought of the peril they ran.

Suddenly the machine began to tumble about in the air as wildly as a scrap of paper in an October wind, steadily losing altitude. The observer soon saw the reason for this: the pilot was wounded, and had lost consciousness. Imagine the sensations of the Staff officer, with his memories of many a tight corner in other campaigns, but nothing like this for long-drawn-out suspense. The pilot half-recovered, and could be seen making efforts to shake off numbness of limb and dimness of eye; and then the machine would steady; and once it even began to climb. Then, after what seemed ages of tortured anticipation, the observer found that it was steadily gliding earthwards. Down through thousands of feet, the earth coming up to meet them apparently quicker and quicker (an illusion, of course). And it landed safely.

Both the pilot and the observer then fainted. The observer, however, quickly recovered, and he handed in his report. The pilot knew nothing until he found himself in hospital.

The spectacle of the battle-front from an aeroplane was amazing. "No Man's Land," an irregular belt of varying width from the sea to Switzerland, the fair earth battered out of recognition; on each side of the lines the earth beaten brown, the shell-holes becoming individually visible a mile or so from the front line; and then, wider and wider intervals of green. The ruined towns and villages like grey graveyards; the barbed wire like blue mist. During a push the scene awakens to dreadful activity. Words fail to describe the flaming horror of an artillery preparation; the shrapnel of a barrage bursting in white puffs that might be a cotton-field in flower; the black blots of a barrage against aircraft.

By the early part of 1917 every aerodrome, whether for bombers, fighting scouts, or for artillery observation craft, had its map-room, the walls of which were adorned with sections of maps, together with the patchwork photographic survey of each showing how it appeared from above. These maps enable pilots to study the country and pick up landmarks quickly, often a matter of critical importance, and much more difficult than the earthman imagines. The Brigade and Divisional Staffs had other maps, and photographic material kept up-to-date by the persistence of our airmen flying high or low, as conditions demanded, over enemy territory, and day after day taking photographs of every acre. Often enlargements of these photographs revealed important changes undetected by the naked eye. A row of bushes, where none existed the day before, usually indicated a new battery camouflaged; but this was a method of concealment that became too crude, and more subtle schemes were devised.

The photographic apparatus employed was far superior to that of the most up-to-date studio or newspaper office of pre-war days. The negatives obtained by splendid instruments were enlarged and printed at marvellous speed. Within an hour of receiving a negative 100 perfect prints of very large size could be produced. The technique of the camera and the darkroom have been greatly advanced by the war; the use of colour screens, in particular, having been brought to a high degree of effectiveness.

Photographs taken from a height of 6,000 feet show such details as barbed wire. Footprints in grass invisible to the eye will sometimes come out in an enlargement.

The expert knows where to look for certain signs; for example, cable trenches and air lines, which in conjunction with railways and tracks come under the head of communications, and may indicate the positions of headquarters, camouflaged batteries, observation posts, and so on. Cable trenches when left open are straight and narrow, when closed "woolly." Air lines are shown by a series of tiny white dots, the displaced earth where the poles have been inserted. A faint track connects them, because the earth has been trodden by the line layers and repairers. Even if the land has been ploughed, an air line can sometimes be detected by the row of dots where the plough has left the soil round the posts undisturbed. In clear weather the shadows thrown by the poles reveal them.

Whether the enemy expected or intended an attack at a given point was revealed by different sets of preparations. In either case it was always of importance that we should know what was in the enemy's mind. Incessant photographic reconnaissance was the principal means of finding out. If the enemy expected an attack he would busy himself with erecting new lines of barbed wire, behind which he would mark out a new line of trenches and dugouts to retire to. All the trenches would be deepened and strengthened. New battery positions would be made, and so on.

On the other hand, an intended attack was heralded by increased artillery activity, an increase in the number of communication trenches; saps pushed forward and linked up; and behind the lines rapid building of light railways. But enough has been said to give a general idea of the aim in view, without technical details, of the infinite complexity of modern warfare.

All the photographs were submitted not only to the Divisional Staffs concerned, but also to company commanders in the case of pre-attack reconnaissance. If there remained any doubt, the matter was settled by sending out a patrol. Precise knowledge was necessary, unless the infantry attack was to be made at a frightful cost of life.

A new German battery might be so cleverly camouflaged as to defy detection until it fired. Then the withered grass or the bleached earth in front was quickly disguised to its original appearance; but this had to be done very cleverly to escape the eye of the camera. Un-usual signs of wear in a road revealed the fact that movements of troops or transport had been made during the night.

Thousands of exposures had to be made by scores of pilots who had to "cover" the ground allotted to them with particular care, since one failure might have grave results. And they had to do their work at the first attempt; for a machine flying across warned the enemy's anti-aircraft artillery, and woe betide the second comer! So the photographic reconnaissance observer had to be highly trained in keeping the precise course and altitude. And this work had to be carried on throughout the entire front. On their part, the Germans were similarly engaged. Our Naval Air Service took photographs of the entire Belgian coast, and inland to a considerable depth. The work went on every day, and the enemy exerted all his ingenuity to hinder it. Many a British airman engaged on this duty "failed to return." One report reads:—

> While exposing six plates, observed five enemy planes. Not having seen our escort since turning inland, pilot prepared to return. Enemy force separated, one taking up position above tail, and one ahead. The other three glided towards us on the port side, as they came opening fire. The pilot was hit in the shoulder. The observer held his fire until the machine behind was very close. Then he fired a tray of ammunition into the pilot's face."

It appears that the observer, realizing that his pilot was badly hurt (he had holes through his chest and both feet), climbed out of his seat to assist. The pilot, half fainting, ordered him back. "The pilot," says the report, "made a perfect landing."

Merely to give the barest sketch of the conditions under which reconnaissance of all kinds was performed needs much space. As the war proceeded, and artillery and bombing became more accurate and intense, methods of disguise were found to keep pace. The art of camouflage became very elaborate, and some of our cleverest artists were called in to help. There were aerodromes, over the sheds and offices of which roads and hedges were cleverly indicated, so that from a height of 10,000 feet, especially if there were the slightest mist, the wayfaring bomber would miss them altogether, and only the camera could detect the ruse.

One of our airmen describing his experiences at the first Battle of Neuve Chapelle, in a letter that appeared in the *Aeroplane*, said:—

> On the first day of the attack I saw little of the battle, as most of the time I was flying in a driving snow-storm and could not see the ground. After a bit my petrol pipe broke, and my engine stopped, and I had to make a forced landing. On the second day

we were up on a rotten old machine, with an engine that runs very badly, and was missing from the time we left the ground. The highest I could get the machine to was 4,700 feet, and then, as I flew towards the lines, I could see our other machines getting it hot from the 'Archies.' They were flying between 7,000 and 8,000 feet, and as soon as I was in range the Germans opened on my machine; and then during the whole of the reconnaissance, which con-sisted of circling about a small area, they didn't give me a moment's peace; and I had shells bursting round my machine the whole time, simultaneously flashes of flame and loud bangs sometimes on one side and then on the other, below the machine, above it, behind, and in front, and some of them bumped the machine about unpleasantly. . . . I have just got down from nearly two hours' reconnaissance, during which my observer was photo-graphing German positions.

As regards your question of the height at which practical obser-vation can be made, given a clear day, after the height of about 6,000 feet is reached, there is very little difference between that and 12,000 feet; and after the first 6,000 feet it would take a very practised observer to tell if he were that height or dou-ble that height. One can see everything perfectly clearly. The other day one of the observers took a lot of photos at 11,500 feet, thinking he was about 6,000 feet, and they came out very clearly.

Facing fire in the air is the same as facing it on the ground. The soldier, in the pursuit of duty, who exposes himself to rifle or gunfire, takes his life in his hands, and knows it. The airman, like the infantry-man, knows that even in the heaviest fire he may escape; but he also knows that he may be the billet of a solitary shot. Again, his machine may be destroyed by one lucky shot finding a vital spot, or it may be scarcely incommoded by a couple of hundred hits. One of the most striking pieces of luck befell Captain G. A. K. Lawrence on September 30, 1915. Out on a reconnaissance in bad weather a shell burst near his machine. To his astonishment its flying did not appear to have suf-fered, and it answered his control perfectly. He finished his task, and returned. The machine had 300 bullet-holes in it. This officer was mentioned in the Honours List for the following:—

He made a reconnaissance on September 21st to points 60

miles inside the German lines, although repeatedly attacked by a hostile machine. On September 25th he attacked and hit a moving train near Lille, descending to 600 feet. On the following day he attacked and drove off a hostile machine which was interfering with our bombing machines. On September 30th he carried out a three-hour reconnaissance in very bad weather. Although his machine was hit by anti-aircraft guns on crossing the German lines on his way out, he carried on and completed his work.

The Flying Services soon claimed the personal devotion of men eminent in science, the arts, and politics. One of the earliest names that became famous was that of M. Raymond, of the French Senate, whose last flight on October, 1914, terminated a short but heroic service career. He was wounded whilst on a flying reconnaissance, but nevertheless managed to land between the French and German lines. He was only rescued after a sharp fight.

While he was being carried away on a stretcher, M. Raymond screwed up his strength sufficiently to report the result of his observations.

Robert Loraine, the accomplished actor, whose clever interpretations place him in the front rank of his profession, served throughout the war as a flying officer. Always keen on adventure, he had served in the Boer war. And he was one of our pioneer aviators, distinguished for numerous plucky flights. Captain Loraine was wounded on November 22, 1914, whilst engaged on an important reconnaissance, by shrapnel when over the enemy's lines at a height of 5,000 feet. He was making a sketch at the moment he was hit. The bullet took him just below the shoulder-blade, traversed the lung, and came out below the collar-bone in front. It was feared he would not recover, but after about three months he was back in France again. He was asked, one day, what he really thought was the most trying experience of his life, and he replied that he gave the palm to the first night of a new play!

The Military Cross was given to Captain McB. Bell-Irving, who, while on a photographic reconnaissance, and severely wounded in the head and half-blinded by blood, steered for the nearest aerodrome, and feeling that he could not last out, landed safely in a small field well within our lines. After giving orders for the safe delivery of his photos, he collapsed. His pluck and skill saved his observer.

Second-Lieutenant F. N. Hudson, although severely wounded in the head, completed his reconnaissance. After recrossing the lines and landing in an aerodrome he lost consciousness. This officer was only eighteen years of age, but had many times driven off enemy machines and twice forced them to the ground.

Captain J. A. Liddell was awarded the V.C. for conspicuous bravery and devotion to duty on July 31, 1915. When on a flying reconnaissance over Ostend-Bruges-Ghent he was severely wounded, his right thigh being broken, which caused momentary unconsciousness. By a great effort he recovered partial control, after his machine had dropped nearly 3,000 feet, and notwithstanding his collapsed state succeeded, although continually under fire, in completing his course, and brought the aeroplane into our lines half an hour after being wounded.

"The difficulties overcome by this officer in saving his machine and the life of his observer cannot be readily expressed," says the official tribute, "but as the control wheel and throttle control were smashed, and also one of the under carriage struts, it would seem incredible that he could have accomplished what he did."

Captain Liddell, be it noted, was flying low in order to give his observer something worth recording in his notebook. This officer was killed on August 31st of the same year.

Second-Lieutenant W. Barnard Rhodes-Moorhouse was awarded the V.C. posthumously for an act of devotion to duty unsurpassed in the annals of the Flying Corps. He paid forfeit with his life; and British aviation lost one of its pioneers and one of its most honoured representatives. In the old days when the Royal Aero Club was a small band of enthusiasts, Rhodes-Moorhouse was one of its leading lights; although his small figure and thin face, with its frequent quizzical smile, and his light voice, gave no immediate evidence of the great spirit within. He was flying in 1909; but took his certificate in 1911. One of his flights was on a Bréguet biplane, with two passengers, from Dinan to England. His wife was one of the passengers. He was a man of great attainments, mellowed by a fine disposition, sterling character, and knowledge of the greater world; and his loss cast a shadow even in those days of general gloom. "Eyewitness," in his first report of the incident of this officer's death, did not divulge his name. He said:—

The raid on Courtrai, unfortunately, cost the nation a very gallant life, but it will live as one of the most heroic episodes of the war. The aviator started on the enterprise alone on a biplane. On arrival at Courtrai he glided down to a height of 300 feet, and dropped a large bomb on the railway junction. When he did this he was the target of hundreds of rifles, of machine-guns, and of anti-aircraft guns, and was severely wounded in the thigh. Though he might have saved his life by at once coming down in the enemy's lines, he decided to save his machine at all costs, and made for the British line. Descending to a height of only 100 feet in order to increase his speed, he was again wounded, this time mortally. He still flew on, however, and instead of coming down at the nearest of our aerodromes, went all the way back to his own base, where he executed a perfect landing, and made his report.

The importance of the service rendered by Rhodes-Moorhouse was apparently overlooked by "Eyewitness," although it was recognized by the authorities, and explained in a dispatch by Mr. Beach Thomas in the following terms:—

He was hit, very badly hit in the thigh and the fingers some time before he came to the low level and dropped the bomb which perhaps did more definite service on a great scale than any bombs let fall during the war. They had the effect of a great strategical move. To maintain speed and take the greatest chance of carrying his message home he flew over the German lines near Ypres at no more than 100 feet, and could see the individual Germans tiring at him. At this part of the course he received two more wounds. Even then he did not descend at the first safe spot, but flew all the way to headquarters. He was cut out of his machine—this was the only method possible—and all the while gave a cool and precise account of his experiences, and how and when he was wounded. It was reckoned that he had flown for nearly three-quarters of an hour after receiving the first wound."

Rhodes-Moorhouse died from the effects of his wounds on April 27, 1915.

In the fighting in Egypt the work of the Royal Flying Corps, performed under most difficult circumstances, often with machines in which the pilots had little confidence, is summarized in the following extract from General Maxwell's dispatch dated February, 1915:—

The French hydroplane squadron and the detachment of the Royal Flying Corps rendered very valuable services. The former equipped with hydroplanes (hydro-aeroplanes) with floats ran great risks in undertaking land reconnaissance, whilst the latter were handicapped by inferior types of machines. Notwithstanding these drawbacks they furnished me regularly with all information regarding the movements of the enemy.

Dispatch of March 1st:—

Part of 30th Squadron R.F.C. carried out daily reconnaissance.

Dispatch of April 9th:—

All this time the oases were kept under constant observation by means of aeroplanes. Very long flights were necessary, and to reduce them as much as possible a system of advanced depots in the desert was started. The credit for originating this system is due to Captain Van Rynefeld, R.F.C., and to Mr. Jennings Bramley, of the Soudan Civil Service, and was first put into practice on the occasion of the flight to Qara (the distance covered was over 200 miles). A Yeomanry reconnaissance sent out at daylight on the 26th found that the position occupied by the enemy on the previous evening had been vacated during the night, but aerial reconnaissance and officers' patrols discovered him in his old position.

On May 17th, it is gathered from other sources, a British aviator left Hilla to reconnoitre the oasis at Bir Meleit, 116 miles away. He failed to find the oasis, and returned. Starting again, he found the oasis, but in flying over it was fired at, a bullet hitting his propeller. He dropped bombs on the enemy, and flew low, raking them with his machine-gun. They dispersed, and Bir Meleit was open to our troops. Before returning, the airman made sure that there was water in the wells, His reconnaissance had lasted eight hours. Another of our airmen dispersed 2,000 enemy cavalry drawn up outside El Fasher. He was wounded in the thigh, and had to steer back with one hand on the rudder-bar.

Preliminary aerial reconnaissance for the battle of the Somme was briefly referred to in Sir Douglas Haig's dispatch of December 23, 1916.

Behind his second system of trenches, in addition to woods, villages, and other strong points prepared for defence, the enemy had several other lines already completed; and we had learned from aeroplane reconnaissance that he was hard at work improving and strengthening these, and digging fresh ones between them and still farther back.... We had good direct observation on his front system of trenches on the various defences, on the slopes above us between his first and second system; but the second system itself in many places could not be observed from the ground in our possession, while except from the air nothing could be seen of his more distant defences.

. . . We were consequently much dependent on observation from the air. As in that element we had attained almost complete superiority, all that we required was a clear atmosphere. But with this we were not favoured for several weeks.

On June 29, 1917, Captain B. L. Dowling and Lieutenant C. F. Lodge were on a reconnaissance when a H.E. shell burst close to the machine, fragments of the shell striking it. Three of the tail booms were cut; one of the propeller blades was blown away; and all the controls, except the elevator, were put out of action. Thus, the machine was in worse case than a ship with engines disabled, and rudderless; for the latter, at any rate, can keep afloat, whereas the aeroplane under the circumstances described could not remain aloft.

In this predicament Lieutenant Lodge climbed out along the right wing in order to operate the aileron with his hand. The machine meanwhile was coming down out of control, but in the last thousand feet Lieutenant Lodge succeeded, and the proper gliding attitude was assumed. Near the ground, however, the machine began to spin. Nevertheless the two airmen kept cool, and by great skill a landing rightside up was effected, in which only the under-carriage was damaged.

In the Palestine campaign our success depended a good deal on the effectiveness of aerial reconnaissance and the prevention of the enemy's. Before Beersheba fell, although enemy machines could not be entirely prevented from coming over, only one reached a region from which he could see the troops preparing to attack the town; and that machine was brought down. The minute photographic survey for the campaign was begun before the battle of Rafa, and the enemy positions at Magruntein Hill were revealed to General Sir Philip Chetwode when the desert column attacked victoriously. When the Turks started to fortify, every redoubt and trench they made was revealed. The Gaza-Beersheba line was continuously photographed, and every change noted.

On the Western Front Major G. B. Ward was piloting one of three machines on photographic reconnaissance when they were attacked by a formation of nine Germans. They beat the enemy off and took the necessary photographs. During the return journey Major Ward turned back to secure some more photographs, and, encountering six hostile machines, he attacked them, bringing one down and driving off the remainder.

Second-Lieutenant B. C. Grimwood, in the Honours List, in the words of the official record, located a strong force of infantry coming up to an attack, and his machine was immediately afterwards hit by a shell which wounded him severely and destroyed his wireless apparatus. His machine was so badly damaged that no expert would have believed it could have possibly held together in the air, but in spite of this and of his wounds he wrote out a message reporting the position of the enemy, and dropped it on divisional headquarters, who were able to put nine batteries on to the target.

Captain C. H. Brewer set out to make a railway reconnaissance, and though the weather conditions became very bad he continued his task. His engine began to fail when he was a long distance over the enemy's lines. By skilful piloting he succeeded in crossing the enemy's trenches, but the machine crashed in "No Man's Land" and turned completely over. Heavy machine-gun fire was opened by the enemy, and, though his jaw was broken, he extricated the observer, who was pinned under the machine and was unconscious, and dragged him to a shell-hole in the face of the enemy's fire.

Lieutenant T. W. Cave, while taking photographs of an enemy area, was slightly wounded by anti-aircraft fire. In spite of this and the enemy's fire seventeen photographs were taken. Later, while he was again taking photographs over the enemy's lines, his machine was attacked by 12 enemy machines. He shot down one of them, after which he took several photographs. On three occasions this officer, in the course of flights lasting four hours or more, ranged a siege battery most effectively on enemy batteries, with the result that several gunpits were destroyed and three explosions were caused.

Lieutenant R. A. Austin, of the Australian Flying Corps, awarded the M.C., was one of two pilots who in one flight photographically surveyed an area of 45 square miles. In another flight he photographed in complete detail an area of 20 square miles, in spite of intense anti-aircraft fire. He once landed in enemy country and rescued another pilot who had been forced to land through engine trouble.

Second-Lieutenant C. F. Ambler, while on photographic reconnaissance, was attacked by seven Fokker biplanes. Putting up a good fight, he was nevertheless twice compelled to retire, but each time he returned, and eventually drove off the enemy and obtained the required photographs.

The brilliant routine work of the Royal Air Force from the time

A German Aviator's End in Mid-Air

of the German advance early in 1918 until the enemy's offensive was shattered, in conjunction with systematic bombing of the enemy's communications, had important results. It upset the enemy's timetable by restricting their Important troop movements to the hours of darkness, and by destroying material. How serious was the position created for the enemy was proved by Staff Orders captured on prisoners, showing that the divisions which the enemy were able to operate with had to be transferred from other parts of the front and rear by night to the scene of operations. On arriving at each stage of their march brigades were ordered to put out police patrols to guard against detection by aircraft, to prevent groups of men forming in the streets or roads, and to camouflage all vehicles. Medical inspection was carried out company by company by regimental surgeons, instead of the sick going to the surgeons' quarters. No bivouac fires were permitted. In the first half of 1918 delay was the thing the Allies had to play for. After that the balance swung round to our favour.

Aircraft may be a two-edged sword if employed against an enemy superior in wit and resource. Sir .Douglas Haig, in his dispatch published on January 8, 1919, tells us of the colossal deception practised on the Germans in July, 1918, when it was desired that the enemy should believe that a big British attack in Flanders was intended.

"Canadian batteries were put into line on the Kemmel front, where they were identified by the enemy. Corps headquarters were prepared, and casualty clearing stations were erected in conspicuous positions in this area. Great activity was maintained also by our wireless stations on the First Army front, and arrangements were made to give the impression that a great concentration of tanks was taking place in the St. Pol area. Training operations in which infantry and tanks co-operated were carried out in this neighbourhood on days on which the enemy's long-distance reconnaissance and photographic machines were likely to be at work behind our lines. The rumour that the British were about to undertake a large and important operation on the northern front quickly spread. In the course of our subsequent advances convincing evidence was obtained that these different measures had had the desired effect, and that the enemy was momentarily expecting to be attacked in strength in Flanders."

CHAPTER 16

Observation Balloons

If the reader has seen an old picture depicting the first use of balloons in warfare at the battle of Fleurus, he will have no difficulty in appreciating the vast difference modern methods have made in the task of the aerial observer. In the old days it was sufficient to ascend in a captive round balloon to a height of a few hundred feet to see the whole of the battlefield spread out below, and to see what was on "the other side of the hill." No important movement could be hidden.

Direction of artillery fire from modern observation balloons came in with the long-range guns that required it; and it improved as their range and accuracy increased. The first method, by captive spherical balloons, was superseded by the kite-balloon used, the author believes, first in war in the Russo-Japanese campaign. It was the invention of Major Sigsfeld, and was made by the German firm of Parseval. It was known variously as the Parseval-Sigsfeld balloon, and as the "*Drachen.*" Of its capabilities there is no need to say more than that it could ascend with two passengers to a height of 3,000 feet under favourable circumstances. Its usual working height, however, was between 1,500 and 2,500 feet; and it was passably steady in a wind of 25 miles per hour. The type now under consideration was in use until 1916, when it was superseded; but with the older form it was possible to observe from greater heights if only one man was sent up.

At the beginning of the war the German Army possessed a very large number of kite-balloons, and the French Army also was fairly well equipped with them. The British had none at all, efforts by the author and others in pre-war days to induce the British Army authorities to adopt them having failed. Up to the time of the war the British relied entirely upon captive sphericals, which were employed in a small way in the South African and in other campaigns, and upon the man-lifting kite. In the technique of both of these the British Army led the way; but improvements in artillery had, early in the century, greatly reduced their value. The spherical balloon could only be used in calm, or nearly calm, weather; the kite required a fresh breeze; neither afforded the steady platform necessary for observation of artillery at the increased ranges of the present century. In the early days of the Great War the British had to rely upon very imperfect aeroplane observation.

Strange to say, even for land warfare the British Army only adopted the kite-balloon after the Royal Naval Air Service had acquired a small equipment; and for many months after force of circumstances compelled the employment of kite-balloons on the Western Front these were supplied and manned by the Admiralty. And, naturally enough, there was endless friction. Moreover, our artillery had to be educated up to the use of the methods of observation thus rendered possible.

But the merit of the kite-balloon made it indispensable, and the number employed at the Front increased as fast as the equipment could be supplied, and officers and crews trained. Then, when this division became overwhelmingly important, the Royal Flying Corps authorities took over all land sections from the Royal Naval Air Service, and started their own training centres in England, although, for a time, Royal Flying Corps officers had to be trained by the Royal Naval Air Service. (The author was for a period occupied with the training of these officers.) Ultimately, the Royal Naval Air Service dealt only with kite-balloons used on ships.

The kite-balloon, or "*drachen*," was superseded towards the end of 1915 by the "streamline" balloon, invented by M. Cacquot, a Frenchman. This afforded a much steadier platform, and could be used in winds up to 40 miles per hour; whilst it could safely be sent up in even stronger winds. Improvements made greater altitude attainable later on. In 1918 a new type of observation balloon was designed by an Italian; it was spherical in form, but was furnished with stabilizing bags.

Both land and sea kite-balloons and the subsequent improved types work on a cable unwound off a motor winch. They carry two observers, as a rule, the equipment being a large-scale map of the district under observation, a telephone, the wire of which was usually separate from the hauling cable, but was sometimes part of the cable itself, binoculars with graticulated lenses enabling the observer quickly to measure the angle between any fixed object and the flash or the smoke of a gun, and thereby to indicate to batteries below the position of new enemy activities by day or by night. The instruments include compass, altimeter, and air-speed indicator (for measuring the velocity of the wind). In addition, the observer officer had to watch the effect of our own shells, and to report to our gunners whether they were "over," or "under," or "right," or "left" of a target.

This work required a capacity to endure the swaying of the basket for hours at a stretch, and experience in making and reporting observations; and these duties often had to be performed under fire or attack by hostile aircraft. It was found necessary by the end of 1915 to accustom observation balloon officers to the use of the parachute, this apparatus offering the only chance of escape from death in the event of the balloon being fired, or from capture by the enemy when the balloon broke away in a high westerly wind. Many exciting escapes, and some regrettable tragedies arose out of these conditions.

At first looked upon as a "soft job," kite-ballooning, by the spring of 1916, became recognized as one of the hazardous and most trying forms of service, whether performed on land, under fire from the German long-range guns employing shell with the clock fuse, or at such imminent risk from aeroplane attack that the occupants of the basket were compelled to wear their parachute harness ready for instant jumping clear from a blazing wreck; or whether employed at sea, searching for submarines under circumstances which practically precluded any chance of rescue in the event of the cable breaking.

As the reader is much less likely to have ascended in an observation balloon than in an aeroplane, a short description of the sensations may be interesting. The observer having entered the basket, the crew of men handling the guy ropes and cables get ready to let up, and the order is given to the winch hands. The balloon, 80 feet in length and about 25 feet in diameter, has so much lift that it unwinds the cable on the drum. Directly the balloon gets clear of the ground, if there is any wind it begins to swing to and fro, and this motion is too much for bad sailors. Up aloft there is no sense of giddiness, and the only discomfort comes from the rolling of the basket and the curious twitches and jerks caused by some winds. Sailors say this is worse than the worst ship.

One's fancies also may roam unpleasantly at times to questions of the security of the gear. Many an aeroplane pilot has told the author that he feels much more nervous in a kite-balloon than in a flying machine. Landing in a high wind may be exciting, and the crew who have to secure the guy ropes are sometimes bowled over. One has been in a basket swinging through nearly 180 degrees. The complete crew, including the motor-winch men and those who have to attend to the silicol plant for making hydrogen, number from 60 to 80.

Part of the training of the observation balloon officer was a course of free ballooning, in order that he might learn how to make use of ballast and valve in the event of the balloon breaking adrift. Londoners became familiar with the spectacle of training sphericals drifting over the city, some of them with as many as eight men in the basket.

By the autumn of 1915 observation balloons were so extensively employed that the Western Front was marked by a long double line of them about three miles behind the respective lines, and extending at intervals of two or three miles from the sea to Switzerland. The author has seen more than forty of these balloons at a time.

With some amusement the sneer of our official "Eyewitness" on September 29, 1914, is here recalled. He wrote:

Recently the Germans have been relying to some extent on observation from captive balloons sent up at some distance in rear of their first line, a method which, whatever its cause, is a poor substitute for the direct overhead reconnaissance obtainable from aeroplanes. As a consequence, the damage being done to us is wholly disproportionate to the amount of ammunition expended by the enemy.

This, beside being an exhibition of deep ignorance, did not excuse our authorities for having no kite-balloons at all at this period, nor for having so few aeroplanes.

A sketch is given in another chapter of the method of squaring the map for artillery observation. For regulating shoots, the "clock" system was also employed. An observation balloon covered a front of about four miles, depending upon local circumstances, and was allotted to a group of guns. As a rule its work lay with heavy artillery, and not with field batteries; never with the latter during big operations. Towards the end of the war, however, it became the custom to move the balloons forward just in rear of advancing infantry, the motor winch simply being driven forward with balloon attached to the cable, and the observer in the basket more or less calmly continuing his duties, which included that of watching the positions of advanced infantry and tanks.

At the Battle of Verdun, and afterwards, the observation balloons on both sides were the objects of fierce attacks. Every great offensive was heralded by an attempt to "blind" the enemy by destroying his bal-loons. On one occasion, at the Somme in 1916, one could count twenty French sausages up and not one German. The French in one day destroyed fifteen German balloons, and this number was surpassed by the British accounting for seventeen in one day. The Allies also at times suffered heavily. Indeed, the pace became so hot that balloon officers abandoned their balloons if a hostile aeroplane succeeded in getting into position for firing, for having got to that stage the result was inevitable. Many a duel between aeroplanes was fought over the defence of an observation balloon. It is not impossible that in the event of another war between highly organized armies observation balloons will be useless.

The Germans had kite-balloons up in the vicinity of Ostend, which month after month were the objects of aerial conflicts. They were well protected by anti-aircraft batteries, and our naval airmen used to attempt their destruction—and sometimes succeeded—by approaching at a great height, and then diving with tremendous speed to effective range, relying upon speed to get clear away before "Archie" could get their range.

An early method of firing kite-balloons was by means of rockets. Aeroplanes were equipped with a number of rockets, which the pilot could easily fire, first getting to very close range in order to secure accuracy. A hit made a small hole in the fabric and ignited the gas. The flames rapidly increased until the whole balloon blazed up. Many kite-balloon officers won honours. Thus Lieutenant K. B. Burburry was mentioned in French Army Orders on September 15, 1915. His balloon drifted towards the German lines, the cable having been cut by a shell. He ripped open the balloon at an altitude of 3,000 feet before dropping out in his parachute, and thus prevented the balloon falling into the enemy's hands.

On June 3, 1916, a German battery in Flanders opened fire on a kite-balloon just as it was about to ascend, the first shell bursting within 10 yards. The cable was immediately cut, and the balloon dragged by the crew at the double for nearly a mile, shells following them all the way. They saved the balloon.

Lieutenant T. W. Nops, on October 21, 1916, was in a kite-balloon with an observer when the balloon was attacked by an aeroplane. Lieutenant Nops opened fire with his rifle, and in the excitement he failed to see that the balloon had been set on fire on top, until the flames spread and the basket began rapidly to fall. Then he helped his comrade out with his parachute, with the result that this officer reached the ground safely. Lieutenant Nops, however, was not in time to save himself. He fell with the basket and was killed.

Second-Lieutenant A. G. D. Gavin, when his balloon broke loose and was drifting rapidly towards the enemy, first saw to the safety of his passenger and helped him out in his parachute. He then destroyed all his papers, and descended by his own parachute, landing under machine-gun fire close to the trenches.

Lieutenant B. G. Porter's balloon and winch were heavily shelled when the balloon was 500 feet up. Six of the ground crew were killed and ten wounded. The balloon being badly damaged, Lieutenant Porter ordered the winch to let it up to 1,500 feet. This was done, and the two officers were enabled to parachute successfully. From the lower altitude this would have been dangerous. The official record adds:

> The presence of mind displayed by Lieutenant Porter saved the lives of his balloon officers, and his cool courage set a fine example to his men.

Two kite-balloon officers were at work one day during the heavy fighting in July, 1918, when the enemy turned two guns on their balloon, and holed it badly. The balloon officers thereupon rang up a 6-inch battery, and told them the exact position of the German guns. The balloon meanwhile was rapidly losing height. But they stuck to their basket, and continued to direct the fire of the British guns; and they had the satisfaction of witnessing the putting out of action of one of the enemy guns before the balloon had sunk too low for further observation. Being then too low for a safe parachute descent, both climbed well up the rigging of the balloon for protection in the inevitable bad bump.

Here an official *communiqué* on the work of the first kite-balloon ship is summarized. It refers to the *Manica*, and her work out in Gallipoli spotting for the *Queen Elizabeth*. The *Manica* was a converted tramp. Within three days of her arrival a Turkish camp was shelled under the direction of the kite-balloon observers. In the following week fire was directed on the Gaba Tepe position, which resulted in the destruction of the barracks. These objectives, of course, were right out of sight of the crews of the guns. On one occasion the observers spotted on the other side of the peninsula a large Turkish transport. The *Queen Elizabeth* was operating, and the bearings of the Turkish vessel were given her. The first shot fell short. A second shot went nearer the mark. Again the direction was corrected; and a third huge shell screamed over. Then, by the telephone of the kite-balloon, came the words "Got her. She's sinking by the head."

Many attacks were made by the Turks on the kite-balloon and its ship, but were unsuccessful. The effect on Turkish shipping was very evident, for whenever the balloon went up all enemy ships hurried off out of range of our big guns. The official record of the *Manica* for the next fortnight is as follows:

April 28th—Two field batteries silenced; several guns destroyed.

April 30th—Chanak shelled; burned for two hours.

May 2nd—Battery of 8-inch guns shelled; three direct hits.

May 8th—Four batteries silenced.

May 12th—House reported to be Turkish headquarters destroyed.

It should be remembered that barely three months before there was not a single kite-balloon in England.

This kite-balloon ship incident should perhaps be included in the chapter on sea aircraft, where a number of references to the work of kite-balloons will be found.

CHAPTER 17

Aircraft and Infantry

Unforeseen, either by aeronautical or military authorities, was the close co-operation between aeroplanes and troops on the ground, which became a big feature of the war and out-sensationed the florid pictures of pre-war fiction. When this method was first employed in Egypt it was supposed to be a casual occurrence, only to be expected where an ill-trained or poorly equipped enemy was concerned. Great surprise, therefore, was caused by its systematic use against the splendidly disciplined and well-armed German infantry on the Western Front.

There is little likelihood that the Germans would have initiated this method of attack, unless we can conceive a situation in which the Allied armies, including their flying services, had become demoralized, and German aviators had secured an unquestioned ascendancy that they certainly never held. For it meant that the attacking craft had to fly down through thousands of feet, exposed to gunfire, and then to face hot rifle and machine-gun fire at close range. At least, that was how it first appeared. It called for daring, even in the first attempt; but to repeat it again and again against a thoroughly awakened enemy was in defiance of all early ideas. The Germans only adopted this style of attack when we had shown them the way. They then put it into effect on various occasions, notably in their big offensive in March and April, 1918.

At first, aeroplane attacks on ground troops were casual, almost unpremeditated. Rapidly, however, the possibilities were realized, and this method of warfare, including all that is known as "contact work," became more and more elaborately organized.

In the Somme battle of 1916, in which the British and French were heavily engaged, the foundations were laid. On July 14th co-operation of aeroplanes with infantry was on a large scale. On August 20th Sir Douglas Haig reported: "Effective co-operation with infantry," and "One of our aeroplanes brought effective machine-gun fire on troops in the trenches." The employment of aeroplane guns against troops on the ground occurred in Egypt also. On September 3rd and 15th our aeroplanes, sweeping along at low altitudes, raked retiring enemy infantry; and on September 30th and October 12th artillery and transport were engaged and often scattered.

The distinction of formulating plans for the systematic co-operation of aircraft and infantry in a push belongs to the French, but the British Third Arm carried it much further. It was called for by the need to ascertain the position of troops during an advance. This was known as "trench registering," and was a natural sequel to subterranean warfare, which effectually conceals men from friend and foe alike, and is one of the factors helping to create the deadlock of trench warfare.

At first aeroplanes flew low over the advanced positions, and reported the results of their observations by dropping messages. Then the necessity arose for quick methods of identifying troops, and providing against ruses by the enemy. Aeroplanes employed on these duties carried special identification marks showing the particular squadron or division, and the troops below also carried distinguishing marks. The machines carried Klaxon horns, and signalled according to a simple limited code. Very lights were also used. And the troops below replied by flags, flares, and mirrors.

When tanks arrived on the scene the deadlock of the trenches was threatened; and advances penetrated to a greater depth. The tanks communicated with other tanks and with infantry by coloured discs and lights.

Thus, three reds meant "Broken down"; red and white meant "No enemy in sight"; the display of a red disc meant "Wire uncut"; and so on.

Defence had to be organized against attacking aeroplanes, and the machine-gunners soon found their time wasted if they simply aimed at the swift-travelling machine. Like anti-aircraft artillery, it was necessary to fire according to a zone system; and also they had to employ incendiary projectiles.

At first the aeroplanes used on these services were any available type, especially scouts and two-seaters that were becoming obsolete through lack of sufficient climbing power. Indeed, not until the autumn of 1918 did specially-designed trench aeroplanes appear. These were heavily-armoured, and in some cases were two-seaters. They had a "ceiling" of no more than about 8,000 or 10,000 feet, and they were not particularly fast. They carried one or two guns, firing through the propeller, for, contrary to the forecast of some experts, and to the actual practice of the Germans at first, nothing was to be gained by a vehicle travelling at upwards of 80 miles per hour firing directly downwards. In such a case the bullets would hit at points many feet apart; whereas by firing along the trenches or anybody of troops the chance of results was much improved. The Sop with "Salamander" was the particular British trench-strafer; it carried armour-plate weighing about 650 lbs.

The general introduction of infantry-attacking aeroplanes led to a curious result, at first, on both sides. The infantryman so attacked saw the hostile aeroplane and feared it. But he seldom saw our own machines; or, if he did, they were tiny unidentifiable specks engaged in, to him, meaningless manoeuvres at a vast distance in the blue. So he got an impression of unhindered enemy aircraft activity, and a Third Arm paralysed on his side. This accounts for letters written home to this effect by British soldiers, and similar letters and entries in German prisoners' diaries. On the British side it occurred at a period, September and October, 1918, when the enemy's Third Arm was completely outclassed.

The French losses on the Somme in 1916 were on a smaller scale than in any previous movement of magnitude. The secret was the accurate timing and placing of the moving artillery barrage protecting the advancing infantry. There was danger of moving it too far ahead and, what was far worse, of not moving it forward enough, and of shelling our own troops. The solution is that already indicated, namely, the "trench-registering" aeroplanes, owing to which in this battle the French advance, whether it was or was not precisely according to programme, always moved forward under the shells of a barrage that preceded it almost exactly 200 yards ahead.

A battalion of Prussian guards was marching up to save the situation at one point, when one of our aeroplanes came down to within 300 feet, and the observer emptied several drums of ammunition into the close ranks. This attack, combined with the artillery barrage, inflicted a loss of 50 *per cent,* on that battalion. But aeroplanes engaged in this manner not only infantry, but cavalry and artillery also.

The low-flying aeroplane, as time went on, participated in the operations in all sorts of unexpected ways. It actually arranged surrenders of parties of the enemy. Sir Douglas Haig reports the first incident of this kind in his dispatch relating to September 26, 1916, as follows:—

On the same day Gueudecourt was carried, after the protecting trench to the west had been captured in a somewhat interesting fashion. In the early morning a Tank started down the portion of the trench held by the enemy from the north-west, firing its machine-guns and followed by bombers. The enemy could not escape, as we held the trench at the southern end. At the same time an aeroplane flew down the length of the trench, also firing a machine-gun at the enemy holding it. These then waved white handkerchiefs in token of surrender, and when this was reported by the aeroplane, the infantry accepted the surrender of the garrison. By 8.30 a.m. the whole trench had been cleared, great numbers of the enemy had been killed, and eight officers and 362 other ranks made prisoners. Our total casualties amounted to five.

The Honours Lists contained a great many incidents illustrating the special work of low-flying aircraft.

Captain G. C. Bailey was awarded the D.S.O. for flying over the enemy's trenches at a height of only 1,500 feet for more than an hour and a half in very adverse weather conditions. He attacked the enemy in the trenches with machine-gun fire, and located 16 active enemy batteries during the flight. On a previous occasion, by the way, this officer and Second-Lieutenant L. S. White attacked on a prearranged plan, and so occupied the enemy that our infantry were able to approach unobserved and without artillery preparation.

On one occasion, early in 1917, three British airmen flew along the main street of Lens on a level with the roofs, and liberally bombed a regiment of Bavarian infantry which was marching on the road of retreat.

Early in June, 1917, the fight for Messines Ridge saw contact work and infantry attack further elaborated. The enemy were completely overwhelmed in the air. On the morning of June 7th, before it was light, General Von Armin's Fourth Army was attacked with great determination by several British squadrons, who bombed and machine-gunned artillery, infantry, and transport, hour after hour.

A British airman attacked an aerodrome from below the level of the sheds, and when a machine-gun opened on him from the ground he dived at it and scattered the crew. Others chased troop trains at a height of 50 feet, and skimmed over the heads of frightened infantry, sending them in wild confusion into the woods. One of our flyers saw a motor-car with five men going along the road towards Menin. He dropped so low that the body of his machine nearly grazed it, and fired his machine-gun. The car ran wildly into the bank and overturned. The pilot saw four gun teams ahead, so he fired on them and dispersed the drivers, and farther up the same road he flew into a column of 500 infantry marching towards the front, and they, too, scattered.

This work was obviously to the liking of our men, who could feel that they really were giving the German his deserts. Mr. Philip Gibbs, writing of that period, says that "a youthful madness took possession of them." The author can vouch for the fact that when ordinary ammunition was exhausted, if a good target presented itself they fired their Very lights at it, sometimes with good results. Despite its manifold dangers, no class of aircraft activity gave quite the same degree of exhilaration as "infantry strafing."

On the Ypres Front in August weather conditions almost completely prevented aerial observation; but our "flying cavalry" were busier than ever, and they engaged machine-gun redoubts, and silenced several strong points.

One of our airmen flying just above the treetops found three enemy machines getting ready to start from an aerodrome. He wrecked them all. Then he found a wagon and horses on a road and shot both horses. He called at a railway station and shot the guard on duty, and finished up by stampeding a column of horse transport. Work on some of the enemy aerodromes was completely paralysed by our airmen, who flew up and down firing into every shed and office, and setting fire to every visible machine.

Captain Richard Williams was awarded the D.S.O. for flying at a low altitude under intense anti-aircraft fire, and attacking and dispersing enemy troops who were concentrating on our flanks. On another occasion, while on a reconnaissance, he landed in the enemy's lines, and rescued the pilot of a machine which had been brought down by hostile fire.

Captain H. M. Probyn, at a critical time when hostile infantry had penetrated our trenches, went up in bad weather and under heavy machine-gun and anti-aircraft fire from guns of heavy calibre, and managed to locate and report with complete accuracy the position and progress of the enemy. To do this he had to fly at a very low altitude, during which his machine was seriously damaged. The following day he carried out another daring and successful reconnaissance of the enemy's lines, bringing back information of the greatest value. These services are recorded in the list of recipients of the D.S.C.

The M.C. was given to Captain S. H. Clarke, who frequently engaged bodies of hostile infantry at low altitude, causing them heavy casualties, and, although continually subjected to attacks from hostile machines and heavy machine-gun fire from the ground, which considerably damaged his machine, completed his work in every case. On one occasion he took some exceptionally successful and valuable photographs of the enemy's wire from a height of 1,200 feet, and he also carried out a number of successful shoots in co-operation with artillery.

An extraordinary adventure befell one of our trench-strafers, who lost his bearings through ascending into some low-lying clouds in order to clear a jammed machine-gun. When he came down again he alighted in a field in order to ask his way of some peasants. While doing this a troop of enemy cavalry dashed out from behind a wood; but as he had not completely stopped his engine he got away in the nick of time. In revenge he then swooped down on the cavalry, firing at them and stampeding them. The officer leading the troop fired his automatic pistol at the machine, but he fell a victim to the airman's gun.

A notice which appeared in the *Times* "In Memoriam" column bears witness to our airmen's work. It read:—

To *An Unknown Airman*, shot down 23rd November, 1917, whilst attacking a German strong point SW, of Bourlon Wood, in the effort to help out a Company of the Royal Irish Rifles, when other help had failed.

Our airmen also did notable work in the successful operations in Italy and Palestine. The Turks were bombed and machine-gunned for a week during their retreat, and the country was covered with the debris of a beaten army.

With the beginning of 1918 there were apprehensions that the Germans would attack in irresistible might, owing to the strengthening of their Western Front armies by the release of numerous divisions from the Russian Front. Throughout the winter, in anticipation of the coming attack, the British Third Arm maintained a relentless offensive against them, especially attending to their lines of communication and aerodromes. On the 1st day of March a big attack was made on their aerodromes in the morning, at the moment when the enemy were preparing to take the air. This was effectively prevented by our bombs and machine-guns; and during their return journey our men did great execution among transport and troops on the march.

When the enemy pressed back our line, and even in places broke it, our low-flying machines did inestimable service by attacking the advancing Germans, who were forced to bring up their divisions rapidly in solid battalions by road or, as far as they could, by rail. Then, our machines flying low over enemy-held country, with no prospect of reaching our lines in the event of engine-failure, were engaged by the hundred on this work, and they seriously delayed the German programme.

Both the enemy and ourselves employed aeroplanes to convey ammunition, and even food, to advanced isolated detachments. In Mesopotamia, when the British were besieged in Kut, they found plenty of grain, but lacked the machinery necessary for grinding it. Mill-stones were conveyed to them by aeroplanes, which, flying low, dropped their cargo on a sandbank. Food and tobacco were also conveyed by this means.

Yet another branch of activity was that of landing spies behind the enemy's lines, and "collecting" them again when their work was done. This went on in France and also in Italy towards the end to an almost unbelievable extent. Parties were landed to destroy important places by bombs.

In the early part of the German retreat in the summer of 1918 the unprecedented amount of co-operation between our aeroplanes and our infantry resulted in numerous acts of conspicuous courage. Lieutenant H. W. Russell displayed remarkable gallantry on August 11th. Being on a low patrol he saw that our advancing troops were held up by a nest of six machine-guns. These he engaged with his own machine-gun, repeatedly diving so low as almost to touch the ground, and eventually silencing the hostile guns, thus enabling our troops to occupy the position. Having expended all his ammunition, he returned to his aerodrome, and, obtaining another machine, his own being almost shot to pieces, he again joined the attack.

Captain G. J. Scaramanga rendered brilliant service on numerous contact patrols, "and the information he brought in materially contributed to the success of our operations." On August 23rd the situation in a certain area was very obscure; whereupon this officer carried out a patrol lasting two and a half hours, and, flying at a very low altitude, he drew the enemy's fire, and so located their troops. Proceeding up and down the line, he was enabled to render an accurate report of the situation. His machine was badly shot about, having forty-four bullet-holes. Later in the day, on another contact patrol, which lasted two hours, he saw two enemy howitzers drawn by eight horses, in retreat; diving, he fired 200 rounds, killing six horses and sixteen men; the rear howitzer was left behind in a ditch. On another occasion, when on contact patrol, he was attacked by three formations of four, six, and seven hostile aircraft respectively at different times; all these he drove off, and completed his patrol. The D.F.C. was awarded in this and in the foregoing case.

Lieutenant S. Turner, on the morning of September 20th, carried out a contact patrol, locating the position of our troops in face of very heavy fire and under adverse weather conditions. Owing to a hostile counter-attack the situation that evening again became obscure, and this officer carried out a second patrol over the same area. Owing to his Klaxon horn being hit he was compelled to descend to a very low altitude to ascertain the position of our troops.

Lieutenant E. C. Willis, on October 2nd, carried out an extremely valuable contact patrol, flying for two hours at an average height of 300 feet. During this flight he assisted in repelling a counter-attack, engaging the enemy with machine-gun fire from a height of 50 feet. His machine was struck by a shell, but notwithstanding this he continued his patrol and sent in three very important reports as to the position of our advanced troops. On his return he made a perfectly good landing; but his machine immediately collapsed, being unable to sustain its own weight on the ground.

On October 1st the Belgian forces that had pushed out beyond Houthoulst Forest had advanced beyond supplies, owing to the terrible state of the roads. The Royal Air Force attached to the Army, and the 5th Group, which was one appointed to co-operate with the Navy, transported through the air 1,000 army rations. The cases were broken up into parcels and packed in earth. They were dropped in places indicated by large white crosses. About 70 machines, in this manner, conveyed 13 tons of parcels.

This chapter cannot be more fittingly closed than with a record of a V.C. The King conferred this decoration on Captain F. M. F. West, who, while engaging ground troops far over the enemy lines, was attacked by seven aeroplanes.

Early in the engagement one of his legs was partially severed by an explosive bullet, and it fell powerless into the controls, rendering the machine for a time unmanageable. Lifting his disabled leg, he regained control of the machine, and although wounded in the other leg he manoeuvred his machine so skilfully that his observer was enabled to get several good bursts into the enemy, which drove them away. Captain West then, with rare courage and determination, desperately wounded as he was, brought his machine over our lines and landed safely. Exhausted by his exertions he fainted, but on regaining consciousness insisted on writing his report.

CHAPTER 18

Sea Aircraft

The Royal Naval Air Service saw a great deal of work with the Army, besides much fighting and patrolling round the coast on ordinary aeroplanes. But in this chapter only incidents connected with sea operations are included, irrespective of the type of aircraft employed. The Naval Service was driven by force of circumstances to trespass on the domain of the Royal Flying Corps. It was impossible to make a sharp division of responsibility. The occupation of Dunkirk and the establishment there of a big aircraft base brought it and the left of the British line into close contact and overlapping.

But the Air Services were unprepared for war on a big scale. Much of their work was determined by circumstances relating to the provision of machines and equipment; and, owing to the administrative policy of the pre-war period, there was considerable confusion. Thus, the Royal Naval Air Service obtained certain types of aeroplanes and engines, the Royal Flying Corps used others. And the time came when a pooling of resources was extremely desirable, not merely to prevent waste, but also to put an end to the absurdity of one half of the Air Service being compelled to put up with inferior aeroplanes and engines. The Royal Naval Air Service had first call on some of the best types. For effecting complete co-operation no machinery existed until the Air Board came into existence in 1917.

The seaplane was, if anything, less on a war-footing basis than the land aeroplane; and even in 1918 the work of our naval aircraft scarcely settled down to routine by established types to the extent possible to army aircraft. Moreover, it cannot be denied that the progress sought in the direction of seaplane technique was less rapid than it might have been had the Royal Naval Air Service been able to confine itself strictly to that department. As it was, many of its finest pilots were lent to the Army, and much of the energy of the Naval Aeronautical Department was diverted to work which should have been entirely in the hands of the Royal Flying Corps.

One aspect of this is brought out in the chapter on Kite-balloons, Further, the R.N.A.S. had fighting squadrons working as far south as the Somme, besides several fighting squadrons north of Ypres, and all the big bombing squadrons until the end of 1917.

It is important to remember that the war found us with not more than a dozen pilots who had any real experience of naval air patrolling, and that the seaplanes of the period, whether German or British, were extremely unseaworthy. We had no big airships, and our squadron of medium and small non-rigids was negligible. Nor had the enemy, in spite of their fleet of Zeppelins, any naval aircraft that affected the naval situation unfavourably for us either in the first six months of the war, or at the Battle of Jutland, or at any later period; although in 1917, and early in 1918, the enemy by giving great attention to seaplanes, and producing fast and high-powered types, made a fair display in the North Sea. This, however, when all things are considered, was much more apparent than effective. The enemy had given up the intention of a fleet action, they had shot their bolt in the matter of naval raids, they had no commerce on the high-seas to protect. We were at all times ready for a fleet action; we were harrying most available parts of their coast except in the Baltic, and we had a huge military and commercial overseas traffic to protect against the submarines round our coast, in the Mediterranean, and in the Atlantic. Moreover, we succeeded in our gigantic task; and to a notable extent our success was aided by our naval aircraft.

Apart from the type of aircraft employed, the onus of all this rested upon the naval aeroplane observers, whose training during the first half of the war was make-shift. Essential things, such as ability to identify a warship at a great distance at a glance, and familiarity with naval methods, they certainly lacked. These were given in some measure later; but the beneficent process was to some extent interrupted by the abolition of the Royal Naval Air Service in the beginning of 1918.

From the very first the submarines had to be dealt with, and before a year of war had elapsed the Royal Naval Air Service, working with hastily contrived appliances, was keeping its end up. The same can be said as regards our measures against German mine-laying.

One of the series of British aeronautical engineering successes which began before the war, and yet shows no sign of ending, was the

SS. type of airship, commonly known as the "Blimp." Never intended to be an airship in the full sense of the term, it nevertheless surpassed the most glowing anticipations as to the possibilities of the small non-rigid type. The idea of it had been working in the brain of Mr. Holt Thomas, who wanted to build the smallest possible "dirigible balloon," driving it by an aeroplane engine in the lightest possible car.

The authorities and most experts, however, persisted in contrasting such a vehicle with the Zeppelin; and naturally, by such a comparison, it was found wanting. It required the emergency of the war and a desperate need to open British eyes. The author believes he is right in attributing to Lord Fisher the perception of the great promise afforded by this type; and at last a trial vessel was made of an aeroplane body with the engine attached—a 75-H.P. Renault in a B.E.2C fuselage with, instead of the biplane superstructure, a small stream-lined gas-bag and ballonnet—the Willows airship, in fact—simplification being secured by utilizing the back-draught from the propeller to fill the ballonnet, according to its needs, through an oblique pipe.

That was the original "Blimp" of March 18, 1915, and its performance exceeded most anticipations. It developed a speed previously un-heard of in small air-ships, attaining to something over 40 miles per hour; and it was the forerunner of the very numerous fleet which, improved and somewhat enlarged, provided us with one of our most useful anti-submarine patrol vessels. And this is to be noted, while the submarine was not very formidable this type was going through its paces, and the crews were being trained ready for the "unrestricted warfare" that later on was launched. Better still, a fuselage and aero-plane engine rendered obsolete by the increasingly exacting demands upon aeroplanes found a useful outlet. There should be a pleasure and commercial future for this division, which may be compared nauti-cally, if not to big ships, at any rate to yawls.

In 1916 the coastal patrol type appeared, with a capacity of 190,000 cubic feet; and a little later the SS Zero of 70,000 cubic feet with a 75-H.P. engine in a "pusher" fuselage. The latter could do 47 miles per hour for nine hours.

Sea aeroplanes of Great Britain included the Short and the Sch-neider Cup types; the latter, the Sopwith machine which won the International Race at Monaco. There were others, of course; and many pre-war experiments began to bear fruit. There was the White (S. White, of Cowes) two-engine machine. The Curtiss transatlantic flying boat was being built in this country.

The Germans, who lacked "Blimps," and laughed at the idea that a small dirigible balloon could be any use in war, had various seaplanes, for which, as for land aeroplanes, they had a valuable asset in powerful water-cooled types of aero-engines. Our own aero-engine industry had been starved, and for some time we were to suffer not so much from the lack of good designs as the means of producing in quantities.

Probably few people were aware of the energy displayed by the enemy in pre-war days. In far-away Fiji German warships were accompanied by seaplanes, and a great deal of work went on by day and by night, the neighbouring British either unsuspicious or, if they ventured to warn their countrymen or the authorities, receiving scant courtesy.

Directly war broke out the Royal Naval Air Service set to work, and they were very soon heard of in connection with the bombing operations and land aeroplane activities elsewhere described.

The first big seaplane effort was the attack on the German fleet lying off Cuxhaven on Christmas Day, 1914. This was a combined marine and aerial attack, the seaplane mother-ships, *Engadine, Empress,* and *Riviera,* supported by light cruisers, destroyers and submarines. On approaching Heligoland they were attacked by two Zeppelins and various warships. The official report stated:—

The attack was delivered at daylight. It was necessary for the British ships to remain in the neighbourhood in order to pick up the returning airmen; and a novel combat ensued between the most modern cruisers on the one hand and the enemy's aircraft and submarines on the other. By swift manoeuvring the enemy's submarines were avoided and the two Zeppelins were easily put to flight by the guns of the *Undaunted* and *Arethusa.* The enemy's seaplanes succeeded in dropping their bombs near our ships, though without hitting any. The British ships remained for three hours off the enemy's coast without being molested by any surface vessel, and safely re-embarked three out of the seven airmen with their machines. Three other pilots, who returned later, were picked up according to arrangement by British submarines, their machines being sunk. . . . Flight-Commander F. E. T. Hewlett is, however, missing.

Flight-Commander Hewlett is the son of Mrs. Maurice Hewlett, who was one of the first Englishwomen to fly, and was the first woman to take up aeroplane manufacture. He landed on the Dutch coast, after spending three hours in the air and losing his way owing to the thick weather. He dropped his bombs on a Zeppelin shed and a warship, but could not see the result.

The Admiralty report, published subsequently, added the following particulars:—

At the beginning of the flight the weather was clear, but on nearing the land the seaplanes met with thick weather and were compelled to fly low, thus becoming exposed to a heavy fire at short range from ships and shore batteries. Several machines were hit, but all remained in the air for over three hours and succeeded in obtaining valuable information regarding the disposition of the enemy's ships and defences. . . .

In connection with this affair the D.S.O. was awarded to Flight-Commander C. F. Kilner and Flight-Lieutenant C. H. K. Edmonds, the D.S.M. to C.P.O. Mech. J. W, Bell and C.P.O. Mech. G. H. W. Budds.

An account of the raid from the lower-deck point of view (a scarcely permissible term in the case of aircraft!) was given in a letter by C.P.O. Budds, published in the *Aeroplane*.

At daybreak on Christmas morning our machine started away to give the Germans a shock. I was mechanic observer on Flight-Commander Oliver's machine. We had a fine time. Every one gave us a warm reception in the shape of bullets, but neither the Fleet nor the land batteries managed to find a mark, although they were near enough. When you can hear the bullets whizzing round in your vicinity I consider that it is quite close enough. . . At all events, we escaped them all not by ordinary flying. The pilot was an absolute marvel; he was bringing the seaplane up and down, right and left; in fact it was all over the place, and the Germans could not find the range.

By this time Dunkirk in our hands, and Zeebrugge occupied by the Germans, had become the scenes of almost incessant air-fighting, which continued to the end of the war. Our hold on Dunkirk was a thorn in the side of the enemy, for it provided us with a naval and an air base, and enabled us to intercept German raiders on their way to and from England. Before the end our bombers made the submarine workshops almost untenable. Many basins were abandoned and sheds were blown to pieces, and wherever the enemy moved his works our airmen followed him. By day small fast machines pestered the German working parties.

The D.S.O. was awarded to Squadron-Commander R. B. Davies and Flight-Lieutenant R. E. C. Peirse, who repeatedly attacked the German submarine stations at Ostend and Zeebrugge under heavy fire, their machines being frequently hit. On January 23rd they each discharged eight bombs in an attack upon submarines alongside the Mole at Zeebrugge, flying down to close range. At the outset of this Flight-Lieutenant Davies was severely wounded by a bullet in the thigh, but he accomplished his task, handling his machine for an hour with great skill in spite of pain and loss of blood. One submarine was damaged, and many casualties were caused among the enemy.

On the 12th of February the biggest aircraft attack then on record was made against Zeebrugge and Ostend, 34 machines starting on this mission from the English coast. One machine failed to reach the objective, and alighted on the sea, its occupant being rescued. Although the weather interfered with the operation, damage was done by the bombs to Ostend Station and to submarine sheds at Zeebrugge.

On March 24, 1915, five naval machines attacked the submarine base at Hoboken, near Antwerp, when Commander Longmore reported as follows:—

I have to report that a successful air attack was carried out this morning by five machines of the Dunkirk squadron on the German submarines being constructed at Hoboken. Two of the pilots had to return owing to thick weather, but Squadron-Commander I. T. Courtney and Flight-Lieutenant H. Rosher reached their objective and, after planing down to 1,000 feet, dropped four bombs each on the submarines. It is believed that considerable damage has been done to both works and two submarines. The works were observed to be on fire. In all five submarines were observed on the slips.

The pilots were subjected to heavy gunfire, and one of them lost his way and landed in Holland.

On the same day a small British steamer, the *Teal*, was attacked by a German seaplane in the North Sea but suffered no damage from the four bombs and a number of steel darts that were dropped on her. The aeroplane was said to have been sent up from a mother-ship. Shortly afterwards two German seaplanes attacked the steamer *Ousel*, and from a height of about 500 feet dropped eleven bombs, the nearest striking the water 25 feet from the vessel. And a fight at sea took place, also, between the steamer *Serula* and two German seaplanes, the captain of the steamer firing at the enemy with a rifle and hitting one of the machines.

On July 27th the *Matin* reported that a French aviator saved a British transport in the Mediterranean. The airman from a great height observed the submarine making straight for the ship. He sent out an alarm by wireless, and then came down and attacked, dropping several bombs. These unfortunately did not strike the submarine, but they compelled it to submerge.

The Admiralty departed from its customary reserve on August 26th to make the following announcement:—

Squadron-Commander A.W. Bigsworth destroyed single-handed a German submarine this morning by bombs dropped from an aeroplane. The submarine was observed to be completely wrecked, and sank off Ostend. It is not the practice of the Admiralty to publish statements regarding the losses of German submarines, important though they have been, in cases where the enemy have no other source of information as to the time and place at which the losses have occurred. In the case referred to, however, the brilliant feat of Squadron-Commander Bigsworth was performed in the immediate neighbourhood of the coast in the occupation of the enemy, and the position of the sunken submarine has been located by a German destroyer.

Squadron-Commander Bigsworth was flying a Henry Farman machine, and when at a height of about 5,000 feet, and about four miles north of Nieuport, he saw the submarine, the crew of which, perceiving him, fired rockets as a signal to the shore batteries, which then opened fire on the aeroplane. Meanwhile Squadron-Commander Bigsworth descended to less than 500 feet and dropped three bombs, the explosions of which made his machine rock violently. When the smoke cleared he saw the submarine was a total wreck, her bows sticking up out of the water. A seaplane then attacked the British machine, which, being unarmed, retired. Squadron-Commander Bigsworth was awarded the D.S.O.

An occasion for Air Service co-operation with the Fleet was given by the German light cruiser *Königsberg* from Von Spey's China squadron. The *Königsberg* was chased into the Rufigi River, on the East Coast of Africa, in November, 1914. There it was impossible for British cruisers to follow, but two colliers were cleverly run in and sunk in

the fairway, effectively bottling the *Königsberg* up. She sought concealment in a thickly wooded creek. Trees were cut down and placed over
her deck and tied to her funnels and masts.

There she lay for months, but the long arm of the British Navy
was reaching out to her. The monitors *Trent* and *Mersey* took the place
of our cruisers, and aeroplanes were sent up to locate the enemy and
direct our guns. Flight-Commander Cull and A. M. E. Boggis went
up in an aeroplane and photographed the *Königsberg* from a height
of 700 feet. This was done under fire, and the machine was damaged. The monitors got to work in July, and aeroplanes piloted by
Flight-Commander H. Watkins and Flight-Commander Cull (with
Flight Sub-Lieutenant H. Arnold as observer) spotted for the guns.
The first-named also bombed the *Königsberg*. The fire of the monitors
was returned by the enemy, but, after operations extending over a few
days, she was destroyed. The official story runs:—

> Flight-Commander Cull and Flight Sub-Lieutenant Arnold
> were spotting on the 11th of July under fire in a biplane, when
> the enemy's fire damaged it so that it descended in a quarter
> of an hour from 3,200 to 2,000 feet. During this time no at-
> tempt was made to return to headquarters at Mafia, although
> it was obvious that this could not be done unless a start was
> made at once. Flight Sub-Lieutenant Arnold continued to send
> his spotting signals the whole time, and when, a quarter of an
> hour later, the machine was again hit and forced to descend,
> Flight-Commander Cull controlled the machine and Flight
> Sub-Lieutenant Arnold continued to send spotting corrections
> to the last, after warning the monitors that they were com-
> ing down, and would endeavour to land near them. The aero-
> plane finally came down in the river, turning over and over.
> Flight-Commander Cull was nearly drowned, but was assisted
> by Flight Sub-Lieutenant Arnold, and both were rescued by a
> boat from the *Mersey*.

A German submarine was destroyed on November 28, 1915, by
Flight Sub-Lieutenant Viney, accompanied by a French officer, Lieutenant le Comte de Sinçay, whilst patrolling off the Belgian coast.
These officers were awarded, respectively, the Victoria Cross and the
Legion of Honour. Flying at about 10,000 feet west of Nieuport, they
saw two submarines side by side on the surface. Rapidly descending,
the airmen could see one of the submarines moving about in zigzags

in order to perplex their aim. The other boat was the easier mark, and they hit it with the first bomb; and they could see with the naked eye that it was much damaged. A second bomb finished it, and the submarine sank.

One day in January, 1916, flying a Nieuport scout, and carrying four 16-lb. bombs, Flight-Lieutenant Simms sighted a U-boat about 10 miles west of Ostend. The airman flew down and observed the submarine signalling and then preparing to submerge. He released his four bombs from a height of 500 feet. Flight Sub-Lieutenant Norton saw Simms drop his bombs, and he dropped one himself when only the top of the periscope of the submarine was visible. The result was not ascertained.

A big combined air raid was made on the morning of March 24, 1916, on Zeebrugge. Sixty-five British, French, and Belgian aeroplanes and seaplanes took part, and dropped, in the aggregate, about 4½ tons of bombs. The air attack was in co-operation with a sea attack; its object, that of driving the enemy destroyers out to sea, was achieved. Outside the harbour the latter encountered the British naval force, and had to turn again. Some of them were damaged, and one had to be turned back crippled. Great damage was done by our bombs, and the German casualties numbered about 350 killed and wounded.

On August 26, 1916, Flight-Commander T. H. England, accompanied by a military officer as observer, flew a seaplane 43 miles inland from the Syrian coast, crossed a range of hills 2,000 feet high, with clouds at 1,500 feet, and after dropping bombs on the station of Horns, returned safely to his ship. The machine was exposed to rifle fire at extremely low altitudes for long periods, and Flight-Commander England showed remarkable pluck, determination, and skill in carrying out the flight under adverse conditions. He was awarded the D.S.C.

Flight-Commander R. J. Bone pursued and shot down a German raider over the North Sea. The British aviator was in an ordinary land aeroplane. He left the aerodrome while the enemy machine was still in sight, and making no attempt to climb his machine steeply, concentrated on keeping the enemy in sight. After pursuing for nearly 30 miles, the superior climb of his machine enabled him to attain a position at 9,000 feet, 2,000 feet above the German. From this position he rapidly overhauled the enemy and endeavoured to make a vertical dive on to him, firing his machine-gun.

The raider replied vigorously. Flight-Commander Bone then manoeuvred to get ahead of the hostile machine, and having succeeded steered straight at him, diving so as to pass below him, and turning with a vertical right-hand bank almost immediately under him. The German pilot turned his machine away a little to the left before they met, and the observer was visible hanging over the right-hand side of the fuselage, apparently dead or severely wounded. The gun was cocked up at 45 degrees to the vertical.

Flight-Commander Bone's speed carried him up to within 15 to 20 feet of the enemy machine, and he had no difficulty in keeping his sights on, firing four or five bursts of about six rounds until the enemy dived steeply, with smoke pouring out of his engine. The propeller stopped in a vertical position, but the machine was under control, and succeeded in landing safely. The fight was over at 2.50 p.m., and as Flight-Commander Bone was powerless to do anything while the enemy remained on the water, and as his engine showed signs of giving out, he returned to give information.

April 25th is memorable in the annals of Lowestoft, for on that day, in 1916, Germany's battle-cruiser squadron honoured the town with a visit, accompanied by two Zeppelin airships. The official reports were as follows:—

About 4.30 on Tuesday morning the German battle-cruiser squadron, accompanied by light cruisers and destroyers, appeared off Lowestoft. The local naval forces engaged it, and in about 20 minutes it returned to Germany, chased by our light cruisers and destroyers.

On shore two men, one woman, and a child were killed; the material damage seems to have been insignificant. So far as is known at present, two British light cruisers and a destroyer were hit, but none were sunk.

A later report stated that two Zeppelins were pursued over 60 miles out to sea. Bombs and darts were dropped, but apparently without serious effect. An aeroplane and a seaplane attacked the German ships off Lowestoft, dropping heavy bombs. Four enemy submarines were also attacked by bombs.

One seaplane came under heavy fire from the hostile fleet, but the pilot, although seriously wounded, succeeded in bringing his machine safely back to land. One pilot who is reported to have attacked a Zeppelin off Lowestoft did not return.

In the course of the fight with the warships Flight-Lieutenant C. Smith, after vainly pursuing a Zeppelin, sighted the German fleet and attacked, dropping bombs to such good purpose that the submarines submerged to get out of the way; and Squadron-Commander D. Oliver flew along the enemy line dropping bombs, although under heavy fire all the time.

In the battle of Jutland, which gave the enemy such a lesson that he never after risked meeting the British fleet, nor apparently ever sought to catch any separate division of it by stratagem, although every opportunity was afforded by our frequent excursions to German waters, saw very little work by aircraft. The principal reason for this was the obscure weather, making aerial reconnaissance impossible save on one or two minor occasions. In the original dispatch from Admiral Jellicoe the only reference to aircraft in this battle was contained in Admiral Beatty's report:—

> I ordered Engadine to send up a seaplane and scout to NNE. This order was carried out very quickly, and by 3.8 p.m. a seaplane, with Flight-Lieutenant F. J. Rutland as pilot, and Assistant-Pay master G. S. Trewin as observer, was well under way: her first reports of the enemy were received at Engadine about 3.30. Owing to clouds it was necessary to fly very low, and in order to identify four enemy light cruisers the seaplane had to fly at a height of 900 feet within 3,000 yards of them, the light cruisers opening fire on her with every gun that would bear. This in no way interfered with the clarity of their reports, and both Flight-Lieutenant Rutland and Assistant-Paymaster Trewin are to be congratulated on their achievement, which indicates that seaplanes under such circumstances are of distinct value.

Zeppelins are also mentioned later, but only as a subject of surmise. None were seen.

Sensational stories appeared in the press at the time, on the strength of real or fictitious interviews with petty officers and men of the fleet, to the effect that the enemy used Zeppelins and aeroplanes in this action. One has heard before of the lively spirit with which Jack Tar will "pull the leg" of a newspaper man. At all events subsequent official reports were explicit: no Zeppelins put in an appearance. And a Zeppelin officer definitely stated to a member of the Allied Naval Commission in German waters after the Armistice was arranged:—

> It is not true that we had Zeppelin reconnaissance on May 31st, the day of the battle. The High Sea Fleet would never have allowed itself to be drawn into action with your Battle Fleet if

we had had aerial observation to tell us how near they were. We planned to have Zeppelins out on that day, but the weather was not favourable. We did have them the day after the battle, but they were of not much use then.

At the end of the battle mist and darkness enabled the German fleet to escape. They naturally did not boast of this afterwards, but it is beyond doubt that our battleships patrolled to and fro for hours in every likely direction, and if the Germans had wanted a fight to a finish they could have had it. Moreover, in the atmospheric conditions then prevailing, reconnaissance by air would have been absolutely useless, either to us or to the enemy.

On November 11, 1916, the Admiralty announced:—

With reference to the attack on Ostend and Zeebrugge, carried out by a squadron of naval aeroplanes on November 10th, one of our machines (Flight-Lieutenant G. G. Hodge) has failed to return. A Berlin official report states that he has been taken prisoner. All the other machines returned safely.

On the 16th seaplanes and aeroplanes made a further attack, causing damage and a big fire; and again on the 22nd of the month. But every few days similar reports were issued, and it would be outside the province of this book to reproduce them.

The Eastern Mediterranean station afforded our airmen plenty of opportunity for adventure. Flight-Commander A. W. Clemson and Sub-Lieutenant J. L. Kerby were awarded the D.S.C. in recognition of their gallantry on February 28, 1917, when they carried out a reconnaissance of Bayak and Damascus in a seaplane. During the flight they crossed two mountain ranges whose lowest ridges are 4,000 feet high, and brought back valuable information.

An action between three British seaplanes and five German destroyers took place on April 23, 1917, off Dunkirk. The leading aeroplane attacked, dropping 16 bombs, one of which went home. The remaining four destroyers scattered, and were attacked by the two other seaplanes, which dropped 32 bombs on them. The leading destroyer was observed to take a list to port and remain stationary. An enemy seaplane now came up and attacked ours, but was easily driven off. So far as our reconnaissance could make out, only four destroyers returned to Zeebrugge, and it is supposed that the other one sank.

A curious minor phase of the new warfare was illustrated on the same day by the capture by a Zeppelin airship of the Norwegian barque *Royal* (Captain Erikssen). Soon after noon, when the ship was outside Hanstholm, they saw a Zeppelin, which came down low and ordered the barque to stop. The sailors left the ship in lifeboats, and the Zeppelin moored on the surface and sent three Germans on board. The prize was taken to Cuxhaven, escorted by the airship. While the Zeppelin was taking possession of the prize the Germans stood ready with bombs in order to prevent resistance.

The bar to the D.S.O. was awarded to Squadron-Commander K. S. Savory, and the D.S.C. to Flight-Lieutenant H. McClelland and Lieutenant F.T. Rawlings, who on July 9, 1917, during an operation against the German Turkish fleet off Constantinople, attacked from the height of only 800 feet and obtained hits on the *Goeben* and other warships. Big explosions were caused, and fire broke out. The War Office was also bombed. The full story of this raid will be found in the chapter on Bombing.

General Smuts relates how on Lake Tanganyika the Germans displayed much foresight in building more powerful ships than either we or the Belgians did, and so dominated 750 miles of frontier. The Belgians after a good deal of trouble got some seaplanes all the way up the Congo right across the African continent. Once the parts were assembled, and the machines were in the air, short work was made of German supremacy on Lake Tanganyika. The German "*askaris*" had a horror of the "Bird," as they called the aeroplane. General Smuts asked a German non-commissioned officer as to his views on the subject. When he was standing on the bank of a river that was full of crocodiles, was the reply, and he saw the "Bird" coming, he was at first on the point of jumping into the river.

On September 19, 1917, a Henry Farman with Flight Sub-Lieutenant Parker and Sub-Lieutenant Greenwood on board, attacked a U-boat near Strati, Mt. Athos, dropping two big delay-fuse bombs, both of which struck the water within ten yards of the conning tower. This was near enough to stun the crew, apart from material damage to the vessel. One 100-lb. bomb bursting eight feet from a submarine will sink her. The submarine attacked on this occasion sank and was not again seen.

Flight-Lieutenants Hobbs and Dickey in a large "America" seaplane, on September 28th, over the North Sea, sighted a submarine on the surface. Having fired recognition signals and received no answer, they dropped one 230-lb. bomb. The submarine fired one shell at them, which burst about 50 feet from the seaplane and tore a hole in it. Three more submarines were then sighted ahead of the seaplane in line abreast followed by three destroyers. All six vessels opened fire on the British seaplane, and three German seaplanes overhead were prevented from joining in the attack by the barrage put up by the destroyers. The seaplane continued her attack on the damaged submarine and dropped a second large bomb, which exploded close to the bow. The submarine immediately sank, and a large quantity of wreckage was thrown up.

One of our small airships out on patrol in September, 1917, came across the torpedoed S.S. *Kouang*, 15 miles south of the Lizard, and escorted her. A submarine was then sighted, and the airship headed towards her and dropped two 100-lb. bombs with delay-action fuses in front of the position where the submarine had submerged. Oil rose to the surface in such quantities as to cover about one square mile, and there is no doubt that the submarine was destroyed.

Flight-Commander Struthers, who was in command of the airship, had by this date on this station spent 970 hours in the air, in recognition of which and of the several occasions when he had bombed submarines he was awarded the D.S.O.

Many pages could be filled with the incidents of our aircraft anti-submarine work. On one occasion two British seaplanes over the North Sea saw a submarine travelling fast on the surface. Two men were seen in the conning tower. The seaplanes came down to about 800 feet, and the leading machine dropped a bomb which burst on the starboard side of the submarine, which heeled slowly over to port and remained in that position. The bow lifted as she stopped and began to sink. The second aeroplane then dropped a bomb which burst in front of the conning tower. A third bomb effected the complete destruction of the enemy.

During an engagement between German, British, and French destroyers on October 27, 1917, 17 enemy aircraft flew over and dropped bombs, wounding six seamen. The aircraft were scattered by our gunfire.

Our large seaplanes and our "Blimps" and C.P. airships patrolling hour after hour in the North Sea, the Channel, and the Irish Sea, or escorting merchantmen, frequently picked up the S.O.S. sent out by torpedoed or threatened ships, and these messages often proved to be the call to action, and at times spelt punishment for the enemy. Sometimes the aircraft arriving on the scene would find nothing left but a boatload or two of sailors or some floating bodies and wreckage.

If the actual number of German submarines sunk by our aircraft was not immense—it was certainly considerable—the success of the work is to be measured also by the number of times it prevented submarines from attacking. The following figures give a slight idea of the extent of these operations. They refer only to one period, April 1 to October 31, 1918.

Total number of hours flown		39,102
Hostile submarines sighted		216
,,	,, attacked	189
Hostile aircraft attacked		351
,,	,, destroyed	184
,,	,, damaged	151
Mines spotted		69
,,	destroyed by aircraft	32
Number of bombs dropped		15,313
,,	convoy flights	3,441

These figures are exclusive of the work in the Mediterranean.

For inshore work the D.H.6, an automatically stable aeroplane, largely used for tuition purposes, was much in evidence; but the more powerful D.H.4 and D.H.9, and the Short and other seaplanes, were our chief strength. Outside the 30 miles limit the big seaplanes and airships did the work. The large flying boat came into use on the East Coast—on a large scale that is—early in 1917. There was the H.I 2, and later the big F type driven by two 350-H.P. Rolls Royce engines.

Some years before the war the Royal Naval Air Service had experimented with torpedoes from seaplanes, and in 1918 special machines each carrying one torpedo were commissioned. In due time, no doubt, we should have employed these against the German fleet itself. The technical difficulties that had to be overcome before the torpedo plane could be considered a success were very formidable. The mere discharge of the huge missile—an 18-inch torpedo and gear weigh 1,095 lbs.—was a tremendous tax on the machine, and usually called for a certain amount of expert piloting. The method of attack was to come down from the clouds at high speed, get close to the target, release the torpedo, and soar aloft again. In one such attack we torpedoed and sank a Turkish transport carrying 3,000 troops.

When the German fleet surrendered, an aeroplane "mother-ship" carrying twenty of these machines met the enemy out at sea, prepared

H.M.S. *Argus* the Aeroplane Carrier

A Ship's Aeroplane Flying Over the Deck of H.M.S. *Argus* Preparatory to Making a Landing

for any event.

Unlike other vehicles, the aeroplane's flight is strictly limited by the amount of fuel it can carry; and long excursions out at sea can only be made at great risk. Even if the floats or the boat under-carriage were satisfactory, there would remain the problem of fuel replenishment. The very big aeroplanes with two or more engines can travel great distances on one load, and our big flying boats did a vast amount of patrol work round the coasts, even penetrating into the Bight of Heligoland. Many years ago the need for providing ships with means of aerial reconnaissance always at hand was seen, and in England and America aeroplanes ascended from specially constructed decks.

Another experiment was the cable-way, by which a light aeroplane provided with a securing contrivance on the top plane came to rest under a stretched cable. The war saw a big development of the aeroplane "mother-ship," some types of which carried a regular aerodrome of appliances, and special arrangements for hauling inboard aeroplanes forced to descend to the water. But this was not enough, and most war-ships larger than destroyers carried one or two scouts that could be flown from a platform over the gun turret, the platform being about 40 feet in length. The machines used in many cases were ordinary fighting scouts provided for the contingency of coming down in the water with air-bags in the under-carriage. These air-bags were inflated by a simple quick operation by the pilot when within 500 feet of the water. The machine having alighted, the air-bags could be "trimmed," so that the machine would float on an even keel.

A vast amount of experimenting was necessary before any of these arrangements could be deemed satisfactory, and lives were sacrificed in trial flights where niceties of fifths of a second had to be observed in the timing. Flight-Commander Dunning lost his life in this way in the autumn of 1917.

Until the summer of 1918 German airships were often able to venture out into the North Sea, but our deck-planes by that time began to make matters too warm for them, and their only security lay in maintaining such a great altitude that our machines were prevented from getting to close quarters while the enemy made for home. This was a special case that demanded special treatment, and in the chapter on Zeppelins will be found a description of the treatment which succeeded in bringing the enemy to book in the case of the last Zeppelin of the war. What developments would have been seen if the war had continued cannot be said, but it is certain that the enemy would have been deprived of the means of aerial reconnaissance in the North Sea.

Some of our Naval airmen had unpleasant adventures through forced landings on the sea, and there were several occasions when they remained afloat for two or three days, sending out wireless calls for help or dispatching pigeons with messages. A big French machine was afloat on one occasion for 80 hours, with a floating anchor out in a rough sea. One day in September, 1918, one of our seaplanes on submarine patrol in the North Sea had to descend about five miles from the Scottish coast. A heavy sea was running, and the machine was in great danger of breaking up. The airmen released a pigeon at 4 p.m. Twenty-two minutes later the bird reached its loft about 22 miles away, the assistance requested was sent, and the crew of the seaplane, who were found clinging to what was now a mere wreck, were rescued.

A patrol encountered some German seaplanes, and the following messages were dispatched by pigeon and received at the base in Flanders:—

Short shot down ten miles NNE. of Nieuport. One Hun down. My tanks shot. French T.B.D. on its way. Send fighters quick.

Then followed another pigeon with—

Message 3. Am shot down. Hit in tank and radiator. Observer shot. Am unhurt; please send small craft."

Message 4. Machine turning over to port. Have jettisoned everything. Am on wing-tip. Sea calm. Machine has seemingly steadied. Nothing in sight. I think machine will float a long time. Send small craft at once. Land 'bus has just made one circuit, but I don't think he saw me. My love to my mother. Tell her I am not worrying. If machine sinks I will swim to a buoy close by.

The crew of a flying boat being in difficulties dispatched a pigeon. There was a strong head wind, against which the bird made very slow progress. He fought his way homeward and passed the coast, but fell dead within a few miles of home. The message was delivered, however, and the crew were saved.

Two acts of bravery incidental to fighting aircraft and U-boats are here included. The Royal Humane Society awarded its medal to Lieutenant J. S. Hodges for his gallant attempt to save Lieutenant Fedden, whose aeroplane came down in the sea 800 yards from the shore on

January 7th. Lieutenant Hodges flew out and dropped into the sea where he supported Lieutenant Fedden for 35 minutes, when a boat reached them. But when landed Lieutenant Fedden was found to be dead.

The King awarded the Albert Medal to Flight-Lieutenant V. A. Watson and the Albert Medal in gold to Air Mechanic H.V. Robinson and Boy Mech. E. E. Steere:

. . . . on the occasion of an accident to one of His Majesty's airships, which resulted in a fire breaking out on board her. Flight-Lieutenant Watson, who was the senior officer on the spot, immediately rushed up to the car of the airship under the impression that one of the crew was still in it, although he was well aware that there were heavy bombs attached to the airship, which it was impossible to remove owing to the nearness of the fire, and which were almost certain to explode at any moment on account of the heat. Having satisfied himself that there was in fact no one in the car, he turned away to render assistance elsewhere, and at that moment one of the bombs exploded, a portion of it shattering Lieutenant Watson's right arm at the elbow. The arm had to be amputated almost immediately.

A.M. Robinson and Boy Mech. Steere, on the occasion of an accident to one of H.M. airships, which caused a fire to break out, approached the burning airship without hesitation, extricated the pilot and two members of the crew, all of whom were seriously injured, and then undipped the bombs from the burning car and carried them out of reach of the fire. As the bombs were surrounded by flames, and were so hot that they scorched the men's hands as they carried them, they must have expected the bombs to explode.

The adventures of the German warships the *Goeben* and *Breslau*, gave us many opportunities of testing the possibilities of naval aircraft. The ships came out of the Dardanelles on January 20, 1918, and from that date until January 29th our aeroplanes made 270 flights over them, dropping 15 tons of explosives, and obtaining sixteen direct hits. Owing to the attentions of our aviators the *Breslau*, steering a zigzag course, struck a mine and sank. The *Goeben* was also damaged by a mine, but she re-entered the Straits and ran lightly aground.

At dawn the following day five of our bombing machines set out and dropped 10 heavy bombs on the estimated position, the light being too bad to see the ship. About noon 14 machines set out, one after another, and dropped bombs; and the same night nine machines visited the *Goeben*. Continuous anti-aircraft fire was directed on our machines from shore batteries and from the *Goeben*. Six heavy bombs were dropped on the ship, and an explosion took place near her. On the following day one of our machines secured a direct hit amidships which certainly did much damage. On one occasion one of our seaplanes had to come down near Lemnos, and on gliding to the surface six shots were fired at her from a submarine. Next day this machine was found by a search party in a seaplane and taken in tow.

Subsequent operations resulted in further hits on the *Goeben* and in damage to boats in her vicinity; but, as we know, she was able to get away, the bad weather interfering greatly with our aerial work, and our seaplanes not carrying anything heavy enough to do material damage to such a heavily-armoured ship.

A Short seaplane sighted a U-boat near our coast one morning. The submarine was about 10 miles away, but figures could be discerned on her deck. The aeroplane made for the spot, coming steadily down to about 1,000 feet, and dropped a bomb just after the submarine left the surface. She then dropped another bomb, and the submarine was not seen again. This probably saved a convoy which was at that moment approaching the spot.

A "regular dog-fight" took place on June 4th, when five British seaplanes set out from an East Coast base on patrol. When near Ter-schelling one of the seaplanes was forced to descend owing to a broken petrol pipe. The others circled round the damaged craft, but sighting five hostile machines, set off in pursuit. They failed to bring these to action, however, and returned to the damaged machine, which was meanwhile being repaired. Two other German seaplanes appeared and were soon driven off.

Probably they went off for help, for ten machines soon came on the scene and offered battle. In the fight between our four and the enemy ten two of the latter were crashed into the sea, one bursting into flames as it fell. A British seaplane was damaged and forced to land in Vlieland. In this fight one of our observers was shot dead. His pilot continued to fly the machine, and was attacked from the rear and below by four of the enemy on one side, and three on the other. He dived and put up a running stern fight with the seven, and he eventually succeeded in breaking clear.

While climbing again to rejoin the other British machines the petrol pipe of this seaplane broke, necessitating a landing 10 miles off the Dutch coast. Thanks to the quickness with which the mechanic made the damage good, the seaplane was able to resume in 10 minutes and joined two of the other British machines. The first British machine which came down and was being repaired had to be destroyed, and the crew swam ashore.

One of our submarines had an exciting encounter with a German seaplane—a somewhat rare occurrence. From the submarine commander's report we read:—

4.36 p.m.—Sighted an aeroplane about 3 miles SSE. and dived to 80 feet. Three minutes later, while at 85 feet, three bombs were dropped right overhead, and very shortly afterwards three more, and five minutes later four more. At 5.30 I decided to come to the surface for sights. Nothing could be seen of aeroplane, but before gun could be got ready a biplane was sighted very close planing down on us at great speed with engine stopped. I steered N. at low speed, and at 6.15 p.m. decided to rise and get gun into action. I got under way on the north course at ten knots with upper deck awash. The biplane was sighted on starboard bow at 6.20 p.m., and we opened fire at 3,000 yards. The biplane immediately sheered off and kept out of range after eighth round, and then kept three miles astern of us. Shortly after, another aeroplane was sighted ESE. two or three miles, and I dived to 80 feet in less than two minutes heading south. At 9.15 p.m. we heard nine distinct explosions in quick succession, and I decided to remain down until dark.

Flight-Commander Pattison was piloting a large seaplane on May 10th, when in rather thick weather he sighted a Zeppelin. The seaplane attacked and the Zeppelin began to rise rapidly, throwing out bombs indiscriminately and discharging a quantity of water ballast. She also threw out a smoke screen. Nevertheless the seaplane hung on, and opened fire, the duel proceeding and taking both craft higher and higher, and the Zeppelin sacrificing every portable article in a vain endeavour to outclimb its assailant.

After about 35 minutes the Zeppelin was in full retreat towards the German coast. Then several enemy destroyers arrived on the scene and opened fire with anti-aircraft guns. They broke the seaplane's oil-pipe, and she had to descend to the water for repairs. This was done sufficiently well with tape to enable her to get away again.

One of our seaplanes sighted two steamers and the conning tower of a U-boat which was obviously getting into position to attack. The seaplane warned the ships, one of which was a hospital ship, and then dropped three 100-lb. bombs on the U-boat about two minutes after it had submerged. In about five minutes more there was a great up-heaval of the sea, and the submarine was not seen again.

Kite-balloons towed by warships proved very useful as a counter to the submarine. One of them in May, 1918, sighted a U-boat. Depth charges were dropped and the submarine was compelled to change its position. An hour later a submarine was observed to break surface and begin shelling a sailing ship. The balloon was towed rapidly to the spot, but meanwhile the towing vessel forced the submarine to cease firing and submerge. Aided by the balloon the towing ship got over the submarine and dropped nine depth charges. The submarine was completely wrecked.

A German submarine escaped on one occasion owing to an ir-ritating mishap. The officers in an observation balloon towed by a destroyer and weathering a net wind of 60 miles per hour, saw a periscope clearly only a mile distant, although it was not visible from the deck of the destroyer. At the very moment of telephoning the presence and exact position of the enemy, the snatch-block taking the balloon cable gave way, thus deranging the telephone; and the submarine escaped.

At the Armistice period fifty British warships were equipped with observation balloons.

CHAPTER 19

Heroic Experimenters

Some of the most daring flights have been far from the battle lines and the sound of the guns. The full story of experimental work during the war will probably never be told. Every flight is, of course, recorded in the Log Books of the aerodromes, where such details as petrol consumption, duration of flight, service of each engine, and other matters are entered. But no one will ever collect all these, and tell the story from the pilots' point of view. Occasionally, however, the veil of official secrecy or the oblivion due to their remoteness from the all-absorbing theatres of the war is pierced, as when some dramatic or tragic event marks another milestone in the death-strewn path of progress.

Every new machine has to be tested in the air. What is more, every new type must be tried; and the general public have very little idea of the number of new types whose unfitness for service has had to be proved by repeated trials in the air by pilots whose names are unknown outside their own immediate circle. Some of these pilots do nothing else. Certainly the work is interesting to the enthusiast; but it is not without peril.

The mere testing of established types entails risks. Thus Lieutenant Harry Fleming, one of the best-known pilots and instructors of 1911-12, was killed in testing a new machine. Lieutenant R. T. Gates, well known to visitors who flocked to pre-war Hendon flying meetings, was killed in the early days of the war during an experimental night flight, one of the many whose lives were laid down to make safer the work of the Zeppelin destroyers of a later period of the war. It would be impossible to give a complete list of similar sacrifices. All that can be done is to mention a few whose names come first to the mind in this connection.

One of the most remarkable occurrences was the last flight, in the summer of 1916, of Wing-Commander Nevill Usborne and Squadron-Commander de Courcy Ireland, both officers of great experience, the former a scientific experimenter, the latter an exceptionally skilful and daring pilot.

Rather than send others, they made the experiment themselves. The contrivance was an entirely new departure in the realm of aeronautics. Now, no matter how careful are the preliminary calculations in such a case, it is impossible to make completely certain that all risk of mishap has been foreseen. In this instance everything that could be tried on the ground had been tried. The experiment was not hurried forward unduly, and every detail and possibility were discussed over and over again. When it was decided to make the practical test it seemed that every danger had been foreseen and guarded against.

The object of the experiment was to secure for an aeroplane the rapid attainment of high altitude, so that on the receipt of warning of the approach of hostile aircraft defending machines could be ready to meet them at or about their level. The means employed was a balloon of sufficient buoyancy to carry aloft an aeroplane with pilot and gunner. Sufficient altitude having been attained, the aeroplane was to be detached from the balloon, the latter thus cut adrift and lost. The aero-plane was suspended from the balloon at two points with quick-release gear. In the experiment De Courcy Ireland was the pilot and Usborne the passenger.

Arrived at a height of several thousand feet the moment came to test the apparatus. But the quick-release gear proved faulty. The experimenters probably conversed for a few moments by signs; and then, apparently, De Courcy Ireland left the pilot's seat and climbed out on one of the planes to make the necessary adjustments. Exactly what then happened will never be certainly known; it is surmised from the evidence collected afterwards that in the act of adjusting the mechanism he was thrown off the machine, which then became un-manageable. Apparently, however, Wing-Commander Usborne climbed into the pilot's seat, and attempted vainly to get the machine into control. The machine with his dead body fell at a considerable distance from the spot where De Courcy Ireland was found.

In 1918 aeroplanes were taken up by our big rigid airships and then released; but success was not attained without unfortunate accidents during experiments.

Another occasion for experiments has been the desire to provide our airmen with means of escape from a wrecked aeroplane or airship.

It is not a difficult matter to descend in a parachute from an observation balloon, or from a spherical balloon, although the first essay is a distinct trial to the nerves. There is, however, but a small element of danger; some performing parachutists have made over 300 descents without more injury than an occasional bruise or slight cut. Provided the apparatus be carefully examined for faulty material or attachments, the only risk is in the nature of the ground upon which the parachute descends. A landing in a tree, for example, may be dangerous, and any confusion with buildings, glass or other, may lead to bruises or cuts. And it is necessary for the parachutist to be a swimmer in case the parachute, drifting helplessly with the wind, descends in a lake or reservoir. A quick-release gear is desirable in any case, for if the lateral motion with the wind be more than five or six miles per hour the parachutist is dragged along the ground.

In the testing of new parachute types there is obviously an element of the unknown, and the war gave occasion for the invention of various quick-opening parachutes, and parachutes packed into smaller compass than those previously employed for show purposes. All these had to be repeatedly tested.

During the war hundreds of safe descents were made from observation balloons set on fire by the enemy, although in a few cases such descents ended fatally. It must always be remembered, however, that descent by parachute is made to avoid either certain death or certain capture.

In support of the argument in favour of carrying parachutes on aircraft innumerable occurrences could be quoted. Take, for example, the Zeppelin airship wrecked in a rain-squall off Heligoland before the war. On that occasion a sudden load of rain-water, combined with loss of buoyancy through chill, caused the ship to take on a downward run. All the ballast on board would not save it; but it is almost certain that if, in addition to the ballast, ten or a dozen of the crew could have descended by parachutes, thus suddenly lightening the ship by half or three-quarters of a ton, the fall would have been checked. The jettisoned crew themselves would probably have been saved by the warships that were standing by.

The utility of parachutes for descent from aeroplane is less certain, because in so many cases it would be impossible to preserve the apparatus intact in the circumstances—whatever they might be—compelling the abandonment of the aeroplane. The value of experiment, however, was obvious; and as a matter of fact, before the war was over we were to see the successful employment of parachutes from aeroplanes in action.

One of the first aviators to put this to the test was Major F. W. Goodden, a pre-war aviator who was employed during the war by the Royal Aircraft Factory for experimental work. Major Goodden lost his life while on another experiment on January 28, 1917.

Captain C. F. Collett on January 13, 1917, left an aeroplane, travelling at 60 miles per hour at a height of 600 feet, in a parachute.

A notable experiment was made by Colonel (now Brigadier-General) E. M. Maitland, the well-known aeronaut who, by the way, was one of the author's companions in the British long-distance record balloon voyage (London to Mateki Derevni, Russia) in November, 1908. Colonel Maitland had made numerous parachute descents, and had reached the stage when, as he confessed one day, "I can no longer do it without my knees shaking while I am getting ready to jump clear." But he was determined to test for himself a fall from a great altitude with a Service parachute of a small size that would come down rather quickly.

He ascended in a balloon with Flight-Commander J. Dunville, one of the leading balloonists in Royal Aero Club pre-war sport, and Flight-Commander Corbett Wilson. Arrived at a height of 10,800 feet, the balloon alone in the immensity of the sky, Colonel Maitland jumped off, disaster having been narrowly averted by Corbett Wilson perceiving in the nick of time a fault in the attachment of the parachute. Picture the scene. Preparations coolly made, one of the crew standing by with the valve-line ready to pull the valve open and let the gas out to check the sudden upward bound of the balloon relieved of the weight of a man. Few words are spoken; a joke or two. The parachutist climbs to the brim of the basket and sits outside.

"Are you ready?"

"Yes."

He jumps clear, and his two comrades gazing anxiously down, breathless until they see the parachute open, quite forget their own case and omit to pull the valve-line.

"That's all right!" both exclaim, as they see the white disc develop against the dull background of the earth. But they continue to watch until they can see it no longer. After Colonel Maitland left the balloon, the latter ascended in 14 minutes to 13,300 feet, a very ordinary rise.

Colonel Maitland descended at a rate of 12 feet per second, which, from so great a height, meant a rather rapid transition from low to high pressure. Indeed while falling and after he landed he felt discomfort. Nevertheless, the experiment was a complete success. The rate of fall could, of course, be reduced by using a somewhat bigger parachute than one of 25 feet diameter; and it is worthy of record here that on one occasion a fall from 10,000 feet occupied 35 minutes. Frau Poitevin took 43 minutes to descend 5,500 feet in a parachute. A parachute about 35 feet in diameter flat, or about 28 feet in diameter arched, will give so much support to a man that with its aid he can fall from a great height without alighting so heavily as to be hurt.

Some time before the war Colonel Maitland made a parachute descent from a height of some thousands of feet from an Army airship piloted by Major Waterlow, R.E., this being the first experiment of this kind.

Testing a quick-opening parachute, Major T. Orde Lees and the Hon. Lieutenant E. Bowen, on November 11, 1917, safely descended from the Tower Bridge, the distance to the water being only 153 feet. A similar experiment was made in August, 1916, by Sir Bryan Leighton, Bart., who, using a quick-opening type of parachute, left an airship going at full speed at a height of only 800 feet, and made a perfect landing.

One of the best-known French aeroplane designers, Gaston Caudron, was killed during an experimental flight on a new war machine. Captain Gordon-Bell, one of our earlier and best-known pilots was killed in France in the summer of 1918, testing a new machine.

In the list of awards issued on January 8, 1918, of the Medal of the Order of the British Empire for services in connection with the war in which great courage or self-sacrifice has been displayed, the following appeared: "*Herbert Sykes, for courage in testing aircraft in spite of severe accidents.*"

Willingness to take risks instead of deputing sub-ordinates for them is a characteristic of the Air Service. Thus two well-known pilots having a certain machine to test, and greatly distrusting it—tossed up for the "privilege." Both took it in turn, however, and they then pointed out certain defects in the design, which were remedied.

Lieutenant Harold Rosher's death is worthy of a place in this chapter. He insisted upon taking the place of a pilot in a newly-repaired machine. It crashed, and he was killed. (*With the Flying Squadron* by Harold Rosher also published by Leonaur.)

CHAPTER 20

Casualties in the Third Arm

How different was the reality of war from expectations was manifested in the casualties in the Flying Services. While aeronautical enthusiasts had been proclaiming the miracles that aviators would perform in war, there were not wanting high military and political authorities who harped insistently upon the danger to the airmen-danger that they asserted would be almost if not quite prohibitive. One voice had proclaimed in the Council Chamber that no one need feel disquieted at the thought of the rumoured preparations by a rival nation to contrive our defeat by air, for every hostile aircraft that ventured over England would undoubtedly be shot down, that we had the necessary armament!

At that time some of the authorities were extravagantly anxious to find an effective answer to aircraft, and in one case, which the reader can verify by referring to the records of the years 1912-1914, this cupidity went to so extreme a length that they were readily imposed upon by a pretended inventor bent on fooling their unscientific minds. But apart from that incident, they were quite sure that the anti-aircraft means at their disposal made operations by aircraft exceedingly difficult. They were wrong.

The first squadrons of British airmen who went to the Front were convinced that they would never see their homes again. Many were, indeed, killed in the first few months; but the casualties were nothing like the expectations based upon the calculations of the authorities already mentioned.

As already said, the strictly military view was that reconnaissance could be made with reasonable safety at a height of not less than 3,000 feet, an opinion that was just as erroneous in its way as the idea that aircraft would inevitably fall victim to gunfire from below.

It is due to the airmen to testify that although, more than other arms of the Service represented in the small British force that first went to France, they felt they were doomed to destruction, there was never a hint of wavering and hesitation. And civilian aviators throughout the land importuned for the privilege of serving their country; and the press to join up became embarrassing.

This was before the first casualty lists were published, or people had any reliable data to form an estimate of the danger of war-flying. Then, when it was discovered that the Royal Flying Corps was not "wiped out," and that many even of the first three squadrons survived the retreat to Paris and the push back again—in short, that the casualties were not nearly so great in the aerial arm as in certain infantry brigades, people went to the opposite extreme and said that flying was the safest job at the Front! There were periods afterwards when the percentage of casualties became heavy; but there was never any diminution in the stream of applicants to join.

Here and there incidents almost justified the view that the airman's work was not excessively dangerous, as when one saw 10 machine-guns pounding away at an enemy aeroplane, so near that the pilot's face was recognizable, and without getting a hit even on the wings of the machine, and our own machines sometimes returned scatheless after being subjected at close range to terrific machine-gun fire.

At the Battle of Neuve Chapelle the casualties among the Royal Flying Corps were heavy. But we must bear in mind the exceptional intensity of the struggle, and we ought reasonably to make a deduction for preventable casualties—some of those due to our own artillery firing at our own airmen. In the early part of the war, through lack of understanding of aircraft on the part of a number of brigade commanders, several of our machines were brought down and the pilots and observers killed. Our airmen knew when they went up that they would be shot at by friend as well as by foe.

Also, in the first year they were much overworked—especially the more reliable and skilful of them. In individual cases pilots have had an average of more than six hours' flying per day for a fortnight at a stretch. Throughout the Service early in the war the average per pilot per day is said to have been five hours' flying—a figure which was afterwards brought down to three hours. Even the latter amount puts a severe strain on the average pilot, so that at the end of three months' war service he ought to have a good spell of leave.

"For the first three months at the Front," said one of our leading aviators to the author, "you are inuring yourself to being under fire continuously in the air. By the end of that time you accept the bursting of shrapnel and high explosives in your vicinity with equanimity. But immediately then you begin to feel worn out, and if you are kept too long at it your work suffers, at first imperceptibly, but afterwards quite badly."

The mileage flown in the early part of the war must be recorded here, because only by the consideration of such facts is one able to appreciate fully the work of our men and the adventures they faced.

Between the memorable flight to France on August 14th till September 10th, Sir John French states in his first dispatch, "a daily average of more than nine reconnaissance flights of over 100 miles each has been maintained." Further details were given by "Eyewitness," an official narrator of events, a few days later.

Up to September 21st the air mileage made by our airmen since the beginning of the war amounted to 87,000 miles, an average of 2,000 miles per day. The total time spent in the air was 1,400 hours.

Some more remarkable figures were given at the end of January, 1915, relating to the French Air Service:—

The whole of the old and new squadrons carried out about 10,000 reconnaissances during eight months of war, corresponding to more than 18,000 hours of flight. In order to form an idea of what was accomplished it is sufficient to observe that these flights put together represent a distance traversed of 1,800,000 kilometres, or 45 times round the world.

These remarkable results were not obtained without grievous losses, which are comparable to, and often more severe than, those of other arms so far as the numbers of killed and wounded and missing is concerned.

Writing on February 2, 1915, Sir John French states:—

During the period under report (about two months) the Royal Flying Corps has again performed splendid service. Although the weather was almost uniformly bad and the machines suffered from constant exposure, there have been only thirteen days on which no actual reconnaissance has been effected. Approximately one hundred thousand miles have been flown. In addition to the daily and constant work of reconnaissance and co-operation with the artillery, a number of aerial combats have been fought, raids carried out, detrainments harassed, parks and petrol depots bombed, etc. Various successful bomb-dropping raids have been carried out, usually against the enemy's aircraft material. The principle of attacking hostile aircraft whenever and wherever seen (unless highly important information is being delivered) has been adhered to, and has resulted in the moral fact that enemy machines invariably beat immediate retreat when chased. Five German aeroplanes are known to have been brought to the ground, and it would appear probable that others, though they have managed to reach their own lines, have done so in a considerably damaged condition.

Continuing on this subject and dealing with the period in which the battle of Neuve Chapelle was fought, Sir John French said:—

There have been only eight days during the period under review (February 2nd till early April) in which reconnaissances have not been made. A total of approximately 130,000 miles have been flown—almost entirely over the enemy's lines.

This was in the winter, be it remembered. The amount of flying in fine weather in the later days of the war, when the strength of the Flying Services had been increased manifold, was almost beyond belief.

The casualties among our flyers seemed light only because most people had anticipated that they would be something like 100 per cent, of the strength. By the autumn of 1915 the proportion of Flying Corps officers killed exceeded the proportionate losses of any other corps, with the exception of particular regiments which, in the fiercer battles, lost nearly all their officers. But as the war proceeded, and German anti-aircraft gunnery improved, the risks run by aviators increased. And the risks, of course, were incurred continually and during the periods between the big "pushes" and raids when the men in the trenches enjoyed a respite.

Direct hits were made on aeroplanes by the middle of 1915 at a height of 15,000 feet, yet in spite of that our flyers would on occasion risk coming down to less than 200 feet, where, if safe from the high-range guns, they were in greater peril from machine-guns.

Everyone will recognize that the work of the airman has its compensations. In the first place it is less monotonous than some services, and—a very appreciable factor—it is of a nature to allow of fairly comfortable night billets. But our flying men, it must not be forgotten, face a certain amount of danger from the day their training is begun at home. Risks are incurred in learning to fly—risks that are not excessive and are slowly but surely diminishing.

There was an ebb and flow in casualties. At one period the much-exaggerated Fokker made fighting in the air hotter, and for a few weeks increased the losses. But it was soon overcome. A more serious situation arose in the spring of 1917, the Germans having by that time put a large number of very fast machines into commission. British casualties were heavy, and on many days the balance of losses was against us. On the other hand, the work accomplished was of vital importance, and our men simply refused to permit heavy casualties to prevent its execution. The casualties were worthwhile; although it could doubtless be shown that some of them might have been prevented had our supplies of the latest machines been unhindered.

The *Guerre Aerienne* calculated for the year 1916 that the Allies carried out 750 bombardments, and that in that year the French brought down 450 enemy machines and the British 250. Eighty-one German observation balloons were destroyed. One authority estimated that in the first three years of the war the Germans lost 2,300 aeroplanes and the Allies 1,400.

During July, 1917, the British Air Services on the Western Front brought down 122 German aeroplanes and drove down 120 out of control. In April the British alone destroyed 110 German aeroplanes and drove down 161, besides destroying 16 observation balloons: and the French destroyed 60 German aeroplanes, drove down 34, and destroyed 5 balloons. In the same month the British lost 147 aeroplanes, in addition to a few shot down by anti-aircraft guns.

During the year July 1, 1917, to June 30, 1918, 2,150 enemy aircraft were destroyed by the British on the Western Front, and 1,083 were driven down out of control. In the same period R.A.F. units working with the Navy accounted for 628 enemy aircraft. Our missing machines numbered 1,186.

From March 21, 1918, to August 15th the French lost 348 aeroplanes (some of the pilots being taken prisoner). In the same period they destroyed or sent down out of control 1,325 enemy machines and fired 147 observation balloons. In August and September 2,451 aeroplanes were brought down in all theatres of war. Of these 1,962 were enemy machines.

On the Western Front from January 1, 1918, to the end of the war, 3,060 enemy machines were destroyed and 1,174 were driven down. The British on the Western Front lost 1,318 machines "missing," and a few others shot down in our lines. The total British Air Force casualties from April 1st to November 11th were:

	Officers.	Other Ranks.
Killed	1,551	1,129
Wounded	2,357	631
Missing	1,512	225
Interned	45	39

(These figures include accidents at home and abroad.)

The casualties in the Flying Services for the whole period of the war, both before and since the amalgamation of the R.N.A.S. and the R.F.C. were as follows:

	Officers.	Other Ranks.	Total.
Killed	4,579	1,587	6,166
Wounded	5,369	1,876	7,245
Prisoners	2,794	334	3,128
Interned	45	39	84
Total	12,787	3,836	16,623

The casualties shown in these totals include all officers and other ranks serving with the Flying Services during the war.

The strength of the Royal Air Force was——

	1914.	1918.
Officers	285	30,000
Other ranks	1,853	264,000
Aeroplanes	166	21,000
Seaplanes	45	1,300
Airships	4	103

Of the 264,000 "other ranks" 21,000 were flying cadets under training.

CHAPTER 21

The Robinson Quality

1

*Let us remember also those who belong to the most recent military arm,
the keen-eyed and swift-winged knights of the air, who have given to
the world a new type of daring and resourceful heroism.*
The King's address to Parliament and Representatives of the
Dominions, November 19, 1918.

No man has more than one life to give, and in readiness to sacrifice that life the heroism of Warneford, or Robinson, or Moorhouse,
or Ball, or West, or Barker, was no greater than that of hundreds in
the ranks—who mere names in the casualty lists—offered all as deliberately. The deeds of our airmen nevertheless make a stronger appeal
to the imagination, for the work of the airman still has the quality of
rarity.

No man flies without being stimulated by it. Upon the man himself depends the quality of the mental and the moral stimulus obtained; but the dullest and the lowest, each in his degree, responds to
the magic touch. Some mysterious chord in us, long asleep, awakens
and thrills to this new experience. What it is, who can say? By few
recognized, by still fewer expressed, is a deep-seated aspiration to fly,
to make the air man's element as it is the birds'.

It is good for man to attain to new and greater powers. He rejoices
in his dominion of the air; and, as a creature of brain and action, he is
there seen in a mist of glory. Directing his craft through the air, and
exposed to perils that will take advantage of any lack of knowledge
or of skill, he lives "above himself." There is no finer sight than a man
flying in a tempest. Conscious of the imperfections of his craft, and
of the mighty and invisible forces around, he keeps fear down, so that

his eye be not dimmed, nor his brain spinning, nor his hand para-lysed. Then is he supremely happy, caring not whether he be alone or whether the eyes of the people be upon him.

It is commonly supposed that no one can be a good aviator who is not capable of banishing all thought of danger from his mind. But with the exception of a type of very unpromising pupil, there is not an airman who does not in every flight realize that it may possibly be his last. This realization does not spoil his flying or his enjoyment, but it makes him careful to guard against any error or weakness. The thought does not prey on his mind: it is no more than recognition of facts, and he is only lightly conscious of it. The majority of people realize, when travelling by railway or steamboat, the possibility of dis-aster. This realization is keener in some matters than in others, and is usually measured by the amount of risk actually run.

It should be very clear to the mountaineer; to the racing motorist; to the trans-Atlantic voyager during the iceberg season; to the aviator. The aviator need not be an exceptionally courageous man: the ordi-nary mortal filled with the desire to live, fearful of personal injury, may become a good flyer. The aviator who ignores the risks is merely fool-hardy. If the much-admired quality of fearlessness means obliviousness to danger it is the "valour of ignorance": if it be indifference to death because life no longer offers any sweetness, it is probably a symptom of mind or body diseased. The author has known one aviator who had this quality; and he soon gave up flying!

Heroism lies not so much in the action as in the decision to per-form the action. Knowing the risk they ran when flying over enemy country of capture after an enforced landing, airmen undertook long journeys, coolly facing this contingency as well as the danger from the enemy. They did more: they deliberately flew low to see in greater detail the enemy's dispositions, or to drop bombs with accuracy, as did Lieutenant L. G. Hawker, D.S.O., when he dropped bombs on the airship shed at Gontarde from a height of only 200 feet; Collett and Marix, who flew over the Zeppelin harbour at Düsseldorf and per-formed their mission under heavy fire; all these acts were heroic in the conception and decision even more than in the performance.

The single-handed combat with a giant airship at night will always appeal as a feat calculated to daunt the stoutest heart. Imagine Lieu-tenant W. L. Robinson's exaltation of spirit when, over London's 250 square miles of houses and millions of straining eyes, on the night of September 3, 1916, he sighted his quarry and fought a running and unequal fight. Imagine his exhilaration when one of his bombs, aimed coolly and truly, struck home, while the air around him was torn by streams of bullets from the raider's guns. His machine almost involved in the flaming ruin of his mighty enemy, and almost out of control, was then two miles high. The victor looped the loop over and over again in sheer triumph.

What a glory belongs to the man who deliberately faces extreme peril realizing that it is not in vain, and that he is doing something of immense importance to the cause! One of the most splendid examples was that of Lieutenant W. B. Rhodes Moorhouse, V.C., who died of his wounds after dropping bombs on Courtrai Station and railway lines. The enterprise was of vital importance. Forty thousand Germans were in full march on our columns. They were stopped dead by Moorhouse's achievement. But that was not all. It was necessary for our commanders to know that the column had been stopped. Lieutenant Moorhouse had flown low and been badly wounded. But he was resolved to return to our lines and make his report; and return he did in a flight of three-quarters of an hour after being dangerously wounded. He could have saved his life by descending behind the German lines.

The airman is in one respect to be envied above the infantryman. He has the inspiration of single combat. Alone in the sky, and shelled by batteries of "Archies," directed with the sole purpose of bringing him down; playing his own hand in a far greater measure than the captain of a ship steaming into action. The infantryman or the gunner under fire is one of a crowd, and he lacks the peculiar thrill of individual combat.

2

Temperamentally, airmen vary enormously. Flachaire refused a commission until he could win the Legion of Honour. Guynemer was naively and simply proud of himself. All the great exponents of it take delight in the art of flying. Thus, Flachaire rejoiced in introducing a new "stunt," a steep spiral ending in a side-slip upwards, performed on a Nieuport.

Some are quiet and modest to a fault; a few have exhibited a manner almost boastful. Most of them at the Front in a very little while settled down to an apparent phlegm, as if their work were quiet, prosaic and humdrum. If the reader has seen a fighting or a bombing squadron prepare to set out, or in the cold dawn witnessed the artillery observation crews get to work, he will readily agree. The absence of excitement; the calm discussion of weather, of engines, of orders. They might have been files of London policemen setting out to take up positions and "beats."

There is an interesting field of study in the various national types of airmen. The British are, in the author's opinion, best, for they combine courage that on occasion can be almost fanatic, with coolness, care for detail and sound groundwork. The British and French were the first to perceive the fact that if you charge directly at an enemy in the air he will sheer off. They were the first—and the British training manuals bear witness to it—to act on the principle that success often comes from the decision to attack and promptness in acting upon it. In his memoirs Baron von Richthofen, the famous German fighter, says of a British airman—

> He is a dashing fellow. He used to come and pelt Boelcke's flying grounds with bombs; he simply challenged one to battle, and always accepted it. *I hardly ever encountered an Englishman who refused battle.*

And it is the author's conviction that among the British there is a more widespread possession of "battle sense." This, even when our men have been handicapped by inferiority of numbers or of equipment, afforded surprise after surprise. It is the same quality that was shown in the destroyer action in the battle of Jutland, in the boarding affair in the Straits of Dover, and in many sea and land fights. Indeed, the aviator is captain of his own small craft, and is continually called upon to make his decisions and act swiftly.

The American when fully trained (until close to the very end of the war, as was only natural, our American friends had still much to learn, a fact that they frankly acknowledged) being of very much the same blood, is of the same order, as the work of the limited number at the Front amply testified.

The French, at their best, are unsurpassed in daring and skill, but are a little inclined to be careless in their groundwork, and apt to be reckless in the air.

The German is not so good on the whole, although there were individuals who were as good in every way as the best of the British or the French. But German airmen as a rule have the faults as well as the good qualities of their nation. They show evidence of over-cramming and barrack-square discipline, which, useful as they may be in some affairs, are a detriment to excellence in the air. It is not to be doubted, however, that the Germans will make aerial mail and passenger-carrying a success.

Speaking of the casualness or carelessness of French aviators, it must not be supposed that these faults are not found among the airmen of other nations. Every squadron commander and instructor will agree that one of their chief anxieties was the contempt for risk which familiarity gave to a large number of aviators—a fault aggravated by slipshod training. Startling incidents illustrating this could be given. Two aeroplanes collided head on under circumstances that left no room to doubt that both pilots for some seconds had either been groping down in their "offices," or else been "looking the other way." Both were killed. How many times has one seen aviators go up without first testing their controls, in spite of repeated examples of the danger thus run.

A British soldier in Belgium, whose letter was reproduced in the *Times* in September, 1915, says:—

The airmen are a new race of human beings. Five of the super-avian birds yesterday evening utterly distracted the Hun batteries along our front. The air spaces above were spotted with shrapnel puffs, regularly, in the proportion of currants to a well-made 'plum-duff' (I can think of no other better illustration), and back and forth passed the hawks with the most perfect and practical indifference. You hear the muffled 'plop' up aloft about eight seconds after you have seen the sparking flash of the bursting shell; you have even seen the graceful rounded curl of the shell-smoke form and change shape before you hear the 'plop.'

When the batteries are really busy you see flash upon flash away up there, four and five together, and soon the flashes merge into a wild confusion of irregular 'plops.' The hawks, if low down, and in great danger, dodge the shells by continually shifting their angle of flight, darting about here and there, and it must need a cool head, and hands and feet, which work automatically, up there.

We have seen flights where it seemed impossible for the hawk to miss a shell, and then, when the hawk had reached safety, we have seen him deliberately turn back and return to the same danger zone. It looks like bravado, but it is not. That hawk had not finished the task he had set himself to finish, so he went back. One hawk did this five times while we watched from the front trench, and when he finally decided to go home to roost, and regained safety, it was great relief to cheer him, and I hope he heard that bottled-up explosion of relief we gave him.

In the evenings, after sundown, by twilight, and against the sunset pinks and yellows, the hawks, from all points of the Hun front, come home to roost. Gliding in, with engines stopped, they swoop in long, gradual slants. And when you think what they have been through, your thoughts break down in a shamed confusion. It does not seem fair, in your ignorance, complete and dense, even to think of their dangers.

Talk about mastery of the air! The air is like the sea, in its unknown dangers which call for certain inborn qualities, and the master of the one can be as easily master of the other. That is just my belief. At any rate, our birdmen treat the Hun birdmen with as much inborn superiority as our seamen do the Hun seamen. If a German hawk ever passes over us, he is a hunted and harried, unhappy thing, which very soon 'scoots' for home and *lagerland*. You never see them at their ease and serene.

Here is a point worthy of consideration. With scarcely an exception, the airmen who had become famous in peace achieved renown in war. The names of Moorhouse, Pégoud, Garros, Védrines, Valentine, and many others, at once occur to the mind in this connection.

3

The men who carried on the war in the air were not at first deliberately selected with a view to any exceptional qualities of body or of mind. Lest there exist any misconceptions on this matter, it will be well to state that admission to the Royal Naval Air Service and the Royal Flying Corps was possible for any youth of suitable age who could pass the medical examination, and the only point In which this examination differed from the ordinary examination for the Army was in the matter of sight: on that item the test was rigorous, yet not more so than it was for candidates for the Royal Navy. Of those who were accepted for the Flying Services, perhaps as many as 20 *per cent*, failed from one cause or another during training, but the failure in a great many cases was not due to inability to pilot a machine.

Later in the war the British Air Services followed the lead of the French in instituting particular physical tests, and afterwards elaborated them, with a view to eliminating men whose nervous reactions were slow, or whose emotional system was too sensitive. While this was a step in the right direction, to make researches towards the end that some ready way may be discovered of detecting the lack of the qualities necessary to the aviator, the tests In question are still in the experimental stage. Rapidly, however, owing to the attention given to the subject by physicians in consultation with airmen, a great mass of useful data is being assembled.

Some of the early tests were too crude. Thus, candidates' nerves were tested by the firing of pistols, unexpectedly, close to their heads. As if the greatest pilot in the world could be expected to recover completely from such a shock in some small fraction of a second! Any aviator close to whom a shell bursts is in absolute bewilderment for two or three seconds at least, and such bewilderment does not necessarily mean permanent loss of control.

The man who has in him the makings of a good flyer is the man who, besides having a stout heart and general physical fitness, possesses self-control and other qualities quite outside the scope of that sort of test. Cautiousness, perseverance, concentration, and other moral qualities might more reasonably be demanded from candidates as a condition of acceptance.

A special form of eye trouble known as hyterophoria began to receive serious attention at the end of 1917. Certain pupils who had passed all the preliminary tests and examinations developed a strange incapacity in landings, and of these a large proportion were found to be suffering from the malady referred to, which may be described as an inability to focus properly and obtain true binocular vision. It is believed that the tension of the nerves natural to the pupil during flight tuition discovered this tendency in those subject to it, and that the tendency was more likely to be found in pupils who had not had a fair share of outdoor life, and in whom the eye muscles brought into play in rapid focusing near and far objects were unexercised.

Successful treatment was discovered, and became known as "eye drill." "Eye drill" of various kinds was also found to be applicable to other disorders, for example, incorrect colour vision and night blindness.

Some pupils are frightened when in their first experience as a passenger in the air the aeroplane is banked steeply for a turn, and they take long to lose this fear. Others, and these are by far the majority, are never anxious; they are perhaps lulled by the absence of any really alarming sensation while the machine is in the air, even when it gets

249

into one of the dangerous positions. As the threadbare witticism has it, it is not the fall that hurts, it's the stop.

Some have been fortunate in experiencing during tuition a fall severe enough, without doing them personal injury, to shatter the machine, and so they were convinced of the tragic possibilities. Others seem never to realize these possibilities, and their imagination is so inactive that while they learn to fly they cannot be said to understand what they are doing while in the air.

So severe is the strain on the nerves of the pilot, and so heavy is his responsibility, that the raising of the age-limit is perhaps a subject for consideration. Some youths of 18 are fit; but the author is convinced that a very large number would have a better chance if they were first given a more generous outdoor education, not of course at the expense of essential indoor study.

This criticism applies to our war methods of selection and training. The Royal Air Force will ultimately have its own aeronautical College, and will take cadets from school at the age of 16 or 17 and train them specially.

Our aviators were drawn from all parts of the Empire, from the wealthy and from comparatively poor and struggling professional and commercial families, from the aristocracy and from the "middle class." A large and most varied assortment passed through the author's hands, including Canadians, Australians, New Zealanders, South Africans, Scotsmen, Irishmen, Welshmen, and Englishmen, boys straight from our Public Schools, others from responsible affairs; there were rubber planters, tea planters, coffee planters, lumbermen, ranchers, a pearl fisher, several officers from the mercantile marine. If the author developed any prejudice for one class, although he would find a difficulty in supporting it by conclusive evidence, it was one in favour of the pupil who, although still a boy, had been engaged in serious pursuits, preferably open-air pursuits. The boys straight from the Public Schools were good, but a rather large proportion of them were too undeveloped in mentality and character. Decidedly they improved after a year or eighteen months of service.

Exceptions to all these generalizations could be quoted. For example, although the poetic and artistic temperaments are not the best for practical flying, the Royal Air Force had successful officers from these classes. It numbered several actors, playwrights, musicians. One has only to recall such names as Robert Gregory and Robert Lorraine.

At a Medical School near London pupils who failed to do well at aerodromes were examined and catechized. In order to obtain data for future guidance a series of questions were put to these subjects, the questions reminding one of the autograph albums in vogue twenty years ago. They included "What Is your favourite amusement?" Who is your favourite poet?" "Have you ever recited or made a speech in public?" "Do you mind solitude?" The intention was to arrive at an understanding of the psychology of the doubtful cadet. The selection of Kipling, or Stevenson, or Fennimore Cooper was supposed to indicate greater promise than one for Shelley or Meredith. A football player stood better with the examiners than a pianist. But it was experimental merely, and one cannot help feeling that at present we are groping our way in the dark,

Upon consideration it was only to be expected that the airmen of both sides in the war should be to some extent in sympathy with each other through the *camaraderie* of the air. The individualistic character of their activities also lent itself to this, a pretty general circumstance of the war, which outlived the bombing raids on London and the Rhine, but suffered a check when German airmen deliberately bombed a hospital base in Northern France in the summer of 1918.

A German aeroplane dropped the following message in the Belgian lines on the 29th of July, 1915:—

For the English Royal Flying Corps. The officer you asked for (13th) was dead when coming down. The bombs are the answer for last night, in which we had much pleasure. Were the German officers dead who came down the 25th, near Hooge?

Lieutenant A. M. Sutherland writing home to his parents said that after his fight with a German airman the latter sent him a message thanking him "for one of the best fights I ever had in the air."

LEONAUR

ALSO FROM LEONAUR
AVAILABLE IN SOFTCOVER OR HARDCOVER WITH DUST JACKET

IRON TIMES WITH THE GUARDS *by An O. E. (G. P. A. Fildes)*—The Experiences of an Officer of the Coldstream Guards on the Western Front During the First World War.

THE GREAT WAR IN THE MIDDLE EAST: 1 *by W. T. Massey*—The Desert Campaigns & How Jerusalem Was Won---two classic accounts in one volume.

THE GREAT WAR IN THE MIDDLE EAST: 2 *by W. T. Massey*—Allenby's Final Triumph.

SMITH-DORRIEN *by Horace Smith-Dorrien*—Isandlwhana to the Great War.

1914 *by Sir John French*—The Early Campaigns of the Great War by the British Commander.

GRENADIER *by E. R. M. Fryer*—The Recollections of an Officer of the Grenadier Guards throughout the Great War on the Western Front.

BATTLE, CAPTURE & ESCAPE *by George Pearson*—The Experiences of a Canadian Light Infantryman During the Great War.

DIGGERS AT WAR *by R. Hugh Knyvett & G. P. Cuttriss*—"Over There" With the Australians by R. Hugh Knyvett and Over the Top With the Third Australian Division by G. P. Cuttriss. Accounts of Australians During the Great War in the Middle East, at Gallipoli and on the Western Front.

HEAVY FIGHTING BEFORE US *by George Brenton Laurie*—The Letters of an Officer of the Royal Irish Rifles on the Western Front During the Great War.

THE CAMELIERS *by Oliver Hogue*—A Classic Account of the Australians of the Imperial Camel Corps During the First World War in the Middle East.

RED DUST *by Donald Black*—A Classic Account of Australian Light Horsemen in Palestine During the First World War.

THE LEAN, BROWN MEN *by Angus Buchanan*—Experiences in East Africa During the Great War with the 25th Royal Fusiliers—the Legion of Frontiersmen.

THE NIGERIAN REGIMENT IN EAST AFRICA *by W. D. Downes*—On Campaign During the Great War 1916-1918.

THE 'DIE-HARDS' IN SIBERIA *by John Ward*—With the Middlesex Regiment Against the Bolsheviks 1918-19.

www.ingramcontent.com/pod-product-compliance
Lightning Source LLC
Chambersburg PA
CBHW032041080426
42733CB00006B/159